CADOGAN

KT-393-247

Bruges

Cadogan Guides
West End House, 11 Hills Place
London W1R 1AG
becky.kendall@morrispub.co.uk

The Globe Pequot Press
246 Goose Lane
PO Box 480, Guilford
Connecticut 06437–0480

Editorial Director: Vicki Ingle
Series Editor: Linda McQueen

Editing: Catherine Charles
Proofreading: Susannah Wight
Indexing: Isobel McLean
Additional Research: Mary-Ann Gallagher
Production: Book Production Services

Copyright © Antony Mason 2000

Book and cover design by Animage

Cover photographs: **front** The Travel Library/Andrew Cowin
                    back The Travel Library/Stuart Black

Chapter title illustrations designed by Kicca Tommasi

Maps © Cadogan Guides, drawn by Map Creation Ltd

ISBN 1–86011–953-0

A catalogue record for this book is available from the British Library

Printed and bound in the UK by Cromwell Press

The author and publishers have made every effort to ensure the accuracy of the information in the book at the time of going to press. However, they cannot accept any responsibility for any loss, injury or inconvenience resulting from the use of information contained in this guide.

About the Author

Antony Mason is the author of over 50 books, which include biographies of great artists, children's atlases, and books on exploration, great civilizations, the Wild West, houseplants, volleyball, spying—as well as travel guides. Having travelled to most parts of the world, he now lives and works in London, but for many years has been a frequent visitor to Belgium. So convinced is he of the virtues and charms of the Belgians that he has married one, and has since felt sufficiently qualified to write the *Cadogan Guide to Brussels, Bruges, Ghent and Antwerp*, and *The Xenophobe's Guide to the Belgians* (1995), designed to cure xenophobes of any misguided prejudices.

Acknowledgements

Numerous people have contributed to the compilation of this book. Many thanks in particular to Anne De Meerleer and her colleagues at the Bruges Tourist Office for patiently answering my questions; to my brother Timothy Mason, my nephew Giles Mason, and Hok Ann Lim for their insights and recommendations; to Dr D.J. Murray Brule, Juliet Phillips, Judith Martin, Harriet Crabtree and Maria Garces for troubling to write to me with their comments. And big thanks also to my wife Myriam and son Lawrence who have shown what an excellent city this is to visit as a family, and contributed their own very useful perspectives.

Last, but not least, many thanks to all at Cadogan Guides: to Vicki and Linda, who steered the book through the planning stages, and in particular to Catherine who has deftly edited the text with both good humour and a rod of iron—much appreciated by this wayward and obsessive author.

Contents

Maps

A Guide to the Guide

The guide begins its journey before you do, with **Travel** and **Practical A–Z** chapters packed with information to plan your trip to Bruges, while **Poetry in Motion**, **History** and **Art and Architecture** fill in the background to what you will see when you arrive.

The Main Attractions chapter lists alphabetically the big places you'll want to see during your stay, which you can visit at your leisure. The four **Walks**, however, divide the heart of the small city into segments, and take you by the hand, showing you the very best Bruges has to offer; the **Walks Introduction** on pp.91–2 tells you more.

For those with more time on their hands, the **Damme** chapter takes you a little way outside Bruges to this charming town which used to be a major port, and was instrumental to Bruges' success in its heyday.

The **listings chapters** cover everything from museums and shops to the wide range of wonderful restaurants and hotels; and the **Language** chapter gives you useful words and phrases to help you decipher signs and menus.

I strongly recommend all travellers through Belgium to devote at least three days to making themselves well acquainted with the interesting antiquities of Bruges. If they have the good fortune to be introduced to the society of the place, they will be willing to stay much longer.

Belgium and Western Germany, Fanny Trollope (1833)

Introduction

In the Gruuthusemuseum in Bruges there is a wooden chest made of slabs of oak, secured by cast iron straps, braces and rivets and an elaborate lock, a solid and workmanlike piece of utilitarian hardware which bears the patina of a long and useful life since its construction 500 years ago. Lift the lid to the 15th century, and you would have seen riches of fairy-tale opulence: embroidered silks from Italy, oriental rugs, ivory carvings, illuminated manuscripts, a lute decorated with marquetry, furs from the Caucasus, bejewelled rings.

This chest might be seen as a symbol for Bruges—a city that today shows a down-to-earth and businesslike face, with a beguiling modesty and human scale, but within hides an interior world of extraordinary riches, recalling the centuries when Bruges was one of the largest, wealthiest and most successful cities in northern Europe, fuelled by international trade that, at the close of its Golden Age, spanned the world.

For a handful of reasons, Bruges lost its pre-eminence to other trading cities in the 16th century, and drifted into a deep slumber that lasted four hundred years; it even dozed through the Industrial Revolution. Perhaps its patron saints were taking the long view for, as it turned out, Bruges' centuries of decline proved to be its saving grace.

Gradually the outside world became aware of a city preserved in a time warp, an unpolished gem barely touched by modernization, with crooked streets, crumbling guildhouses and palaces, and stone bridges over mirror-still canals that reflect the spires and towers of a medieval skyline.

During the 19th century British enthusiasts of neo-medievalism—spurred by the revivalist vogue that produced the Houses of Parliament, William Morris and the Arts and Crafts movement—flocked to Bruges, and took an active part in restoring it. Meanwhile, Symbolist poets and artists wandered its misty canals and dank medieval alleyways in a mood of delicious melancholy, and turned the city into a metaphor for *fin-de-siècle* decay. Georges Rodenbach's macabrely romantic novella *Bruges-la-Morte* was a runaway bestseller. Now tourism really began to pick up, as visitors came in search of the heart-rending gloom. This mood was still all the rage in 1908, when George W. T. Omond wrote in his travelogue-cum-history, *Belgium*: 'Bruges is a city of the dead, of still life, of stagnant waters, of mouldering walls and melancholy streets, long since fallen from its high estate into utter decay.' This could be read as a compliment.

In fact, the city was not so much dead as a Sleeping Beauty, but today we come to the story rather late in the plot: she has already been kissed by the prince, whose name is Tourism; and he has exacted a price. Bruges is now the most visited city in Belgium after Brussels, which means coachloads of tourists, the trample of thousands of feet, the gaze of countless eyes. The tourist industry is continuing where the 19th-century neo-medievalists left off, gradually smoothing away the authentic grime and decay of the old medieval fabric.

As yet another coachload cuts a path through the city centre toward the multilingual tourist menus on the Markt, it can sometimes seem as if Bruges is becoming a museum city, a sanitized replica of its former self, but if you allow yourself to fall into this frame of mind, you alone will be the loser, for Bruges has genuine and unique charms. This intimate, pocket-sized city is indisputably one of the most remarkable urban heirlooms of Europe.

You could get a fair taste of this on a day trip. The triumphant collection of medieval art in the Groeningemuseum and the panoramic view from the top of the belfry would alone justify the visit. But there is far more to Bruges than you could ever hope to see in such a short time. This is a city that yields itself gently. Stay a few days, so you can see all the key sights, but then also enjoy ambling along the medieval streets on a more relaxed agenda, catching the canal views at different times of the day and in different weathers, passing the time of day in the many excellent bars, cafés and restaurants.

Be fair to Bruges: its famous charms are real enough, but you may have to give the city time to reveal them.

Travel

Bruges (Brugge in Flemish) is in the north of Belgium, about 100km northwest of the capital, Brussels, and 14km south of Zeebrugge on the coast. Most visitors travelling by air will arrive at Belgium's main international airport, Brussels Zaventem. From there they can travel on to Bruges by train, bus, hire-car or taxi. The international airports in London and Paris also have reasonably convenient connections to Bruges. Many visitors from the continent of Europe will arrive by car, but it is worth noting here that Bruges is a very small city. If you intend to visit the city alone, a car is of little practical value. In fact it is more of an encumbrance.

By Air

Flights to Brussels, 'the capital of Europe', tend to be heavily booked; if you are on a tight schedule, book early. **Zaventem Airport** is 14km from Brussels' city centre.

From the UK

British Airways, ℡ (0345) 222 111, *www.british-airways.com*
Sabena, ℡ (020) 8780 1444, *www.sabena.com*
British Midland, ℡ (0870) 60 70 555, or (01332) 854 854, *www.british-midland.co.uk*

BA and Sabena, the Belgian national airline, have up to seven flights daily from London Heathrow, and daily flights from London Gatwick, Birmingham, Bristol, Edinburgh, Glasgow, Leeds, Manchester and Newcastle. Sabena also runs a daily service (except Sat) from London City Airport. British Midland flies direct from Heathrow and 10 regional airports across the British Isles.

The full **London–Brussels** fare for unrestricted economy travel is around £330 return. However, if your journey includes a Saturday night APEX return fares drop to about £135–£145, or even to £64 for low-season (winter) flights with a restricted timetable (plus £25.90 airport taxes, payable when you purchase your ticket).

The flight from London to Brussels takes 60–70mins. Since the check-in time is usually one hour before takeoff, you will spend almost as much time in the departure lounge as in the air—except at London City Airport, where the minimum check-in time is just 15 minutes (but here the airport taxes come to £34.50).

From Ireland

Aer Lingus, ℡ Dublin (01) 886 8888, *www.aerlingus.ie*

Up to five flights a day direct to Brussels from Dublin. Prices start at IR£92 for low-season Apex fares, if your stay includes a Saturday night (plus IR£14 airport taxes).

From North America

There are direct flights to Brussels from just about all the major gateway cities in the USA. Prices vary enormously, but the round-trip price quoted by airlines for New York–Brussels is around $350–400 in the low season (winter), and about $800 in the high season (summer)—plus additional airport taxes of about $40. Numerous agencies in the USA offer more competitive prices through charter flights or consolidated fares on scheduled flights; look in the travel pages of your Sunday newspaper, or surf the net. Canadians are rather less well served: travellers have to take a two-stage journey, changing in the USA or in Europe to continue to Brussels.

From Australia and New Zealand

Qantas, ✆ (02) 995 70111, *www.qantas.com.au*

Air New Zealand, ✆ (0800) 737 000, *www.airnewzealand.co.nz*

There are no direct flights to Brussels. Travellers from Australia and New Zealand are normally advised to fly to Paris, London or Frankfurt and then to take an onward flight to Brussels with a local carrier, or to travel direct to Bruges by train. Prices quoted by **Qantas** for Sydney–Brussels return, start at about A$1900 in the low season, but much cheaper deals can be struck with local travel agents, or indeed at Qantas Travel Centres. The same applies to flights from Auckland with **Air New Zealand**, where low-season return fares cost around NZ$2500.

transport from Brussels Airport

Trains for Bruges leave from Brussels Gare Centrale/Centraal Station and Gare du Midi/Zuid Station in the city centre (*see* 'from Brussels to Bruges by train' below).

Taxis from Zaventem Airport to Brussels city centre cost between 1,000 and 1,400 BF, but taxis with an orange and white aeroplane sticker in the top right-hand corner of their windscreens offer special reduced rates, usually 25% off. It's far cheaper to travel by train. Special train services leave the airport three times an hour from around 5.40am to 11.40pm, and connect with the Gare Centrale/Centraal Station. The journey takes 20 minutes. A second class return is 90 BF, rising to 120 BF on weekends.

By Sea

Hoverspeed, ✆ (08705) 240 241, *www.hoverspeed.co.uk*

P&O Stena Line, ✆ (0990) 980 980, *www.posl.com*

P&O North Sea Ferries, ✆ (01482) 377 177, *www.ponsf.com*

SeaFrance, ✆ (08705) 711 711, *www.seafrance.com*

The completion of the Channel Tunnel in the early 1990s has put the cross-Channel ferry business into a state of turmoil. Several lines have been discontinued. The abolition of duty-free sales within the European Union in 1999 has further undermined the margins of the operating companies, so the future of cross-channel services is likely to remain unsettled for some time. The resulting price war may hold advantages for travellers, but they also have their work cut out to find the best deal of the moment, and to follow the ever-changing scenario of routes and shipping lines.

Three ports are convenient for Bruges. Zeebrugge is the nearest at 14km, closely followed by Ostend (27km). Calais in France lies 120km to the west, linked by a new motorway over the polders.

All the services listed below take cars, as well as foot passengers.

Hoverspeed operates a fast-ferry 'SeaCat'—a giant trimaran—**Dover–Ostend**. In summer there are six crossings a day (seven on Sat) starting at 7.30am (Sat 4am) and finishing at 11.30pm. If you catch the early morning ferry, you can expect to pay around £125 for a 5-day return for a car and two passengers. Peak mid-afternoon rates for the same type of ticket are closer to £175; for peak-season standard return fares (for journeys of longer than five days), expect to pay £290. Foot passengers pay £25 each, regardless of crossing times. The ferries depart from the Hoverport at Dover's Western Docks, which can be easily reached from both the M2 and M20 motorways. The crossing takes about 2hrs.

Ostend is about 20 minutes' drive from Bruges. For foot passengers there are also local rail services to Bruges from Ostend Station, which is located close to the Hoverspeed terminal; it is a 13-minute journey to Bruges, with three trains per hour, costing 110 BF single. Unfortunately, because the SeaCat is a fairly lightweight craft, this service is liable to cancellation in poor weather, although alternative routes are offered.

Thanks to improved road links, following completion of the Channel Tunnel, it is well worth considering the **Dover–Calais** route. The E40/A16 is now open all the way from Calais to the Bruges turn-off (on the E40/A10); the drive should take no more than 1½ hours. P&O Stena Line and SeaFrance run the only surviving traditional ferry service (large ships), with up to 15 departures a day; the crossing takes 75 minutes. A standard return should cost about £150, rising to close on £300 in the summer. But there are much cheaper rates for five-day return fares, and in the low season a day return can be bought for as little as £15. SeaFrance 'guarantees the lowest fares from Dover to Calais', so in principle will always be marginally cheaper.

Hoverspeed runs a hovercraft service from Dover to Calais (sometimes replaced by a SeaCat service). A five-day return for a car and up to five people can cost as little as £59, but usually ranges between £105 and £185. The high season standard return is £298. The crossing takes just 35mins. The hovercrafts cannot operate in rough weather.

P&O North Sea Ferries operate an overnight service between Hull and Zeebrugge (departs 6.15pm, arrives 8am). Standard foot passenger fares (with reclining seats) start at around £66 rising to £83 in summer. For those with a car, a five-night return ticket (must include a Saturday night), can be bought in the winter months for £171 and in summer for £210; up to four people may travel. The equivalent standard fare prices are £272 rising to £335. Allow an additional £35 or so per person for the use of a cabin.

By Train

via the Channel Tunnel

Eurostar, ✆ (0990) 186 186, or (01233) 617 575, *www.eurostar.co.uk*

The Channel Tunnel, one of the great marvels of modern engineering, has transformed Britain's links to mainland Europe, and helped to overcome not only a geographical barrier, but also a mental one.

To reach Bruges by train via the Channel Tunnel, you first have to go to Brussels. The total journey time from London to Bruges is about four hours.

The rail company operating the Channel Tunnel passenger service is Eurostar. Trains depart from Waterloo Station in London, and take 2 hours 40 minutes to reach Brussels, arriving at the Gare du Midi/Zuid Station. There are usually eleven departures a day. It is also possible to board the train at Ashford, in Kent, from where the journey to Brussels takes 1 hour 40 mins. In either case, be sure to check in at least 20 minutes before departure, or you simply will not be allowed on board.

Prices are on a par with Eurostar's direct competitor—air travel—and vary between £129 for a standard economy fare to a full fare of £219. However, it's well worth asking about any special deals that might be running. In the winter, a weekend return can be bought for as little as £79, if your stay includes a Saturday night.

from Brussels to Bruges by train

Bruges station/train information, ✆ 050 38 23 82.

There is a direct train link between Brussels and Bruges, leaving from both the Gare du Midi/Zuid Station and the Gare Centrale/Centraal Station (which are on the same line). There are two trains an hour, running from about 5am to 11pm. The journey takes an hour   provided that you take the intercity train, and not one of the slow ones that stops at every conceivable station along the way. Trains arrive in Bruges at Stationsplein, about 1.5km from the city centre.

Belgian rail fares are very reasonable, by UK standards at least: a single from Brussels to Bruges costs 380 BF (first class 580 BF). There are reductions of 40 per cent for return/round-trip fares at the weekend (generously considered to be Fri–Mon); additional passengers in groups of up to six can expect reductions of 60 per cent.

Children under 12 travel free (provided that there are no more than four qualifying children to each fare-paying adult)—a policy introduced in February 2000 to discourage car-use.

If you intend to cycle in Bruges, you can purchase a rail ticket that includes cycle hire from Bruges Station under the '*Trein + Fiets*' scheme (*see* 'By Bicycle', below).

other railway options

Some Eurostar trains also stop at Lille (called Rijsel in Dutch), in northeastern France, 60km from Bruges. Local trains connect to Bruges, and take 1hr 15mins. There is also a connecting bus service between Lille and Bruges, operated by Eltebe of Bruges (✆ (050) 32 01 11).

Trains from Charing Cross Station in London link up with the Hoverspeed SeaCat service from Dover to Ostend, and from there with trains on to Bruges. This route is a bit slow and cumbersome, requiring a courtesy bus to the port at Dover, but it is economical, with prices starting at £29 return for a three-day excursion, or £46 return for five days.

Tickets are available at major UK railway stations, fax the railway operator, Connex South-Eastern, ✆ (01233) 617 803, or contact Hoverspeed (*see* above).

From elsewhere in Europe—Paris, Amsterdam, Schiphol (Amsterdam's airport), Rotterdam, Düsseldorf, Cologne—you can reach Brussels on one of the super-fast 'Thalys' TGV (*train à grande vitesse*) services, a Belgo-French-Dutch-German initiative. Twice a day the Thalys service runs directly from Paris Nord to Bruges via Brussels, a journey of 2hr 25mins (departures at 7.55am and 5.55pm).

There is also a direct train service between Antwerp and Bruges, one per hour, taking 1hr 15mins.

By Bus

From the UK

Eurolines, ✆ (0990) 143 219, *www.eurolines.co.uk*

The service between Bruges and London (via Calais) takes eight hours, but operates only during the summer (*June–Sept*); ring Eurolines for alternative destinations, such as Ostend or Brussels. A return ticket to Bruges for an adult costs about £50. Coaches depart from Victoria Coach Station in central London.

There are also daily buses from Scotland and Liverpool/Manchester to connect up with the overnight ferry from Hull to Zeebrugge, with an onward bus to Bruges.

By Car

via the Channel Tunnel

Eurotunnel, ✆ (0870) 240 2995, *www.eurotunnel.co.uk*

Eurotunnel (formerly known as Le Shuttle) transports cars on purpose-built railway carriers between Folkestone and Calais. The UK terminal is situated off junction 11a on the M20. The journey time is a mere 35 minutes platform to platform; once in France you can reach Bruges in under an hour on the newly completed E40/A16 autoroute.

The standard economy fare on Eurotunnel for a car (and any number of passengers) is £169 return, though this may rise to over £200 in the summer months. There are cheaper rates for travelling between 10pm and 6am, and special rates for five-day breaks. Day-trip return crossings can cost as little as £29. At busy times of the year, it's advisable to reserve space in advance, although you can turn up and wait.

Border Formalities

UK citizens and other EU countries just need a valid passport (with at least three months' validity after your planned return) for stays of up to 90 days. Americans, Canadians, Australians and New Zealanders also just need valid passports, but no visa. Strictly speaking you are supposed to be able to produce your passport or identity card at any time, so keep it with you.

All duty-free shopping for travellers within the EU was abolished in July 1999. In fact, since EU customs controls were relaxed in 1993 there has been virtually no restriction on the amount of alcohol, tobacco and perfume you can bring back to the UK, provided that it is in quantities deemed reasonable for personal use.

The guidelines are as follows, per person: not more than 800 cigarettes or 200 cigars; 10 litres of spirits, 20 litres of fortified wine or 90 litres of wine; 110 litres of beer; 90gm of perfume; plus other goods valued at £420 per person. Quantities above these may be judged to be for commercial purposes, and subject to UK duty and VAT.

US and Canadian citizens are restricted to the familiar limits of 100 cigars, 200 cigarettes and 1 litre of alcoholic beverages. There are no currency restrictions for travellers entering or leaving Belgium.

Maps

The maps in this book will provide all the detail that you need for this small and compact city. Other single-sheet maps are available free in hotels, or found in the tourist office brochures; the Bruges tourist office has also posted one on its internet site (*see* p.28). For a wider view, the Michelin road maps are reliable and fairly comprehensive. No.409 covers the whole of Belgium; No.213 covers northern Belgium in slightly more detail.

By Car

driving in Belgium

To drive a car in Belgium, you'll need a valid EU driving licence—or your own national licence, or an international driving licence—plus valid insurance and your vehicle registration documents. It is advisable to take out an additional insurance policy to cover your car against the cost of breakdown and rescue while abroad. You are required by law to carry a warning triangle and a fire extinguisher, and are expected to have a first-aid kit. Your headlights should be adjusted for driving on the right-hand side of the road, but they do not need to be yellow. Seatbelts are obligatory in both the front and rear seat, and children under 12 must be seated in the rear, if space is available.

The roads in Belgium are well maintained, and the motorway network is free of charge. The speed limits are 120km/hr (75mph) on the motorway, 90km/hr (55mph) on major country roads and 50km/hr (30mph) in built-up areas. (If you are caught speeding by police they may issue you with a ticket there and then; this has to be paid within 48 hours.) Drinking and driving is against the law (you'll be over the limit after more than one drink) and liable to severe penalties.

Belgium once had a reputation for having some of the worst drivers in Europe. It was not entirely unfounded. Driving licences were only introduced in the early 1960s, at which point the government handed them out liberally to anyone over the age of 18 who applied for one. Practical driving tests were introduced for the first time during the 1970s and the situation has improved somewhat since then, but Belgium still ranks fourth for accident rates among European countries with the most dangerous roads, and there are weekly reports of major pile-ups, usually involving heavy goods vehicles. The main problem is that most Belgian drivers seem to have no concept of stopping distance. Cars in the outside lane of the motorway are liable to chase each other nose-to-tail at speeds well over 120km/hr.

Another warning: *priorité de droite* (priority for vehicles coming from the right) is alive and unwell in Belgium. On unmarked roads (but not on major thoroughfares and motorways) vehicles may come shooting out from the right quite legally without looking—provided they do not hesitate. Junctions where this is not permissible have white dog-tooth marks across the road at which drivers must give way.

Belgian drivers are only just coming to terms with roundabouts (remember to go anti-clockwise). According to government legislation, drivers on all roundabouts now have priority and those approaching the roundabout must give way—but beware of drivers who still have not abandoned the old habit of *priorité de droite*, and roundabouts that have not yet been properly marked up with the white dog-tooth marks showing priority.

By law, vehicles must give way to pedestrians wanting to cross at a marked pedestrian crossing, but the concept is fairly new to the Belgians. Proceed with care and use your mirror: if you break suddenly for a pedestrian you are liable to receive a shunt from the rear from the driver behind (the problem of stopping distance again).

parking in Bruges

Bruges is a small city, and highly conscious of its limited capacity for traffic. The authorities have therefore acted to restrict traffic within the city limits. It makes sense: this is a very walkable city, and few people actually need a car to get around within it. Parking in the centre is therefore at a premium. If you are planning to stay in a hotel near the centre, ask whether the hotel has its own parking, or what parking arrangements it can offer.

There are a few small public car parks near the centre. These are well signposted from outside the city (*vrij* means spaces available), but they can be awkward to reach because of circuitous the one-way system, tend to fill up early in the day (especially in summer), and are pricey (about 350 BF per day). Alternatively, there are several very large car parks to the south and west of the city which are less expensive. The nearest to the centre is the underground car park at 't Zand (around 215 BF per day); there is another at the railway station (20 BF per hour, 100 BF per day), and another near Katelijnepoort. If you are on a day visit, the best advice is to head straight for one of these outlying car parks, and walk into the centre (no more than 20 minutes). To encourage you more, the car park at the railway station offers a free use of the public (De Lijn) bus service into town.

Parking meters (for example, on Steenstraat) are for limited duration of up to three hours only. There are also 'Blue Zones', where drivers can park for free for the duration indicated, if they display a parking disc (obtainable from service stations). Both these parking facilities can be used free and for unlimited hours overnight (7pm to 9am) and on Sundays.

Almost everything in Bruges takes place within the oval ring of canals that traces the path of the old city walls. This is no more than 3km across, so it takes no longer than 40 minutes or so to cross the entire city on foot. Walking is the best way to get around, and because of the low volume of traffic it's pleasant and pretty safe.

Two words of warning, though. You will find pedestrian crossings painted across the road, but do not assume drivers will stop at them, though they are obliged to by a law passed in 1996—on 1 April, a joker's day in Belgium as elsewhere. Given enough distance, they will probably reluctantly give way once you are on the crossing. Also: bicycles are permitted to go up one-way streets the wrong way.

Many of the city streets are paved in cobbles—nice to look at, but hard on the feet after a while. Bring a stout pair of walking shoes, with thick soles.

By Bus

Bruges has its own public bus service, called De Lijn, which links the centre with outlying districts. The main bus stops are at the railway station, and in the centre at the Markt, Wollestraat and the Biekorf (City Library) on Kuipersstraat. Information about the services is available from the kiosk outside the railway station, and from the Tourist Information Office (*see* p.27). Tickets cost around 40 BF, and a one-day pass (for unlimited travel on city buses) is available for 110 BF. Alternatively, for 220 BF you can buy a Stadskaart, valid for 10 journeys.

By Taxi

Taxis are available from stands at the railway station (℗ 050 38 46 60) and at the Markt (℗ 050 33 44 44). These are ordinary saloon cars with 'Taxi' written on the top. They cannot be hailed from the street. Fares are expensive: 38 BF per kilometre within the city, twice this outside the city limits, plus add-ons—but you can be fairly sure the price quoted is honest. It is normal to add 10–15 per cent as a tip, or round up to the nearest 50 BF.

By Bicycle

Because of Bruges' restrictive traffic policies it is a pleasant place to cycle around. Bruges' railway station (baggage hall) offers bicycles for hire under the '*Trein + Fiets*' scheme (℗ 050 30 23 29), and there are other **bike-hire shops** in the centre, such as 't Koffieboontje, 4 Hallestraat (beside the Belfort tower), ℗ 050 33 80 27; and Eric Popelier, 26 Mariastraat (south of Sint-Salvatorskathedraal), ℗ 050 34 32 62. Prices range from about 250 to 350 BF per day, or 70 BF per hour. Some hotels even provide bicycles.

Note that bicycles are permitted to travel in both directions on one-way streets, but you are not allowed to ride through pedestrianized areas. The tourist office (*see* p.27) publishes a useful leaflet (with route map) called '5 x by bike around Bruges' (i.e. five times around Bruges by bike).

You will be provided with a bicycle lock. Use it! Bicycles tend to walk in Bruges if left unattended.

Quasimodo, 7 Leenhofweg, 8310 Brugge 3, ℂ 050 37 04 70, ✆ 050 37 49 60, a sympathetic local tour company run by Lode and Sandi Notredame, offers a **daily bicycle tour** with English commentary called 'Bruges by Bike', covering 8km and some of Bruges' less-visited backwaters. Tours depart from the Burg (*mid Mar–Sept 10am (be there by 9.50am); 650 BF per adult, 550 BF for anyone under 26*); the price includes cycles and wet-weather gear. Helmets and babyseats also available. Reservation essential.

By Canal Boat

A boat-trip on the canals offers a picturesque introduction to Bruges—but is madly popular and attracts long queues in summer. All the starting points are along the canal to the south of the Burg, mainly close to Blinde Ezelstraat and the Vismarkt. Trips last approximately 30 minutes (*Mar–Nov daily 10–6; Dec–Feb weekends, school and public hols only; 190 BF for adults, 95 BF for children 4–11*).

On damp days take an umbrella, even if it is not actually raining: the bridges drip copiously. Also, take some small change to tip the boatman as you get off.

By Horse-drawn Carriage

Trundling over the cobbles in a horse-drawn carriage seems an appropriate way to view this pre-automobile city. The carriages leave from the Markt (*Mar–Nov 10–6; 1000 BF per carriage for 30 minutes, 500 BF per 15 minutes extra*). They carry up to four passengers and tend to ply a short circuit between the Markt and the Begijnhof in the south of the city.

There is also a folksy 'horse tram' (*pèèrdentram*), which makes a 45-minute journey across the southwest of the city, from its starting point on 't Zand square to the Minnewater lake (*all year from 10am; 200 BF for adults, 100 BF for children 4–11*).

Sightseeing Tours

The **Sightseeing Line** runs a 50-minute 'CityTour' by minibus, passing the main sights, with a well-prepared recorded commentary through headphones in a choice of seven languages. The buses run throughout the year, leaving from the Markt (*on the hour from 10am; last bus Dec–15 Mar at 4pm, 16–31 Mar 5pm, April–June and Sept–Oct 6pm , July–Aug 7pm; 380 BF for adults, 250 BF for children*).

The tours are professional and user-friendly, and not a bad option if your time is limited, or the weather is inclement, or you just can't face walking any further.

Specialist Tour Operators

Short breaks are part and parcel of Bruges' tourist industry, and a number of companies provide packages that combine transport and accommodation. These may offer significant reductions in overall cost compared with booking the separate elements yourself—particularly if you take advantage of such features as 'fourth night free' or 'kids go free' (free accommodation for children, if sharing with parents). But even if it's not all that much cheaper, buying a package allows you to hand over to one single company all the bother of the booking, ticketing and scheduling.

The Belgian Travel Service, Bridge House, 55–59 High Road, Broxbourne, Herts, EN10 7DT, ✆ (01992) 456 156, ✉ (01992) 44 44 88, *belgian@bridge-travel.co.uk, www.belgiantravel.co.uk.* This is easily the most active and expert agency in the field, providing a full range of travel-and-accommodation packages (or just accommodation), to suit all budgets.

Great Escapes, 27–31 West Street, Storrington, West Sussex, RH20 4DZ, ✆ (0845) 0700 999, *www.greatescapes.co.uk.* Trips (in conjunction with Hoverspeed) tailored for travellers crossing the channel by car. (Part of Allez-France Holidays.)

Leisure Direction, Image House, Station Road, London N17 9LR, ✆ (020) 8324 3041. A full range of 'city breaks', for travellers by car, train and air.

Travcoa, PO Box 2630, Newport Beach, CA 92658-2630, ✆ (949) 476 2800. Luxury coach tours with guides and lectures.

Maupintour, 142 Research Park Drive, Suite 300, Lawrence, Kansas 66049-3858, ✆ (913) 843 1211. Gardens and treasures of Belgium and Holland.

Practical A–Z

Belgium: Key Facts and Figures

Belgium is a small country. At 30,520 square km, it's not much bigger than Sicily or Wales. You can drive from north to south in less than three hours. Its population numbers just over 10 million. There are cities in the world with more people but Belgium nevertheless has one of the highest average population densities, at 331 inhabitants per square km. Brussels, the capital, accounts for one-tenth of them, with a population of about 950,000. Antwerp has 486,000, Ghent 231,000, Charleroi 207,000, and Liège 196,000. Bruges is a comparative tiddler with 118,000.

The northern part of Belgium is Flanders, inhabited by the Flemish, who speak Dutch. The southern part of the country is Wallonia, home to French-speaking Walloons. Brussels is primarily French speaking, but is more or less surrounded by Flemish communities. There are also two German-speaking cantons on the German border.

There are five Flemish provinces, and Bruges is the capital of West Flanders (West-Vlaanderen). It is also one of a famous trio (with Ghent and Antwerp) of historic Flemish trading cities that in the past have relished a strong sense of autonomy. This heritage is still evident today. And if you detect a prosperous, buoyant mood in Bruges, this is not simply the product of its formidable income from tourism: in the last decade or so, Flanders has developed one of the most vibrant and successful economies of the entire European Union.

Children

The first thing you notice about Belgian children is how well behaved they are. Belgium has a comparatively close-knit society, where traditional values are maintained not only by parents but also through the kindly guidance of ever-present older cousins, aunts, and grandmothers. Just about all children go to the local state-run school, which therefore has the strong backing of Belgium's mighty middle classes. If a child is unacceptably disruptive, the parents will soon be under pressure to do something about it. For all that, this is a child-friendly society, where children are broadly welcomed and generally well catered for. Restaurants happily accommodate children. If in doubt try the fondue restaurants (*see* **Food and Drink**, pp.157–170), where they actually cook the food themselves; this will keep them entertained.

Few of Bruges' attractions are specifically geared to children. They will enjoy climbing the spiral staircase of the Belfort, being deafened by the carillon bells, and gazing at the miniaturized town spread out below. Sightseeing Line's bus tours (with headphones) are good for a pain-free whirl around the main sights. The canal trips are also fun. Try giving them a map and make them navigate a walk around the medieval streets. They may also enjoy the jumble of exhibits at the Folklore Museum (Museum voor Volkskunde), and a gallop through the medieval art (much of it spectacularly grisly) at the Groeningemuseum. Lastly, there are several theme parks in the surrounding region, such as the Boudewijnpark, accessible by bus from the city centre:

Boudewijnpark and Dolfinarium, A. Debaeckestraat 12, ✉ 8200 Brugge (St Michiels), ✆ 050 28 28 28 (*open May–Aug 10–6; Easter and Sept 11–6; dolphin shows also in Mar and Oct; adm adults 560 BF, children 480 BF*). Just off the A17 to the south of Bruges, an entertaining amusement park with a big wheel, water shoots, crazy golf, etc. The dolfinarium presents a show that demonstrates the remarkable intelligence and agility of these creatures. You can reach the park by bus (nos. 7 and 17) from Biekorf and Kuipersstraat in Bruges city centre.

Climate and Packing

Belgium shares a similar weather pattern to the UK—that is to say there are glorious summers of endless sunshine, and there are summers when it never ceases to rain. The average temperature in Brussels is 16°C in summer and 3°C in winter. In winter, however, temperatures can be noticeably colder than in Britain, sometimes dropping to –20°C if the wind is blowing from the Baltic; and the entire north of the country can be shrouded in an eerie cold fog for days.

The best weather occurs between April and October, with mid-summer temperatures sometimes in the 30s. But all the seasons have their merits—even winter—and, as any Belgian knows, in filthy weather, you can always retreat to a restaurant and eat well. Clear, ice-cold winter days can be invigorating; the low-pitched sunlight gilds the old stonework, while lakes and canals may be thronged with skaters and sprawling children, like a scene from Bruegel. In December Bruges' central square, the Markt, hosts a merry Christmas market serving hot spiced wine around an improvised outdoor skating rink. In spring daffodils carpet the open spaces in the Begijnhof, a famously beautiful sight. Keep warm by wearing several layers, which can be judiciously removed according to conditions—in winter, Belgian homes, hotels and restaurants can be heated to hothouse temperatures.

The dress code in Belgium is fairly relaxed. Generally people dress casually, but with attention to detail. Belgians appreciate elegance, but take a dim view of pretension or impracticality.

Three further tips: remember to pack some sturdy, sensible and stout-soled shoes for walking. Take a small umbrella to fend off uncertain weather (although cheap umbrellas are widely available, e.g. in the shops in Steenstraat). Lastly, more surprisingly perhaps, take some mosquito repellent if you are staying in Bruges in the summer months (May onwards): the canals provide a favourable habitat.

Crime and Police

You are unlikely to encounter crime in Bruges. This is the kind of city where you can walk safely day and night. But there are always the exceptions—pickpockets, opportunists, vandals, drunks, tourists. Don't drop you guard.

If you are the victim of crime, go straight to the police (Politie). Most officers speak English, and you can expect a sympathetic hearing. Remember that you have to report theft to the police within 24 hours of discovery in order to claim insurance. Note also that you are obliged to carry your passport or other form of identity at all times, and this is the first thing the police will ask to see. (They can check it, but they are not allowed to take it away from you.) If you are arrested for any reason, you have the right to insist that your consul is informed (*see* 'Embassies and Consulates'). Proper legal representation can then be arranged.

The main police station in Bruges is at 7 Hauwerstraat, ✆ 050 44 88 44.

Disabled Travellers

Bruges is never going to be an easy city for the disabled—all those cobbled streets, steps and staircases, and narrow pavements. But the tourist office (*see* p.27) is making significant efforts to accommodate people of restricted mobility where it can; it also supplies a special guide for the disabled that all the Flemish provinces are obliged to publish. Furthermore, the Belgians generally show greater respect, sympathy and patience towards the disabled than many of their European counterparts, and their welcome, and offers of assistance where required, may help to compensate for the absence of lifts and ramps in museums, restaurants and public offices.

A number of organizations can provide useful information about travel in Belgium for the disabled. These include:

Radar (The Royal Association for Disability and Rehabilitation), 12 City Forum, 250 City Road, London EC1V 8AF, ✆ (020) 7250 3222. General travel advice, accommodation listings, and information about specialist holidays.

Holiday Care Service, 2 Old Bank Chambers, Station Road, Horley, Surrey, RH6 9HW, ✆ (01293) 774535. Accommodation advice.

SATH (Society for the Advancement of Travel for the Handicapped), 347 Fifth Avenue, Suite 610, New York, NY 10016, ✆ (212) 447 7284, *www.sath.org*. General travel advice.

Travel Information Center, Moss Rehab. Hospital, 1200 West Tabor Road, Philadelphia, PA 1914/3099, ✆ (215) 456 9600.

Doctors and Pharmacies

Belgium has an excellent medical service, with first-class modern hospitals and well-trained staff. Under the Reciprocal Health Arrangements, visitors from EU countries are entitled to the same standard of treatment in an emergency as Belgian nationals. To qualify, you should travel with the E111 form; application forms are available from post offices in the UK. With an E111 you can claim back about 75 per cent of the cost at the local Belgian sickness office; it is advisable, therefore, to take out personal health insurance as well, which permits you to claim the entire cost on your policy. Note that you will be expected to pay for all medicine and treatment in the first instance, the cost of which can be claimed back later, provided that you have the correct documentation; ensure that you have a receipt (*Getuigschrift voor verstrekte hulp*).

Hotels have a list of doctors and dentists to whom their guests can apply, but a trip to a pharmacy may be sufficient for minor complaints. Pharmacists have a good knowledge of basic medicine and are able to diagnose: if in doubt, they will recommend that you visit a doctor, and can provide you with details.

A list of **24-hour duty pharmacies** is posted on every pharmacy door, together with a list of doctors on call. For emergency numbers, *see* p.20.

Doctors on night call during the week: ℗ 050 51 63 76

Doctors on call at weekends (Fri 8pm–Mon 8am): ℗ 050 81 38 99

Hospitals: AZ Sint-Jan, 10 Rudderhove, ℗ 050 45 21 11; AZ Sint-Lucas, 29 Sint-Lucaslaan, ℗ 050 36 91 11; Sint-Franciscus Xavieriuskliniek, ℗ 050 47 04 70.

Electricity

The current is 220 volts, 50 hertz. Standard British equipment requiring 240 volts will operate satisfactorily on this current. Plugs are the standard European two-pin type. Adaptors are available locally, but it is easier to buy a multi-purpose travelling adaptor before you leave home. Visitors from the US will need a voltage converter in order to use their electrical appliances.

Embassies and Consulates

The following embassies are in Brussels:

Australia: 6 Rue Guimard, 1040 Brussels, ℗ 02 231 05 00

Canada: 2 Avenue de Tervuren, 1040 Brussels, ℗ 02 741 06 11

Republic of Ireland: 89 Rue Froissart, 1040 Brussels, ℗ 02 230 53 37

New Zealand: 47–48 Boulevard du Régent, 1000 Brussels, ✆ 02 512 10 40

South Africa: 26 Rue de la Loi, 1040 Brussels, ✆ 02 230 68 45

UK: 85 Rue Arlon, 1040 Brussels, ✆ 02 287 62 11

USA: 27 Boulevard du Régent, 1000 Brussels, ✆ 02 508 21 11

Emergencies

The basic emergency number is ✆ **100**. There should always be at least one English-speaking operator on call.

Accident emergency/ambulance/fire/rescue, ✆ 100

Police emergency, ✆ 101

Red Cross Ambulance, ✆ 050 32 07 27

Emergency anti-poisoning centre, ✆ 070 245 245

Festivals and Events

Belgium has an extensive calendar of events: some are age-old ceremonies and pageants, widely advertised and drawing large crowds; others are religious festivals, including some of disturbing fervour; others still are entirely local excuses for an annual knees-up and binge. Bruges is no exception: it holds one annual pageant of national importance, the **Heilig-Bloedprocessie**, and has a busy timetable of other cultural events.

Ascension Day The *Heilig-Bloedprocessie* (Procession of the Holy Blood) is Bruges' principal festival, and takes place annually on Ascension Day (40 days after Easter, a Thursday, usually in May, but 1 June in 2000). Following an 800-year-old tradition, the holy relic (*see* p.84) is paraded through the streets, accompanied by medieval interpretations of biblical scenes, which were traditionally presented by the city's craft guilds and trading associations. Tickets (about 400 BF) for the grandstand are available from the tourist office from 1 March onwards.

2nd weekend in July *Cactusfestival*, a three-day (Fri–Sun) open-air rock concert held annually in the Minnewater Park. It attracts a range of interesting, medium-ranking bands. More details are available on the website *uc2.unicall.be/cactus/festival*.

21 July The *Nationale Feestdag België* (Belgian National Holiday), a public holiday, is celebrated with such events as a Big Band concert and shows in the parks.

Late July–Aug	The month-long *Klinkers Festival*, a '*culturele zomer-happening*' of world music, jazz and cinema takes place in the parks and other open-air venues.
End July–early Aug	For about two weeks, the celebrated *Flanders Festival* of classical music comes to Bruges as part of its six-month round of Flemish cities. Concerts take place in the Provinciaal Hof in the Markt and the Ryelandtzaal, as well as several of the churches. For details, and tickets in advance, contact the tourist office (*see* p.27).
15 Aug	In a solemn, and touching procession, the *Blindekensprocessie*, a large candle (16kg) is taken from the chapel of Onze Lieve Vrouw van de Blindekens to Onze Lieve Vrouw ter Potterie, fulfilling a pledge made in 1304 to the Madonna of the Blindekens to deliver the menfolk home safely from the Battle of Pevelenberg.
Last 10 days in Aug	The *Reiefeest* (Festival of the Canals) takes place once every three years (2001, 2004). From about 9pm, spectators walk between various points on the illuminated canals to see a series of historic tableaux.
Late Aug	The *Praalstoet van de Gouden Boom* (Pageant of the Golden Tree) takes place every five years (2001, 2006). A huge costumed procession, first held in 1958, tells the story of Bruges up to the 15th century, its myths and legends, culminating in a re-enactment of the spectacular parade for the marriage of Charles the Bold to Margaret of York in 1468. (The Golden Tree was a bejewelled trophy awarded at jousting tournaments held in the Markt.)
2nd weekend in Sep	*Open Monumenten Weekend* (Heritage Weekend). A range of historic houses, private collections, gardens and businesses throw open their doors for a day. Ask for details at the tourist office.
About 2 Dec–2 Jan	A *Christmas market* takes place in the Markt in the centre of town, beside a temporary open-air ice rink.
6 Dec	The feast of *Sinterklaas*. St Nicholas, aka Santa Claus, walks the streets and markets and enters schools in his guise as the Bishop of Myra. He is usually accompanied by his jolly sidekick, the blacked-up and decidedly un-PC Zwarte Piet. Many Belgian children receive their main Christmas gifts, as well as traditional *speculoos* biscuits.

Guided Tours

In July and August the tourist office (*see* p.27) organizes daily guided tours, leaving from their headquarters in the Burg at 3pm (*150 BF per head, children under 14 free*); reserve your place in advance. The tour lasts about two hours.

Guides can also be hired through the tourist office, for individuals and groups (*maximum 25 people; 1500 BF per guide for two hours, 750 BF for each extra hour*).

Alternatively, you can subscribe to a DIY tour with a Walkman, supplied by the tourist office. Hire for the day costs 300 BF (plus a deposit of 1000 BF). Two people can share one machine.

Tours are also offered by the **Sightseeing Line** (*see* p.13) and **Quasimodo** (✆ 050 37 04 70) who also organize bicycle trips to Damme, and informative and relaxed mini-bus day-trips beyond Bruges: one called 'Triple Treat' takes chocolates, waffles and beer as its main themes; the other, the 'Battlefields Tour' visits the First World War trenches around Ypres: sympathetically done and highly recommended. Price 1500 BF, under 26-years-old 1200 BF; includes picnic lunch.

Insurance

All travellers are strongly advised to take out insurance as soon as they book their tickets. Insurance packages for European travel are not expensive compared with the total cost of a holiday, or the cost of replacing stolen goods or paying any medical bills yourself (*see* 'Doctors and Pharmacies', p.19). Standard packages include insurance to cover all unrefundable costs should you have to cancel, compensation for travel delays, lost baggage, theft, third-party liabilities and medical cover.

Language

Belgium has two main languages: Dutch and French. (The third official language is German.) Dutch is the language of Flanders, the provinces that stretch across the north of Belgium, which includes Bruges. In the past, people referred generally to this language as Flemish (*Vlaams*); there are broadly varying dialects within Flanders, but the basic standard language, taught in schools—and shared with the people of the Netherlands—is Dutch (*Nederlands*), and this has now become the preferred name for the language of Flanders.

The Flemish are generally reluctant to use French. There are strong historical and emotional reasons for this. French, the language of southern Belgium, was imposed as the language of the ruling classes by the Burgundians in the 14th century, and by the 19th century the French-speaking population held political and economic sway over the Flemish to a degree that can justifiably be called oppression. French, therefore, became the language of oppression, an issue that is still deeply resented to this day. As it happens, the language boot is now definitely on the other foot: Flemish and Dutch are in the ascendant, partly as a result of the decline of heavy industry in the French-speaking south and the growing strength of modern light industries and ports in the Flemish-speaking north, and partly because to succeed in administration it is now essential to be bilingual.

Remarkably few French speakers have made the effort to be conversant with Flemish, while a larger proportion of the Flemish have learned French. The result is that the Flemish have now gained the upper hand in the civil service in central government, as well as in public services such as the post office and railways. But they are not inclined to be magnanimous to the French-speakers in victory.

So there is no point brushing up your French for a visit to Bruges. If the locals are going to speak a foreign language it will be English. They might know some French, but will only use it as a last resort, and speak it as though they have some unpleasant taste in the mouth. (For a basic guide to Dutch, *see* pp.186–192.)

Media

The main Dutch-language newspapers in Belgium are *Het Laatste Nieuws*, *De Standaard* and *De Morgen*. But since you are reading this guidebook, the chances are you will not be a Dutch speaker. Rest assured: Bruges is well supplied with English-language newspapers, such as the British broadsheets and the *International Herald Tribune*, sold at newsstands. Most hotels have cable television with a full range of channels piped in from the UK and the USA. In fact, you might find a rather depressing familiarity in the fare on offer.

The local free 'what's on' paper is called *Exit* (available in the tourist offices and in many hotels and restaurants). It's in Dutch but, even if you know no Dutch, it doesn't require too much lateral thinking to get the gist of it.

Almost all films shown in cinemas in Flanders are in the original language, with subtitles, and not dubbed.

Money and Banks

The currency of Belgium is the Belgian franc (abbreviated to BF, BEF, BFr or simply F), divided into 100 centimes. At the time of writing, the exchange rate is just over 65 BF to £1, or 35 BF to US$1. There are coins of 50 centimes and 1, 5, 20 and 50 BF, and notes of 100, 200, 500, 1000, 2000, 5000 and 10,000 BF.

Belgium is also one of the 11 European Union nations that have adopted the common currency called the **euro**. However, euro-banknotes and coins will not replace local currency until 1 January–1 July 2002. Until then Belgian currency will remain in circulation, but all prices are quoted in both Belgian francs and euros, mainly to get people used to the concept. Euros are also used in credit card statements. The exchange rate has been fixed at 40.33 BF to one euro.

You will find no shortage of banks offering exchange facilities; there are several in the central square, the Markt. **Banking hours** are not absolutely rigid but are usually 9.30–12 and 2–4, although some larger branches do not close over lunch. Exchange bureaux (labelled *Wissel*) have extended opening hours, including weekends; their rates of exchange and commission charges vary, but may compare favourably with banks for traveller's cheques and currency notes. The tourist office in the Burg (*see* p.27) also has an exchange desk.

Cards: Visa, Mastercard/Eurocard, Cirrus and Switch cards can be used to draw cash from banks, but usually only through automatic cash dispensers, which means you must come armed with your PIN code. Visa, Mastercard/Eurocard, Diners Club, American Express and a handful of other leading cards are all widely accepted in shops, restaurants, hotels and petrol stations, but you should always check this first: you are sure to find the occasional surprising exceptions.

Traveller's cheques are widely accepted not only for exchange, but also in lieu of cash.

American Express, 100 Boulevard du Souverain, 1170 Brussels, ✆ 02 676 26 26 (lost cards: ✆ 02 676 23 23 or 02 676 21 21)

Diners Club, 151 Boulevard Emile Jacqmain, 1210 Brussels, ✆ 02 206 97 99 (lost cards: ✆ 02 206 9800)

Mastercard/Eurocard/Visa, 159 Boulevard Emile Jacqmain, 1210 Brussels, ✆ 02 205 85 85 (lost cards: 070 34 43 44)

Opening Hours

The standard opening hours for **shops** are 9–6, but many bakeries, small shops and tobacconists open at 7.30am. Shops that close for lunch usually remain open until 7 or 8pm. On Sundays, supermarkets and high-street shops are closed but *pâtisseries* and other specialist food shops open in the morning to cater for the tradition of Sunday lunchtime indulgence. In the summer many tourist-oriented shops in Bruges are open on Sunday. For **bank** opening hours *see* 'Money and Banks', above; for **post offices** *see* below.

The public **museums** and **galleries** are open over the weekend; watch out for Tuesdays in winter (1 Oct–31 March), which is the day of closure for several museums and churches, including the Groeningemuseum. The churches have frustratingly idiosyncratic opening hours, particularly in winter.

Post Offices

The main post office is on the western side of the Markt, close to the Belfort: 5 Markt, ✆ 050 33 14 11, open 9–5.

Stamps are also available from tobacconists and shops selling postcards; however, for reliable information about the cost of postage, it is best to ask at a post office.

Public Holidays

Belgium has a generous number of public holidays. On these days all banks and post offices are closed, as are many shops, bars and cafés. When a public holiday falls on a Sunday, the following Monday is often taken as a public holiday in lieu.

1 January	New Year's Day (*Nieuwjaar*)
March/April	Easter Monday (*Pasen*)
1 May	Labour Day (*Feest van de Arbeid*)
May	Ascension Day (6th Thurs after Easter) (*Hemelvaart*) Whit Monday (seventh Mon after Easter) (*Pinksteren*)
21 July	Independence Day (*Nationale Feestdag*)
15 August	Assumption (*Maria Hemelvaart*)
1 November	All Saints' Day (*Allerheiligen*)
11 November	Armistice Day (*Wapenstilstand*)
25 December	Christmas Day (*Kerstmis*)

Public offices and institutions are also closed on 15 November (Dynasty Day) and 26 December (Boxing Day), and on 11 July, the Festival of the Flemish Community, called *Gulden Sporenslag* (recalling the Battle of the Golden Spurs).

Religious Affairs

About 90% of Belgians are Roman Catholic. However, the Church is not a dominant feature of Belgian society; it provides the context for all the major rites of passage, but less than 25 per cent of the population attends Mass regularly. That said, the Flemish tend to be more observant than their Walloon counterparts in the south of Belgium. The British have a long historical connection with Bruges, and the Anglican Church and United Protestants still hold regular Sunday services in the old chapel of the candlemakers' guild, the *Kapel 't Keerske*, also called *Sint-Pieterskapel* (1 Keerstraat). The tourist office publishes a list of church opening times, and a schedule of the services held in each.

Telephones

Telephoning in Belgium presents few problems. If you are staying in a hotel, the switchboard can connect your call, but this is usually far more expensive than using a public telephone. These take 5 BF and 20 BF coins, but if you intend to make a lot of calls a 'Telecard' is a good investment. Telecards are available from tobacconists, newsagents, post offices and public transport ticket offices and cost either 200 BF for 20 units or 1000 BF for 105 units. They can be used in any public telephone bearing the Telecard sign; telephone boxes showing a row of foreign flags on the window can be used for international calls. The illustrated instructions in telephone boxes are easy enough to follow, and a liquid-crystal display tells you how many units you have left on your card.

In Belgium, area codes are now an integral part of every telephone number, so for Bruges numbers you need to dial the whole number (including 050) as listed in this guide, even within Bruges itself. From abroad, the country code for Belgium is 32, and if you are calling Bruges you should then dial 50 instead of 050.

To make an international call from Belgium dial 00, then the country code, then the area code without the initial 0, then the number. The country code for the UK is 44, for Ireland 353, for the USA and Canada 1, for Australia 61 and for New Zealand 64.

Telephone enquiries: © 1207.

Time

Belgium is on Central European Time and is one hour ahead of Britain throughout the year. For Belgian Summer Time (two hours ahead of Greenwich Mean Time), clocks go forward one hour on the last Sunday of March, and back one hour on the last Sunday of October. This means that in mid-summer, evenings are very long. In the summer Belgium is seven hours ahead of US Eastern Standard Time, ten hours ahead of California and eight hours behind Sydney.

Tipping

On the question of tipping, relax. Except in the few circumstances mentioned here, it is not generally expected. In restaurants a 16% service charge is usually included in the bill, along with 21 per cent TVA (Value Added Tax), and so additional tipping is not expected—but if service has been noticeably good a further 5% or so would be appreciated. If you have had table service at a bar or café, it is usual to leave any small change (say 20 BF for a small order), but this is not essential.

Service is included in hotels, so there is no need to tip porters or staff providing room service. In taxis it is usual to round up the total by 10–15 per cent, but note that in metered taxis the tip is included in the fare. Attendants in public lavatories will expect 10 BF or so; minimum charges are posted at the entrance, and the attendant herself will usually be there to enforce it.

Toilets

Public toilets (*heren* for men, *dames* for women) are usually kept scrupulously clean by dedicated middle-aged women with their own brand of hearty chat; for this service you are obliged to pay around 10 BF. In central Bruges there are toilets in the same courtyard as the tourist office in the Burg, and more in the courtyard of the Halle, beneath the Belfort (belfry) in the Markt. Most Belgians will freely make use of facilities offered by bars and cafés, but it is considered polite to act as a legitimate customer by buying a drink in passing.

Tourist Information

The main tourist office in Bruges is in an imposing building in the Burg, the centrepiece of historic Bruges. The staff can offer all kinds of advice about what to see and when, and about special activities and guided tours; they will also make hotel reservations for you. They publish a useful illustrated brochure about Bruges. But be warned: in the high season, this office becomes very busy.

Toerisme Brugge, 11 Burg, B-8000, Bruges, ✆ 050 44 86 86, ✉ 050 44 86 00, *toerisme@brugge.be* (*open April–Sept Mon–Fri 9.30–6.30, Sat–Sun and holidays 10–12 and 2–6.30; Oct–March Mon–Fri 9.30–5, Sat–Sun 9.30–1 and 2–5.30*).

There is also a smaller tourist office at the railway station, ✆ 050 38 80 83, open similar hours to the above. This can be handy for hotel reservations.

The Belgian tourist board has offices in London and New York, which can supply you with information before you leave home. In Britain, it now calls itself Tourism Flanders–Brussels, and is located in Docklands, east London.

Tourism Flanders–Brussels, 31 Pepper Street, London E14 9RW (*open Mon–Fri 9–5*). Automated telephone service, ✆ 09001 887 799 (calls cost 60p per minute).

Belgian Tourist Office, 780 Third Avenue, Suite 1501, New York 10017, ✆ (212) 758 8130, ✉ (212) 355 7675.

Alternatively, visit the Bruges website, which contains virtually the same information as the tourist office brochure: *www.brugge.be*. Further information on Flanders generally can be found the Tourism Flanders–Brussels website at *www.toervl.be*.

Weights and Measures

Belgium uses the metric system and continental clothing sizes. Below are some conversion factors for the most common metric units. For clothing and shoe sizes it is best simply to ask in the shop and get an assistant to measure you.

1 centimetre (cm)	= 0.39 inches (in)	1in	= 2.54cm
1 metre (m)	= 3.25 feet (ft)	1ft	= 305cm
1 kilometre (km)	= 0.621 miles	1 mile	= 1.61km
1 hectare (ha)	= 2.47 acres	1 acre	= 0.4ha
1 litre (l)	= 1.76 UK pints or	1 UK pint	= 0.57 litre
	2.11 US pints	1 UK gallon	= 4.55 litre
		1 US pint	= 0.47 litre
		1 US gallon	= 3.78 litre
1 gram (g)	= 0.35 ounces (oz)	1oz	= 28.3g
1 kilogram (kg)	= 2.2 pounds (lb)	1lb	= 0.45kg

Poetry in Motion

Lace

Since the 16th century the wealthy of Europe—men and women—have decked themselves in lace: lace cuffs, lace collars, lace caps, lace handkerchiefs, all fashioned in exquisite patterns wrought from hours of painstaking labour. Lacemaking has always been a cottage industry, but in the old days it was also a pastime for women from virtually every social rank, notably by the hundreds of women living in the *béguinages* (*see* p.107) and convents of the Low Countries.

Various lacemaking techniques have been used over the centuries. In the 16th century it was essentially a form of embroidery; a hundred years later, the dominant technique was needlepoint (point lace), which had evolved in Venice. Bobbin lace developed during the 17th century in Genoa and Milan, as well as in Flanders, where the main centres were Brussels, Mechelen and Bruges. The bobbin technique is the one most widely seen today, especially in Bruges.

Handmade bobbin lace is extremely slow to make, requiring thousands of carefully planned movements of the bobbins and pins. The intricate patterns are created by moving the threads attached to the bobbins around the pins, which are pressed into a cushion. Complex lace calls for more than a hundred separate threads and bobbins. With the Victorian passion for lace with everything—from women's collars and lappets (ribbon-like hair adornments) and even underwear, to dining-room tablecloths and bedlinen—production grew exponentially in the 19th century, but by this time much of the demand was being met by lacemaking machines. Bruges lace was originally made from linen from the flax fields of central Flanders, but at this time cotton took over.

Postcards seen in Bruges today show smiling elderly women sitting outside their cottages in the sunshine (for better light), quietly clicking away at their bobbins. However, there was once a more pitiful side to lacemaking: Bruges' textile industries were never mechanized, and during the 19th century unemployment soared. Lace was seen as a way to earn at least some income, and thousands of women and children laboured long hours to produce lace by hand, usually for a pittance. Girls as young as five in orphanages and convents were taught to make lace as a training for a profession, and they received no payment at all. By 1840 there were over 10,000 lacemakers in Bruges out of a total population of 45,000. The number dwindled only in the last 30 years of the century, as Victorian fashions became less flouncy.

Fine lace production has been further undermined in recent decades by cheap imports from the Far East, but in Bruges the tradition lives on—as a hobby and as a cottage industry. Genuine handmade lace is available in the more respected outlets, where the staff will be happy to reassure you of its provenance; it should also come with a quality-control label. Handmade lace is always expensive: expect to pay at least 1000 BF for a table doily. Cotton lace is more robust and less pricey; linen lace is much finer, and a larger piece with a complex design can cost many thousands of Belgian francs.

If you want to find out more about the process involved, you can watch lace being made at the Kantcentrum (Lace Centre, *see* p.78), where demonstrators pass the afternoon magically conjuring their intricate patterns out of nothing more than yarns, bobbins and pins. Collections of lace can be seen at the Kantcentrum, and also in the Arentshuis (*see* p.131).

Guido Gezelle

Guido Gezelle (1830–99) pops up time and again in Bruges, a mysterious figure to English speakers, few of whom have ever heard of him. In Flanders, however (and to all Dutch speakers), this is equally surprising, since he is one of the leading figures of 19th-century Dutch literature, and one of its most popular poets.

Guido Gezelle was a priest as well as a poet, and almost all his work is suffused with religious wonderment. He is best known as an observer of nature, looking at reeds in a river, cherries on a tree or birds bringing up their chicks in a nest, and transforming these small details into symbols that reflect the extraordinary variety of the world and the infinite imagination of God.

In English translation his verse seems rather insubstantial, anodyne even, but in Dutch it has a powerful, melodic cadence, exploiting the cut and thrust of Dutch clicking consonants and chewy vowels coupled to poetic innovation. This is clear even if your Dutch is minimal. The following verse is from a poem about a bird's nest, from which the hatchlings have just emerged, and are now bouncing around on the twigs in a way that makes the poet burst out laughing.

> *Een meezennestje is uitgebroken,*
> *dat, in den wulgentronk*
> *gedoken,*
> *met vijftien eikes blonk;*
> *ze zitten in den boom te spelen,*
> *tak-op, tak-af, tak-uit, tak-in, tak-om,*
> *met velen,*
> *en 'k lach mij, 'k lach mij, 'k lach mij bijkans krom.*

Gezelle was also famous for reasserting Dutch (or Flemish, in this case) as a valid literary language, at a time when French predominated in Belgium as the language of education and culture.

Guido Gezelle was born in the modest little house that is now his museum, on the eastern edge of the city (*see* p.135). He was the eldest of five children; his father was a gardener, and his mother came from a farming family. He spent his childhood in the neighbourhood, and at the age of 16 went to a junior seminary school in Roeselare to begin studies for the priesthood. By the age of 18 he was writing and publishing poetry. He returned to Bruges to complete his studies at the Bishoppelijk Seminarie, where he was ordained in 1853. He developed a strong belief that the unity of religion and poetry (and art generally) could achieve a revitalization of Christian culture, as it had done in medieval times. He learnt to speak perfect English—he always retained a close bond with the English community in Bruges—and travelled frequently to Britain. In fact, one of his early ambitions as a priest was to become a missionary for the Roman Catholic faith in Britain (he hoped for a rapprochement between the Anglican and Roman Catholic churches).

His first post was as deputy rector of the English Seminary on the Potterierei (now the Sint-Leocollege), where English Catholics were trained for the priesthood. Then from 1865 to 1872 he was parish priest at the Sint-Walburgakerk, just over the canal to the west. At this time he also began to broaden his cultural and journalistic endeavours, launching *Rond den Heerd* (Around the Hearth), the first of three cultural magazines that he founded. (One of these, *Biekorf*, still exists today.)

His work (often written under pseudonyms) had a strong Flemish-nationalist bent, which was supported by several of Bruges' leading figures. However, his attitude brought him into conflict with the Francophile cultural elite, who accused him of being obsessed by Flemish issues to the point of 'fetishism'. His work for the English community, many of whom were Roman Catholics, drew much praise and thanks, but malicious rumours that a close relationship with the mother of an English family had exceeded the bounds of discretion persuaded his seniors to transfer him, and Gezelle was appointed parish priest at the Onze-Lieve-Vrouwekerk at Kortrijk (Courtrai).

Gezelle remained in Kortrijk for the next 27 years. During this period he developed as a poet, helped to found the Flemish Academy of Language and Literature, and personally collected thousands of Flemish words, sayings and proverbs. He also joined in the general vogue for folklore revival, and gradually came to be seen as a leading figure in the Flemish Movement. He translated Longfellow's 'Hiawatha' into Flemish (1886) to great acclaim, and published his two most celebrated collections of poems, *Tijkrans* (A Crown for the Year; 1893), and *Rijmsnoer om en om het jaar* (A Wreath of Rhymes Roundabout the Year; 1897).

Driven by great energy, he also maintained broad contacts and correspondence with literary and religious figures and former pupils. In 1899 he was invited back to Bruges to translate some theological works, and also took up the post of Director of the Engels Klooster (English Convent), with its attached convent school for English girls, in Carmersstraat, close to his birthplace. Already in declining health from diabetes, he became ill during one of his trips to England, this time to visit a sister convent set up at Haywards Heath. Shortly after his return to Carmersstraat, he died, on 27 November 1899.

It is not easy to gain an appreciation for Gezelle's work unless you can read Dutch. However, there is an excellent dual-language text of *The Evening and the Rose*, with English translations set beside the Dutch (*see* p.196), which reveals the unusual charm of his work. Gezelle's poetry does not range widely across life's broad experiences, but within the narrow focus that he set himself it excels, and is cherished for its calm and innocent wonder, and its radiant spiritual balm.

Football

Bruges is not all history: it also has a famous football club, Club Brugge, champions of the Belgian league in recent years. Support incites great passions, and at the time of crunch matches the gentle streets of Bruges are occasionally the scene of skirmishing fans and riot police anxious to put their training to good use. In February 1999 rioting fans of the Brussels club Anderlecht ran amok during a match against Club Brugge, hurled seats on to the pitch, caused play to be suspended, and did an estimated one million BF damage.

In fact Bruges has two teams: Club Brugge and Cercle Brugge, archrivals, both founded back in the late 19th century, and both in the Belgian first division. **Club Brugge** (the blue-and-blacks) was founded in 1890 and had links with the Socialists, still maintaining strong working-class support today. **Cercle Brugge** (the green-and-blacks) was founded in 1899 by old boys of the Xavier Institute, a Jesuit school (close to the Gruuthusemuseum), which had a strong British contingent from the 1860s.

Since 1975 the two teams have shared the new **Jan Breydel** (Olympiapark) **Stadium** in Sint-Andries, a southwestern suburb of Bruges (the only stadium in Flanders to host the European Championship in 2000). Of the two, Club Brugge has had a better record in recent years, dominating the league in the late 1970s, and four times champions in the 1990s. The glory days for Cercle Brugge were the 1920s, but it hangs on in at the lower end of the first division. When the two teams clash for a local derby all the emotions of football tribalism emerge, demonstrating that Bruges is, after all, a European city just like any other.

The British in Bruges

Britain has had close links with Bruges for over a thousand years. Flemish mercenaries took part in the Norman Conquest of England in 1066, and English wool became the mainstay of Bruges' high-quality textile industry. During the Hundred

Years' War (1337–1453) Flemish loyalties wavered between England and France, and Flanders might even have become an English possession. During the Reformation, hundreds of English Roman Catholics fled to Flanders; English monks and nuns joined Flemish religious institutions, or set up their own—a trend that grew during the continued religious tensions of the early 17th century.

The future Charles II, son of the beheaded Charles I, took refuge in Bruges in 1656. Initially, after the Battle of Worcester (1651), he had gone to the court of King Louis XIV in France, but in 1656 Oliver Cromwell made a treaty with France, and Charles became persona non grata. From a new base in Cologne he made an agreement with the Spanish king Philip IV, then barged his way uninvited into the Spanish Netherlands.

Charles was persona non grata just about everywhere he went, mainly because he, and his entourage of some 70 officials and household staff, plus 800 soldiers and camp-followers, were almost universally penniless. His close coterie of advisers had lost their estates in England, and were dependent on hand-outs from supporters on the Continent, who became decreasingly generous as the prospects of Charles's restoration faded. It was a hard game to play. Charles was a flamboyant, affable aristocrat in his 20s, with a reputation for grand living to uphold, and a string of mistresses. Cromwellian spies lurked, reporting back on the antics of the English exiles in lurid detail. 'Fornication, drunkenness and adultery are esteemed no sins amongst them,' reported one. Charles was desperate for money: funds promised by the Spanish king were sporadic and quickly consumed, shopkeepers would no longer give him credit, and he was forced to sell his silver and his horses.

A further cause of disapproval was the fact that Charles was a Protestant; the Council of Flanders was outraged to learn that Protestant services were held for his entourage, and declared that it would permit services only for Charles and Charles alone, in the privacy of his own chambers. Meanwhile, against a backdrop of politicking, negotiations, and failed hopes of English rebellions, Charles contrived to have a jolly enough time. For much of his stay, his base in Bruges was the previously grand Huis de Zeven Torens in Hoogstraat, close to the Burg, but it was rented unfurnished, and furnishing it caused yet another worrying drain on funds.

He and his youngest brother, Henry, Duke of Gloucester, liked to spend time at the three archers' guilds (two of these, the Schuttersgilde Sint-Sebastiaan and Sint-Joris, survive; *see* pp.134 and 136), practising shooting and carousing, and in 1656 he founded the First Regiment of Foot Guards at the Schuttersgilde Sint-Sebastiaan, as his personal guard—a regiment that after 1815 was renamed the Grenadier Guards. But as the numbers of his soldiers swelled to five regiments, and then found themselves idle and unpaid, they turned to begging and robbery, and terrified the locals. This continued until 1657, when Cromwell attacked Spanish possessions in northern France, and Charles' troops, led by his more austere younger brother, James, Duke of York (the future James II), were sent into action.

Charles apparently found some female company in Bruges. Lord Taafe wrote to him to recommend a Mademoiselle d'Imercell of the Brussels court, but added, 'if your Majesty be libre, which Mme Renenbourg saies you are nott, having gott a new wan at Briges.' The Brussels court nonetheless regularly lured Charles away from Bruges, and in the summer of 1658 he finally moved, first to Brussels, and then to Hoogstraten on the Dutch border. Oliver Cromwell died later that year, and England soon tired of the turmoil and lacklustre quality of the Commonwealth; Charles was invited home as king in 1660.

A strange footnote to this story appeared in 1963, when a Flemish fisherman, Victor De Paepe, was arrested off the coast of England. He claimed that in 1666 Charles II, as a way of repaying Bruges' hospitality, had granted 50 of its fisherman the right to trawl English coastal waters. This was strongly denied by the British government, and the matter faded from the headlines. But in 1999 newly released documents showed that the British might have lost the case if De Paepe had pushed it through the courts, for it appears that such a charter does indeed exist.

A new breed of British visitor arrived after 1815: tourists on their way to see the battlefield of Waterloo, just south of Brussels, which became an attraction even before the thousands of bodies had been removed. Many of the visitors stopped off at Bruges on their way through, and were pleasantly surprised.

They also found Bruges remarkably cheap. Many impecunious middle-class families, unable to maintain standards in Britain, relocated to Bruges. In his *Tour through Belgium* (1816), James Mitchell remarked that over 40 British families were already resident in the city, enjoying cheap rents—a good house with garden, coach house and stable for £25 a year, 'a mere nothing'. But he also pointed out that 'the main secret of the economy of living... is this, that a family may here, where they are unknown, lower their style of living without hurting their feelings.'

This is what brought the writer Fanny Trollope (1780–1863) and her family to the city. She had taken up writing in an effort to escape the debts incurred by her barrister husband, Thomas; in 1827 they had been forced to flee the threat of debtors' prison by going to the United States. After four years in Cincinnati she produced *Domestic Manners of the Americans* (1832), a critical exposé of a hypocritical, slave-owning society—successful in Britain, but not much appreciated by the Americans. She followed this up with a travelogue called *Belgium and Western Europe* (1833), an account of a journey she took in the company of two of her sons, Henry and Hervieu. But in 1834 her husband's creditors were again pressing hard and they fled Britain once more, this time to Bruges, where they rented a villa to the south of the city called, rather grandly, Château d'Hondt.

Here she embarked on a Gothic novel, *Tremordyn Cliff*, which was coloured by the laudanum she was taking to sustain her strength as her family collapsed into ill health. Henry died of tuberculosis aged 23 on Christmas Eve 1834, and her husband, Thomas, who had become unsociable and reclusive—probably as a result of taking mercurous chloride (in calomel) for headaches—died in October 1835. Both are buried in the Protestant section of a cemetery to the south of Bruges, near the Katelijnepoort. After her husband's death, however, the threat of imprisonment was lifted, and Fanny was able to return to England where the youngest of her six children, Anthony Trollope, was about to embark on his career as one of the great 19th-century English novelists.

Bruges by now had also attracted a handful of English antiquarians and art collectors who were to have a profound effect on its subsequent history. They included the print collector John Steinmetz; the architect and painter William Brangwyn (*see* **Main Attractions**, p.78); Thomas Harper King, a pupil of the great neogothic designer Augustus Pugin; the architect Robert Chantrell; and the art historian James Weale, who did much to establish the fame of the great Bruges artists of the late Middle Ages, such as van Eyck and Memling. They were avid supporters of Bruges' restoration, and helped to see a number of the key historic buildings saved and then embellished in neogothic style. They also laid the foundations for the collection in the Gruuthusemuseum.

By 1870 the English community in Bruges numbered some 1200, and warranted its own schools and church. The Anglicans used the old church of the Carmelite nuns (now the Josef Ryelandtzaal) in Ezelstraat. The Catholic community was larger: there was a Catholic girls' school at the Engels Klooster in Carmersstraat, and Catholic boys could go to the Xavier Institute in Mariastraat, where they were taught by British brothers. The former trading house of the Genoese merchants in Vlamingstraat was used as an English reading room, and English was widely spoken in the town. Today more British people come to Bruges than ever before, but they come as tourists and, by and large, are utterly unaware of the important role their compatriots have played in the evolution of the city.

Bruges-la-Morte

> *How sad Bruges seemed in the late afternoon. And how he loved it thus! It was for its melancholy that he had chosen to come and live here after the great disaster.*

Bruges-la-Morte, Georges Rodenbach (1892)

On the death of the Belgian writer **Georges Rodenbach** in 1898, at the age of 43, there was talk in Bruges of erecting a statue in his honour. However, the suggestion was greeted with an outcry by many of the great and the good—including Guido Gezelle—who felt strongly that Rodenbach's most famous work, the novella *Bruges-la-Morte* (Bruges the Dead; 1892) had done a shameful disservice to their city. Yes, it had put Bruges firmly on the tourist map by being such a literary success, but it had painted such a gloomy, sickly, decaying, moribund image of Bruges that the people who actually lived there, and those who were actively trying to restore and renovate it, felt irked and offended by it. In the end, a small plaque was put up at a corner house (No.8) on Jan van Eyckplein in 1948, 50 years after his death—but his family had to pay. It has since been removed.

What was all the fuss about? *Bruges-la-Morte* is certainly a curious book: evoking a mood of unremitting lugubriousness, it tells the story of the 40-year-old, hypersensitive and fastidious widower Hugues Viane, who settles in Bruges to nurse his sorrow. He feels that this misty, silent city chimes with his own misery over the loss of his young and beautiful wife, with whom he had shared perfect love until she was so cruelly taken from him by illness some five years previously.

At his house on the Rozenhoedkaai, with only the aged and pious housekeeper Barbe (Barbara) for company, he creates a shrine to his dead wife, where he preserves precious mementoes of her: photographs and long tresses of hair cut from her corpse. On his walks in the gloaming, he regularly visits the Onze-Lieve-Vrouwekerk, and the tomb of Mary of Burgundy, herself cut down in her prime.

One day on leaving the church he encounters a woman in the street who bears an uncanny resemblance to his dead wife—so close a resemblance in fact, that he is convinced that she must be some kind of reincarnation of her. He stalks this woman, and discovers that she is a dancer at the Stadsschouwburg (Municipal Theatre) in Vlamingstraat, and that her stage name is Jane Scott. He meets her, and realises that she could assume the role of his dead wife, as the living embodiment of his memories. They become lovers, and he visits her frequently at her lodgings before setting her up in a house of her own—much to the shock of this moralistic and pious city.

But soon the differences between Jane and his dead wife become apparent: for her part, Jane finds Hugues a mystery, and cannot fathom quite why he behaves as strangely as he does. He never reveals the secret behind his infatuation, and after several months the relationship starts to fall apart: although Jane resembles his dead wife in almost every detail physically, and has been prepared to play the demure and sweet-natured lover, in reality she is more boisterous, fun loving, hardhearted and slovenly.

Hugues is already distressed by this dichotomy, when Barbe, his faithful servant, is informed of her employer's sinful relationship by a relative, a nun at the Begijnhof. Barbe refuses to accept what she is told—were it true, she would be morally obliged to leave his employment. Meanwhile, Jane has become heartily sick of Hugues' cheerlessness. She threatens to leave, and when Hugues crumbles before the fear of losing her, she realizes that she has him in her power, and could have access to his evident wealth.

On the day of the *Heiligbloedprocessie* (the Procession of the Holy Blood) she determines to enter his house for the first time, on the pretext of coming to see the procession. Hugues relents, and invites her to dine with him. When Barbe hears this, she immediately realizes that the guest is Hugues' mistress, and she resigns. Hugues descends into despondent gloom. When Jane arrives and flaunts her presence to the public by sitting ostentatiously in the window to watch the procession, he is mortified. But when she barges into his shrine to his wife and plays flippantly with the tresses of the dead woman's hair, his rage turns to blind fury, and he strangles her with the very same tresses. Hugues then slumps into a chair in shocked disbelief as the last bells of the procession fade into the distance, seemingly ringing out the words 'Morte…morte… Bruges-la-Morte'.

Gothick and ridiculous it may seem today, but *Bruges-la-Morte* deserves its reputation as a masterpiece of Symbolist fiction. Its sustained mood of *fin-de-siècle* melancholy is achieved with admirable elegance. It was also, in its day, highly experimental: for Rodenbach, Bruges itself was one of the main characters in the plot, and the mood of the city helps to shape what happens. This was the essence of its Symbolism, painting a reality that is not concrete, but formed by mood and perception. 'I wish to imply this,' Rodenbach wrote in his Foreword, 'that it is the town which directs all that occurs there.'

To this end, he insisted that the novella should contain photographs of the city:

> …the quays, deserted streets, old dwellings, canals, the béguinage, churches, a goldsmiths' shop producing church treasures, the Belfry— so that those who read this work may themselves feel the presence and the influence of the city, experience the contagion of the waters, and be conscious of the long shadows of the high towers as they fall across the text.

It was, in fact, the first time photography had been used to enhance fiction in this way. Rodenbach wasn't making everything up: for those inclined to see it that way, Bruges no doubt was gloomy, claustrophobic and moralizing in the 1890s. But the people of Bruges did not appreciate being stigmatized by such labels, especially by an outsider who knew the city only as an infrequent visitor, and who lived in Paris and wrote in French. And they haven't fully forgiven Georges Rodenbach yet.

History

Way back in time, before history began, when the coast of Flanders was inhabited by sprites, sea-creatures and giants, the North Sea washed in and out of these indeterminate flat lands, creating a patchwork of islands amid the marshes. The Romans passed this way, having conquered Belgium in a bitter war that led Julius Caesar to declare: '*Horum popularum omnium fortissimi sunt Belgae.*' ('Of all these people [the Celts or Gauls], the Belgae are the most courageous.')

Remains of a Gallo-Roman settlement have been found in Bruges, but it was probably little more than an isolated trading outpost on the northern periphery of the empire, a crossing point on the road linking Oudenburg to the west and Aardenburg to the east. After five centuries of stable rule, the Romans withdrew to defend their homelands from the Barbarians pushing in from the east. They ceded northern Europe to a Germanic tribe called the Franks, who had settled as Roman mercenaries in Belgium around Tournai (Doornik, in Dutch), 50km south of modern Bruges.

The Frankish leader, Clovis I (*r.* AD 481–511), founded the Christian Merovingian dynasty (*c.* 500–751), and Tournai became the hub of an empire covering much of France and Germany. It was during this era that Christian monks spread through the Frankish empire as missionaries. Among them was Saint Eloi (or Eligius, *c.* 588–660) from Limoges, and Saint Amand (*c.* 584–679) from Poitou, who are said to have brought the faith to Bruges. It may be true: it's hard to judge whether Bruges by this date was a significant place on the map, or just a cluster of daub and wattle huts inhabited by shell-fishers and salt-makers.

The Split

The development of Bruges still lay 100 years in the future, but events were afoot that would shape the destiny of Flanders, right down to the modern age.

The Merovingian kings ruled until AD 751, when they were ousted by **Pepin the Short**, who founded the Carolingian dynasty (AD 751–987). Pepin the Short's son, born in Liège in AD 742, was one of the great kings of this transitional period of European history. He was called **Charlemagne** ('Charles the Great', *r.* AD 768–814), and under his rule the Moors were pushed back from northern Spain, and the Frankish kingdoms were extended into Italy and southern Germany.

Charlemagne saw himself as the heir to the Roman Empire, and the Pope obliged by crowning him Emperor of the West in AD 800. But after his death his heirs squabbled and the Frankish Empire splintered. Under the **Treaty of Verdun** in AD 843 the River Scheldt (or Schelde), which flows across the middle of Belgium between Tournai and Antwerp, marked the border between lands assigned to rival grandsons of Charlemagne—the German king **Lothair I** (AD 795–855) and the French king **Charles the Bald** (AD 823–77). Charles took West Francia, to the west and north of the Scheldt, and Lothair took lands to the south and east. His kingdom became known as Lotharingia, later Lorraine.

The division of the Frankish empire along the Scheldt was not simply geographical, but was also linguistic. In late Roman times, when the Franks had settled in the north of Belgium, the south was occupied by Romanized Celts called the Wala— later the Walloons—whose language evolved out of Latin to become French. Hence, this was a political and linguistic divide which, broadly speaking, still exists today. Paradoxically, however, the part assigned to France was Flemish speaking, while the French-speaking half fell into the orbit of East Francia, which evolved into Germany. The history of Belgium was now to follow two different threads for five centuries.

Baldwin Iron-Arm

One catalyst for the collapse of the Frankish Empire was the growing frequency of raids by the Vikings, whose shallow-draft longships penetrated deep inland on the rivers to sack the monasteries. With their centralized power now dissipated, the Franks were unable to coordinate a response, and local warlords rose to fill the vacuum. One of these was Baldwin (d. 878), a man of such ruthless courage that he was nicknamed 'Iron-Arm'. He challenged the authority of the French king, Charles the Bald, and ran off with his daughter, Judith.

Judith was something of a problem daughter. She had been married to Ethelwolf of Wessex, in England; after his early death she married her step-son, Ethelbald (father of Alfred the Great), but this relationship was judged to be incestuous, and she had to leave England in a hurry. By this time she was all of 17 years old.

For her father, running off with Baldwin Iron-Arm was about the last straw. The couple had to seek refuge in Rome, where Pope Nicholas I managed to bring about a reconciliation. In AD 862 Charles gave Baldwin a rather back-handed reward: he put him in charge of the Viking-ridden northern territory, and created for him the title Count of Flanders. The long and testy relationship between the Counts of Flanders and their overlord, the French king, was to continue the way that it had been forged.

Baldwin built a castle, or *steen*, at Bruges, a large square island in the marshlands of the River Reie. He set up a palisade, dug a ring of canals around his island, and founded a chapel that was soon to be dedicated to **St Donatian** (or Donatus), a 4th-century Roman missionary in France whose remains were brought here. The shape of this island can still be discerned from the old canals and quays, with the Sint-Annarei in the east, the Spiegelrei to the north, the Groenerei to the south, and the Kraanrei (since drained) to the west. From the outset, the distinction between existing rivers and man-made canals in Bruges was blurred: the very word *rei*, used in Bruges to mean canal or quay, derived from the River Reie.

Initially Baldwin Iron-Arm's Bruges was a stronghold against the Viking raiders, but it also grew as a trading outpost. The Counts of Flanders became rich by taxing trade, at river crossings, bridges, crossroads, town gates and markets. In return, merchants received their protection. Through trade, Bruges soon began to develop its web of international connections.

A series of Baldwins now ruled over Flanders. **Baldwin V**, who came to power in 1036, had a daughter called **Matilda**. The story goes that she caught the eye of **William, Duke of Normandy**, the future conqueror of England, on a visit to Bruges. She, however, fancied Brihtic, Earl of Gloucester, who was also in Bruges at the time, but spurned her. Furious also to be rejected, William grabbed Matilda in the street, spanked her on her bare bottom, threw her into the mud and then rode away. Such outrageous behaviour might have resulted in war, but Matilda would have none of it. Instead she insisted on marrying William, and a long and stable union was forged.

Although Bruges was made capital of the County of Flanders in 1093, the niceties of chivalry still lay some way off in the future. In 1127 **Count Charles the Good** was murdered while saying his prayers in the church of St Donatian. He was, it seems, a genuinely good man, who strove to protect the poor from exploitation, and generously handed out alms and clothing during the very severe winter of 1124. News of this savage death spread rapidly across northern Europe (such were Bruges' trading links already). His killers were the ambitious Erembald clan, whose powers he had strived to curtail. The result was a spate of reprisals, after which **Derick** (or Thierry) **of Alsace** was appointed the new Count in favour of the first choice of France, William Clito. It was a measure of Bruges' independence from France, which Derick affirmed by granting the city its first charter—a guarantee of its autonomy.

In around 1127 a new set of defensive walls was built around the city, covering an area now demarcated by the Sint-Annarei to the east, the Augustijnenrei to the north, the Dijver to the south and the Speelmansrei to the west. Bruges was already an established trading centre, but a stroke of luck transformed its fortunes. In Roman times the town had direct access to the sea, but the coastal lowlands

What's in a Name?

The origin and meaning of the name Bruges, or Brugge, remains a mystery. Although *brug* means bridge in Dutch, and there are plenty of these in the city, it is thought unlikely to be the true derivation. More favoured is the theory that it comes from the Norwegian Viking word *bryggja*, meaning a landing place, perhaps conflated with the old word for the River Reie, Rugja. The name Bruggia first appears in print on coins struck in AD 864.

were constantly vulnerable to silt. By the late 11th century Bruges' access to the sea had become more or less blocked off by silt, largely the product of land reclamation which affected drainage. Bruges had begun to turn to overland trade. Then a mighty storm in 1134 caused massive inundation along the coast, and left behind a deep inlet called the Zwin. This provided Bruges with a natural harbour, accessible at Damme, 7km to the northeast. A canal between Bruges and Damme was dug in 1180, so that goods could be unloaded at Damme and transferred to barges and taken to the city centre. The silting of the Zwin remained a constant concern, however, and regular dredging began in the following century.

By the 13th century Bruges was one of the wealthiest cities of northern Europe. It was a key player in the London Hansa (trade association) and had close links with the **Hanseatic League**, the powerful association of seventeen northern European (mainly German) trading cities. The city's merchants exchanged Flemish cloth for wool, lead, tin, coal and cheese from England; pigs from Denmark; wood and fish from Scandinavia; leather goods, oranges, lemons and pomegranates from Spain; wine from Germany and France; furs from Russia and Bulgaria; silks and oriental spices from Venice and Genoa; exotic animals from North Africa. Each year, from the third week after Easter to Whitsun, Bruges held a month-long trade fair, one of the great mercantile events of medieval Europe.

But the key trade of Flanders was **textiles**. Wool was imported and turned into cloth by the weavers of Bruges, Ghent and Ypres (Ieper in Dutch). There were over 4000 weavers in Bruges alone. The finest, fleeciest wool came from the chalk pastures of England, and the deft skills of the Flemish weavers turned this into the finest cloth available. After 1282 only cloth made with English wool could be graded as first class. 'All nations of the world are kept warm by the wool of England,' wrote Matthew of Westminster in the 14th century, 'made into cloth by the men of Flanders.' This trade created an interdependency between Flanders and England, much valued on both sides. It was also a political hot potato, because Flanders was a part of France, and England and France were continually at loggerheads. And, because of its heavy dependence on one sole product, Flanders was

The Bourse

Bruges proudly boasts that it produced the first stock exchange in Europe. From the 12th century merchants would buy and sell shares and credit notes in and around an inn on Vlamingstraat (corner of Grauwwerkersstraat). The inn was owned by a family called Van Ter Beurze, hence the origin of the term by which many European stock exchanges are known: *beurs* (Dutch), *bourse* (French), *borsa* (Italian), *Börse* (German), *bolsa* (Spanish). There is another theory, also plausible: the merchants called the square where they met and did business by the medieval Latin term *bursa*, meaning a purse. The innkeeper then adopted the name Van Ter Beurze, referring to the location. One of the few languages that did not adopt the term *beurs* was English. 'Exchange' was preferred, and the London Royal Exchange was first established in 1566 by Sir Thomas Gresham—who had been Queen Elizabeth's ambassador in Flanders.

always vulnerable to economic and political turmoil. In addition, because the merchants so closely controlled and regulated the weavers, this gave rise to a constant undercurrent of social friction.

By and large Flanders was left to its own devices, and Ghent, Bruges and Ypres became virtually independent city states. This often put the Counts of Flanders in an awkward position: on the one hand they owed their allegiance to France, and on the other hand the economic wealth of their people depended on the ability to control trade, and relationships with England. Power ebbed and flowed.

By the late 13th century the French feared that Flanders was slipping from their grasp, and vigorously reasserted their authority. The patricians of Bruges supported this move and pledged their allegiance to the French king, but the craft guilds and the populace deeply resented the erosion of privileges and the presence of large numbers of French troops sent in to impose order. The city was split into two opposing factions: the patricians and supporters of French rule were called the *leliaerts* (after the *fleur de lis* or lily, the French royal emblem); the Flemish masses were called the *clauwaerts* (from the claws of the Flemish lion).

In 1280 a *clauwaert* uprising, the **Moerlemaye Revolt**, was brutally crushed. In 1297 the king of France, **Philip the Fair** (i.e good-looking rather than fair minded; *r*. 1285–1314) annexed Flanders, a move opposed by the Count of Flanders, **Guy de Dampierre**. As France reinforced its army, Bruges was fortified with a new and larger set of defensive walls and ramparts 7km long—the 'Brugse Vesten'—the line of which can be traced today by the outer oval ring of canals around the city. (The city gates were completed a century later.)

On 29 May 1301, amid considerable tension, Philip the Fair came to Bruges on a state visit to reassert French authority. The nobility and wealthiest merchants turned out in their finery, the opulence of which surprised the French Queen, Joanna of Navarre, who commented famously: 'I thought I alone was Queen, but I see that I have 600 rivals here.'

To add insult to injury, the citizens of Bruges were asked to foot the bill for Philip's ostentatious reception. Bruges was seething. Two leaders emerged at the head of this *clauwaert* resentment: **Pieter de Coninck**, a weaver, and **Jan Breydel** (or Breidel), a butcher. Early in the morning of 18 May 1302 the rebels massacred all supporters of the French and French troops—and anyone who was unable to pronounce in convincing Flemish the shibboleth '*Schild en Vriend*' (shield and friend). Some 1500 died in what has been euphemistically called the '**Bruges Matins**' (Brugse Metten).

This revolt in Bruges stirred up a widespread rebellion in Flanders. Later that year, on 11 July, Flemish volunteers led by Jan Breydel—and armed with little more than lances and staves—took on the full might of the French army on the Groeninge Plain near Kortrijk (Courtrai). Bruges fielded the largest contingent of 2380 men. The French had massively superior and better equipped forces, led by a cavalry of gloriously caparisoned knights, the cream of French chivalry, but the Flemish prepared the marshy ground well, laying branches that acted as traps. The battle began with a devastating attack by the French archers. Thinking they were on the verge of victory, the heavily armoured French knights charged in, but soon became completely bogged down. Now helpless, they were picked off one by one by the Flemish pikemen, who took no prisoners. This humiliating rout became known as the **Battle of the Golden Spurs** (Gulden Sporenslag), because the Flemish victors collected 700 pairs of golden spurs, which they exhibited triumphantly in Kortrijk Cathedral.

As a result of this battle, Flanders enjoyed a brief spell of independence, but French forces mounted a counterattack which included the indecisive **Battle of**

Battle of the Golden Spurs

The Flemish 'national' holiday is 11 July, the anniversary of the Battle of the Golden Spurs in 1302. The battle struck a great and symbolic blow for Flemish independence, although power was clawed back by the French in subsequent decades. It remains a highly emotive symbol, but its significance has shifted: it is now taken as a symbol of Flemish autonomy from the French-speaking Belgians. Events commemorating the battle are often underscored by Flemish 'nationalism', promoting a separatist agenda.

Pevelenberg in 1304, followed by the **Treaty of Athis-sur-Orge** in 1305, by which the Flemish had to pay reparations and disarm. The humiliation of the Battle of the Golden Spurs remained a sore wound for the French, and their victory over the Flemish at the **Battle of Cassel** in 1327 turned into a vengeful massacre. By 1329 Flanders was under French rule once more. The policy of crushing suppression ruthlessly led to a period of instability and confusion throughout Flanders, which coincided with the outbreak of the Hundred Years' War, and the emigration to England of large numbers of weavers.

The Hundred Years' War (1337–1453)

English claims to French territory, plus their trading interests in Flanders, led to a protracted series of military confrontations with France known as the Hundred Years' War. The trigger was the death of the last French Capetian king in 1328, after which the English king **Edward III** (r. 1327–77), the maternal grandson of Philip the Fair of France, reckoned he had a good claim to the French throne—at least as valid as Philip's nephew, **Philip de Valois**, who became Philip VI.

The aristocracy of Flanders naturally sided with the French, so England responded with sanctions: all wool exports to Flanders ceased. Since English wool was the foundation stone of the Flemish textile trade, this had a rapid and profound effect and the wealthy Flemish wool merchants were faced with ruin. In 1338 a brewer from Ghent called **Jacob van Artevelde** led a successful rebellion against the French authorities, put the Count of Flanders to flight, and invited **Edward the Black Prince** (1330–76), son of Edward III, to become the new Count. Edward III arrived in Flanders with an army, and proclaimed himself king of France in Ghent in 1340. But Jacob van Artevelde became dictatorial, and was murdered by rioting Ghent citizens in 1345. **Louis de Male**, Count of Flanders (r. 1346–84), reasserted control, and even extended his domain by seizing Brabant, the province to the south containing Leuven and Brussels.

Peace conferences between the English and the French were held in Bruges in 1374 and 1375. The **Duke of Lancaster** distinguished himself by 'rioting... revelling and dancing', which left the city with a bill for £20,000, resentfully described as '*horribles expenses et incredibiles*'—but little else was achieved. Meanwhile, Ghent and Bruges went to war over a canal. When the people of Ghent refused to pay for an extravagant tournament, Louis de Male enlisted the support of Bruges by the promise of a canal link to the sea. Work on the canal began, but was stopped at the intervention of troops despatched from Ghent deeply anxious about trade competition. From 1381 to 1382 **Philip van Artevelde** (son of Jacob) led an uprising in Ghent and defeated Bruges in battle. Count Louis was forced to flee, taking refuge in an old woman's hovel.

The Flemish Origins of Cricket

No one knows for sure the origin of the name of the great English game, but by one theory it comes from the Flemish expression '*met de krik ketsen*', to hit with a stick. When Flemish weavers emigrated to England in the 14th century, they may have taken with them a stick-and-ball game, which they called '*krikets*' for short.

At this point Louis appealed for help from his son-in-law, **Philip the Bold** of Burgundy, who was married to his daughter Margaret. Assisted by a massive French army, Louis was able to crush the Flemish rebels at the **Battle of Westrosebeke** in 1382. **Charles VI** of France then reaped final revenge for the Battle of the Golden Spurs (80 years earlier) by sacking Courtrai. In the shake-out Bruges was forced to hand over many of its privileges, and 224 rebels were publicly executed in the city.

The 14th century was tumultuous, punctuated by civil strife, as well as by a famine due to crop failure from 1315 to 1317, and the plague that killed 24,000 in 1349. But paradoxically it was also a time of great prosperity for Bruges—perhaps its greatest. Its population stood at about 40,000—comparable to London and Paris. In the next century it became the centrepiece of the splendid and lavish Burgundian empire, but it was already being eclipsed by trading rivals, and by growing competition in textile manufacture from England and Holland. Bruges retrenched by specializing in luxury products, such as tapestry, paintings and illuminated books, which found a ready market among the wealthy within its walls and beyond. But at the height of its glory, the writing was already on the wall.

The Burgundian Period (15th Century)

In 1384 Louis died, and **Philip the Bold**, Duke of Burgundy, became Count of Flanders. Bit by bit, through negotiation, marriage and conquest, the Burgundians took control of a vast territory, split into two distinct areas: the Burgundy region of central eastern France, and the area covering most of modern Belgium plus the Netherlands—the 'Low Countries'. Its capital was Dijon, in France.

Philip the Bold was the brother of Charles V of France. As a member of this ruling Valois family, he and his heirs had a close stake in the throne of France. They also ruled over one of the wealthiest regions in Europe. Bruges prospered. It played host to merchants, bankers and moneylenders from 17 countries—Spaniards, English, Scots, Germans, Venetians, Lombards, Tuscans, Basques. Visiting merchants enjoyed a comparatively relaxed commercial environment, where there were few restrictions to buying and renting property, or to trading. The Venetians were the first to open a trading house of their own, in 1322, thus becoming the first foreign 'nation' in Bruges, and a regular postal service ran between Bruges and Venice, covering 1100km in seven days.

As the Hundred Years' War rumbled on, the aspirations of the Dukes of Burgundy became a cause for fierce conflict within France. **Charles VI** (r. 1380–1422) succeeded his father to the French throne; known as Charles the Mad, he was of unsound mind, and control of France seemed up for grabs—a prize contested by the Dukes of Orleans and Burgundy.

Now events became really complicated. In 1407 the Duke of Burgundy, **John the Fearless**, had Louis Duke of Orleans murdered, plunging France into civil war. John then negotiated with the English, offering to support **Henry V**'s claim to the French throne. Henry thereupon opened up a new campaign with his famous victory over the French at **Agincourt** in 1415.

As the English laid siege to Paris, John the Fearless, Duke of Burgundy, got cold feet. He attempted to negotiate with the new Duke of Orleans, but was himself murdered. In revenge John the Fearless' son, **Philip the Good** (r. 1419–67), gave his open support to the English, and had soon forced Charles VI to sign the **Treaty of Troyes**, in which Henry V was named as Charles' successor to the French throne.

But it was not to be. Henry V died just two months before Charles, and the throne went to Charles' son, **Charles VII** (r. 1422–61). The French then launched a new campaign, inspired by **Joan of Arc** (1412–31), and eventually pushed the English out of their lands.

Philip the Good had come to power at the age of 23. During his long reign Bruges enjoyed an era of unprecedented splendour. The Prinsenhof, an extensive palace in the city, became his main residence, and in 1429 Bruges became the capital of all the Burgundian domains, supplanting Dijon.

One of Bruges' great landmark events took place in 1430 when Philip the Good married **Isabella of Portugal** (his third wife). He had despatched his court painter, Jan van Eyck, to make a portrait of her to help make up his mind, and liked what he saw. Her arrival in Bruges and the celebration of her wedding was accompanied by one of the most stupendous beanfeasts of the medieval era. It was also marked by the foundation of the prestigious **Order of the Knights of the Golden Fleece**.

It was the greatest honour to be appointed a knight of the order, a title reserved for high-ranking nobility, even kings (Edward IV of England became one). Originally there were 23 knights, but membership expanded over time to 51. The basic idea was to uphold Christianity and the ideals of chivalry, and to settle any disputes between this ruling elite at the semi-religious conventions, called 'chapters', which were held at various locations within the Duchy of Burgundy. Bruges hosted three

The First Printed Book in English

One of the guests at the marriage of Charles the Bold and Margaret of York was the governor of the English Merchant Adventurers, a resident of the city since 1442. His name was **William Caxton**. He became the personal secretary to Margaret of York, who despatched him to Cologne to learn about a new-fangled invention called printing. Back in Bruges Caxton set up a press and produced the *Recuyell of the Historyes of Troye* in 1474—the first printed book in English, dedicated to Margaret of York. Two years later Caxton returned to England, and set up his press in Westmister. After his death his work was continued in Fleet Street by Wynkyn de Worde, who had been his assistant since the pioneering days in Bruges.

chapters: in 1431 in the church of St Donatian, in 1468 in the Onze-Lieve-Vrouwekerk, and in 1478 in the Sint-Salvatorskathedraal. In the latter two churches, the painted escutcheons of the knights can still be seen above the choir stalls where they sat.

The emblem of the order was a chain, with a sheep suspended as a pendant—a reminder of the Golden Fleece won by Jason and the Argonauts in the Greek myth, and a potent symbol, both of shining courage and of the importance of the wool trade. Wagging tongues suggested mischievously that it was also symbolic of the golden pubic hair of a Bruges beauty called Maria Crombrugghe, mistress of Philip the Good.

Bruges was by now a truly international city. Philip the Good was the richest man in Europe and his court was the height of European fashion, attracting some of the greatest men of the times—including composers, writers and painters. This was a dazzling period for Flemish art. **Jan van Eyck** worked and died in Bruges, and painted the *Adoration of the Mystic Lamb* here (now in Ghent Cathedral). **Hugo van der Goes** spent his last years in Bruges, whilst **Hans Memling** spent most of his working life in the city.

Philip died in 1467 and was succeeded by his son, **Charles the Bold** (r. 1467–77)—also known as Charles the Rash. The following year he married Margaret of York (his third wife), sister of Edward IV of England. This marriage was the second great highlight of Bruges' Burgundian age, celebrated with processions, feasts and jousting. The fountains flowed with wine, and at a lavish celebration at the Prinsenhof guests were wowed by such wonders as a choir of singing goats, a whale that opened up to reveal forty performers, and a vast pastry containing a whole orchestra.

Through this marriage, relationships with England could barely have been closer. When **Edward IV** was forced into temporary exile from 1470 to 1471 during the **Wars of the Roses**, Charles undertook to shelter him in Bruges. But Charles was not a popular ruler: he raised taxes, rashly renewed aggression against France, now under **Louis XI** (*r.* 1461–83), and was killed at the **Battle of Nancy**. Louis XI then seized the French part of Burgundy for France.

Charles' only heir was his daughter, **Mary**, who was thus left with just the Burgundian lands of the Low Countries. Aged only 20, she faced opposition from the Flemish cities and, to pacify them, she was obliged to give them greater powers of autonomy. Her rule was also undermined by subversion orchestrated by agents of Louis XI, who had plans to coerce her into marriage with his own son. But Mary's mother, **Margaret of York**, had a scheme to thwart the French: in 1477 she arranged a marriage between Mary and the 19-year-old **Archduke Maximilian I** (1459–1519), a member of the ruling German-Austrian Habsburg family, and future Holy Roman Emperor—as the heirs to the eastern Frankish kingdom liked to call themselves, in the style of Charlemagne.

Maximilian and Mary had two children, **Philip the Handsome**, and **Margaret of Austria**. Then, in 1482, aged just 25, Mary died when she fell from her horse while hunting, and her broken ribs punctured her lungs. She was buried in a splendid tomb in Bruges' Onze-Lieve-Vrouwekerk. Maximilian now assumed regency over the Burgundian Low Countries. He made himself deeply unpopular in Bruges by attempting to reduce the privileges of the citizens, while also increasing taxes. This triggered a revolt in 1488, and he was placed under house arrest for 21 days in the Craenenburg, overlooking the Markt. To show they meant business, the rebels executed his treasurer, **Pieter Lanchals**, in the square below. Maximilian hastily agreed to the terms for his release, which included pledges to respect Flemish privileges. But this promise was ignored by his father, **Emperor Frederick III**, who marched on the Flemish cities and brutally crushed all signs of revolt.

It was a critical turning point. From now on Bruges began its slow decline. Maximilian moved his court from Bruges to Ghent, and insisted that all foreign merchants leave. Although they returned in 1492, the damage was done. More vitally, dredging on the Zwin was not vigorously pursued, and the rising salt made access to the city ever more difficult. Sluis, 10km beyond Damme, had now became the avant-port, but even here the Zwin was choking.

Bruges had to concentrate on more localized trade. Antwerp's star was rising, and Bruges' key trading 'nations'—Germany, Italy and England—as well as many of its old merchant families, relocated. In 1505 the **Fuggers of Augsburg**, one of the most powerful merchant and banking families of Europe, shifted their business to Antwerp. The die was cast. Only the Spanish stayed on, maintaining a profitable trade in light textiles using Spanish wool. In the early decade of the 16th century some 5000 houses were standing empty in the city.

Emperor Charles V (1500–58)

In 1494 Maximilian became Holy Roman Emperor and passed control of the Low Countries to his son, Philip the Handsome. Two years later, Philip married Joanna of Castile, and they ruled Castile (effectively Spain) together for just one year (1506) before Philip died. This was enough, however, to assure the succession of their son, Charles V, to an unprecedentedly vast kingdom.

Charles V was by far the most powerful ruler of Europe in his day. Born in Ghent, he grew up in Mechelen and always regarded the Low Countries as his homeland. However, events and his restless energy took him much further afield, and for most of his reign the home countries were governed by his sister, **Mary of Hungary**.

In 1517 Charles took over the Spanish throne on the death of his grandfather. Then in 1520 he assumed the crown of Holy Roman Emperor after the death of Maximilian—taking with it Austria and Germany, Burgundy and the Low Countries, as well as the kingdoms of Naples and Sicily. He put down rebellions in Spain, defeated the Turks under Suleiman the Magnificent, and in Italy he fought the French under **François I** (*r.* 1515–47), his long-term rival, whom he succeeded in capturing at the **Battle of Pavia** (1525). As part of the settlement, under the Treaty of Cambrai of 1529, France was finally forced to give up its control of Flanders, after 685 years.

Meanwhile **Hernán Cortés** conquered Mexico (1521) and **Francisco Pizarro** conquered Peru (1532) in the name of Spain, bringing in not only vast new territories but also huge quantities of gold. The Age of Exploration was also an age of extravagance, fostering a get-rich-quick mentality in which huge sums were speculated on trading expeditions—to the Americas or the Far East—and the gains were spent lavishly on fancy buildings, paintings, banquets and feasting.

At home, land reclamation schemes, using dykes and windmills, began to push back the sea from the flat lands of the north, while the gardens of the Low Countries became the envy of Europe. Tapestry, pottery and glass were produced and exported, and the linen industry also took off, notably in Ghent and Kortrijk. By the 1560s Antwerp's population had risen to 100,000, but Bruges' had dropped to 30,000. Its merchants did not take up the opportunities which the era offered.

Religious Strife

Charles' reign coincided with the remarkable advances of Renaissance learning and art in northern Europe. The great humanist **Desiderius Erasmus** acted as adviser to Charles and went on to play a leading role in the development of

Leuven/Louvain University. Charles' own physician, **Andreas Vesalius** (1514–64) is now regarded as the father of modern anatomy. At the same time Bruges also emerged as an intellectual crossroads, a centre for humanism that brought together notable thinkers of the day such as Erasmus, the English humanist **Thomas More**, and the Spaniard **Juan Luis Vivés**.

The new thinking promoted by the Renaissance, however, smacked to some of subversion, and its most feared and controversial manifestation was **Protestantism**. **Martin Luther** posted his 95 theses to the church door of Wittenberg in 1517, and the course was set: the Reformation spread among the dissident German states and in the northern Netherlands. It was the one challenge that Charles was not equal to.

Bruges, with its open-house traditions and intellectual tolerance, welcomed the Reformation, but the potential for incandescent conflict quickly emerged. Condemnations for heresy were recorded as early as 1523, and the first execution took place in 1527 when a Protestant was burnt at the stake in the Burg. This became a regular activity in the city for the next 50 years. Meanwhile the people of the Low Countries were taxed heavily for the privilege of being part of Charles' mighty empire. It was, after all, expensive to run. When Ghent rebelled in 1540, Charles personally saw to a crushing suppression—a rude shock from their favourite son. Bruges escaped less vengeful treatment when it was brought to heel in 1548. In 1555, exhausted by his struggles, Charles announced from his palace in Brussels that he was abdicating: he gave his Spanish crown to his son Philip and the crown of the Holy Roman Empire to his brother Ferdinand.

The Low Countries did not take kindly to the fact that, shortly after the beginning of his reign, **Philip II** decided to rule at arm's length, from Spain. 'I would prefer to lose all my domains and die 100 times than rule over heretics,' Philip, a fanatical Catholic, is quoted as saying. He meant it, and the **Inquisition** was sent to the Low Countries in 1559 in order to apply its ruthless answer to Protestantism. All unconventional thinking came under the Inquisition's scrutiny, and Bruges stood in the firing line: many of its citizens had rejected the Roman Catholic faith in favour of Calvinism.

When heavy taxes were imposed to finance Philip's extravagant wars, resentment in the Low Countries boiled over into rebellion. Good citizens and Catholics were caught up in this mood, as well as the Protestants. The Low Countries had been placed under the governorship of **Margaret of Parma** (daughter of Charles V), who bore the brunt of increasingly vociferous criticism. The opposition found a champion in **William of Orange** ('the Silent'), whose forebear had been rewarded for his loyalty to Charles V with substantial estates in the Netherlands. William formed a **League of Nobility**, which appealed for moderation in the treatment of Protestants. Their petition, however, was roundly rejected by Margaret's advisers.

In 1566 the resentment of Calvinist Protestants turned to violence. Throughout the Low Countries they vented their pious wrath on the churches, vandalizing the interiors in an orgy of iconoclasm. More moderate forces recoiled in horror and swung back in favour of Margaret. William of Orange and the Governor of Flanders, Count Egmont, tried to find a compromise, but as events slipped out of control William withdrew to Germany.

Philip's answer was to send the **Duke of Alva** with 10,000 troops to restore order. He was assisted by the Inquisition, which set up the **'Council of Disorders'** (also known as the 'Council of Blood') and handed out 8000 death sentences; Count Egmont was among the victims. From 1568 William began a military campaign against Spanish rule, aided by a navy of privateers called the Sea Beggars. After several false starts, William gained the upper hand and took the towns of the Low Countries one by one. Facing mutinous troops and angry creditors, the Duke of Alva fled in 1573. William entered Brussels in triumph in 1576 and won Amsterdam in 1578. Protestants took over in Ghent in 1578, then invaded Bruges. The abbeys of Bruges were closed, the monks persecuted and expelled—three Franciscans were burnt at the stake—and many of the churches were ruthlessly swept clean of their remaining ornament. By 1581 Protestants had taken over all the city's churches.

However, Protestantism had many fierce critics in the southern half of the Low Countries—essentially modern Belgium. Here the bulk of the population clung more steadfastly to Roman Catholicism, and did not believe it shared a destiny with the Protestant provinces of the north—the modern Netherlands. Indeed, Catholics were now being persecuted in the north.

In 1578 Philip of Spain sent **Alexander Farnese, Duke of Parma**, into the south at the head of a large army, and he was rewarded by a series of capitulations in the French-speaking provinces. Many of these then signed the Union of Arras in 1579, declaring their allegiance to Spain. In response, the Protestant northern provinces—called the United Provinces—declared their independence and appointed William of Orange as their *stadhouder* (governor). The Duke of Parma pressed on north, retaking Bruges after a long siege in 1584, and Antwerp and

Brussels in 1585. Hundreds of citizens from Bruges fled to Holland, joining a flood of refugees from Flanders that would help fuel the Dutch Golden Age of the next century. Most of Flanders and the French-speaking provinces was now back in Spanish hands, and these lands became known as the Spanish Netherlands, with Brussels as the capital.

By this time Bruges was in dire economic straits. A canal driven through to Sluis in 1562 had already been defeated by the silt, and much of the city lay in ruins.

Just before his death in 1598, Philip II handed the Spanish Netherlands over to his daughter, the **Infanta Isabella** (1566–1633), and her husband, **Albert, Archduke of Austria** (1559–1621). The news was received with great joy in Brussels, and Isabella entered the city amid celebrations, sumptuously dressed and riding on a saddle studded with diamonds and rubies. The Spanish, however, still aspired to regain the United Provinces—but they insisted that only Catholicism would be tolerated. In 1601 Isabella refused to change her shirt for the duration of her husband's siege of Ostende; the siege lasted three years—and *isabelle* is now a colour, a sort of yellowy brown. The **Twelve Years' Truce** of 1609 sealed independence for the United Provinces, at which point a further 100,000 Protestants from Flanders emigrated across the border.

Europe's Battleground: the Spanish Netherlands (1579–1713)

For a while the Spanish Netherlands enjoyed a period of peace and prosperity. The mood is caught by the ebullient paintings of Rubens, who was court painter to Isabella and Albert. But Europe was overshadowed by the **Thirty Years' War** (1618–48), in which Protestants contested the power of the Catholic Habsburgs. Isabella and Albert took the opportunity to take up the cudgels once more against the United Provinces, which drove them into an alliance with the French in 1633. The lasting result was that **Philip IV of Spain** (*r.* 1605–65), desperate to be able to turn all his military strength on France, signed the **Peace of Münster** in 1648, which gave formal recognition to the independence of the United Provinces. The terms of the treaty allowed the United Provinces to stop all traffic through the mouth of the River Scheldt, which ran through territory now controlled by them. Antwerp's and Ghent's access to the sea was sealed off and their fortunes doomed until Napoleon lifted the ban 150 years later.

For Bruges, there was some optimism during this turmoil. In 1613 a new canal was opened to connect the city with Ghent, which had direct access to the sea via a canal completed in 1547. Then in 1622 a canal was opened to Ostend. This proved fortuitous when the Scheldt was closed under the Peace of Münster. In 1665 a new mercantile dock, the Handelskom, was opened in the north of Bruges and the canal to Ostend was widened. Trade picked up, but Bruges was a mere shadow of its former self. Meanwhile, the old city walls were updated to current military thinking and converted into large earth ramparts.

Spain's conflict with France was a running sore throughout the 17th century, and inevitably the Spanish Netherlands were drawn into it. When **William III of Orange**, *stadhouder* of the United Provinces, became king of England in 1689 by virtue of his marriage to **Mary**, Protestant daughter of James II, the stage was set for a major big-power conflict.

The first phase was the **War of the Grand Alliance** (1690–7), designed to put an end to the expansionist exploits of **Louis XIV** of France. In the Spanish Netherlands the conflict was inconclusive, with a series of sieges by Louis' forces— including, temporarily, of Bruges. France came out the loser in the war, but Louis' antics were not over yet. In 1700 Charles II of Spain died—the last of the Spanish Habsburgs. Charles had no direct heir, so he passed the crown of Spain to **Philip, Duke of Anjou**, the grandson of Louis XIV. Louis leaned upon Philip to hand over the Spanish Netherlands to France, but such a solution was unacceptable to either England or the United Provinces of the Netherlands, who greatly feared the French domination of Europe.

The result was the **War of the Spanish Succession** (1701–13). England, the Netherlands, Austria and many German states formed an alliance against France, and the brilliant generalship of the **Duke of Marlborough** and Prince Eugene of Savoy drove the French out of the Spanish Netherlands, but not before the armies had raged across Flanders. Ghent and Bruges changed hands twice, while the allies won two victories on Belgian soil: at Ramillies (1706), near Namur, and Oudenaarde (1708), southwest of Ghent.

At the end of the war France was left in tatters. In the **Treaty of Utrecht** it renounced its claims to the Spanish Netherlands, which passed into the hands of **Charles VI**, the Habsburg Emperor of Austria, and became the Austrian Netherlands. This high-handed reassignment of ownership was bitterly resented in some quarters.

The Austrian Netherlands (1713–94) and the Age of Napoleon

Charles VI of Austria had no male heir, so in 1713 he announced a 'pragmatic sanction'—eventually accepted by most of the European powers—that the succession would pass into the female line through his daughter **Maria Theresa**. However, when Charles died in 1740 the European powers disregarded this arrangement and Maria Theresa had to contend with the **War of the Austrian Succession** (1740–8), a complex conflict in which rivalries between France,

Britain and the United Provinces of the Netherlands were played out across most of Europe, as well as in North America. Bruges was occupied by French troops from 1744 to 1748. Maria Theresa emerged from the war with her succession affirmed, and the Austrian Netherlands then enjoyed several decades of prosperity.

In 1741 Maria Theresa put these provinces in the hands of her enlightened brother-in-law, **Charles of Lorraine** (1712–80), who set up a dazzling court in Brussels, famed for its generous and elegant hospitality and its ceaseless round of masked balls and merrymaking. The sedate neoclassical style was adopted for ambitious building projects, and spread as far as Bruges, where the old medieval Waterhalle on the Markt was pulled down and replaced by a stately neoclassical building in 1786.

Industry was transformed by investment; new roads connected the cities and linked Brussels to Vienna. But while the aristocracy partied, draped in voluminous lace and eating off the finest European porcelain, the poor faced crowded, insanitary conditions exacerbated by high levels of unemployment. In Bruges, this was the era when the greatest number of almshouses were created.

Charles of Lorraine died in 1780 and Maria Theresa died five months later, to be succeeded by her son, **Joseph II**. He was in many ways a child of the Enlightenment, and introduced various reforms—in education and administration, as well as freedom of worship—which allowed Protestants to build churches, to become full citizens, and to take up public office. He ordered the destruction of old city walls (emblems of the past): Bruges' walls were pulled down between 1782 and 1784, with the exception of the city gates. Monasteries that served no social purpose were also closed—an edict that hit Bruges particularly hard since it had accumulated a large religious community with over 1000 monks and nuns.

For all Joseph's good intentions, his reforms were interpreted in Belgium as the unwelcome meddling of a despot. He simply went too far and too fast: he tried, for example, to streamline Austrian government by centralizing power in Vienna; and in 1784 announced that German was to be the official language of the empire. With the Age of Enlightenment came the rumblings of intellectual discontent.

A vociferous opposition arose, composed of two quite different tendencies: on the one hand there were the liberals who wanted to expel the Habsburgs in favour of a democratic, modern state; on the other there were the Catholic conservatives and aristocracy, who looked back nostalgically to the *ancien régime* of Maria Theresa. The latter were led by **Henri van der Noot**, who, following an insurrection in 1788, became the main voice of the opposition. This was in stark contrast to the fervently radical political atmosphere which carried the French Revolution the following year.

Nonetheless, the Revolution in France inspired an uprising in Belgium, and when this was crushed by the Austrians at Turnhout, the whole country rose to the call in what has become known as the **Brabançon Revolt**. In January 1790 the provinces agreed to form their own Congress, with Van der Noot as its prime minister, and they unilaterally proclaimed an independent United States of Belgium, which was readily recognized by England, Holland and Prussia.

But events were about to overtake this first attempt at Belgian nationhood. In February 1790 Joseph II died, to be replaced by **Leopold II** (*r.* 1790–2) who immediately despatched troops to crush the revolution and returned Belgium to the Austrian fold. However, in 1792 the French Revolutionary Armies went to war against Austria and quickly scored a success at Jemappes (near Tournai). They had enthusiastic supporters in Bruges, who greeted the victory by demolishing the statues of the Counts on the Stadhuis as the carillon in the Belfort rang out the **Marseillaise**. Austria expelled the French in 1793, but the following year the French Revolutionary Armies under **Marshal Jourdan** finally scored the decisive victory at Fleurus (near Charleroi), thus ending Austrian rule in Belgium.

The French were welcomed by many Belgians as an army of liberation—one that heralded the advent of a modern state in which merit, not family connections and wealth, would be rewarded. Initially the French proceeded carefully, wisely respecting the power of the Church and Belgian autonomy. But to many of the more radical French revolutionaries, Belgian Catholicism was anachronistic and a hindrance to change.

In October 1795 Belgium was absorbed into France and religion was suppressed. The churches were closed: many were vandalized and appropriated as stables, warehouses and factories; others were auctioned off as state property. This was the fate of many churches and abbeys in Bruges, while its fine old church on the Burg, St Donatian's, was demolished in 1799. This, as well as the humiliation and hounding of the priesthood, caused deep resentment.

It was relieved to some extent in 1800 when, under the rule of the **Consulate**, priests were released from hard labour, returned from exile and began holding services in private houses. Meanwhile citizens held 'dry masses', without priests, in the ruins of the churches. The Concordat in 1801 between **Pope Pius VII** and **Napoleon** saw the beginnings of a slow return to normality.

Despite his charisma as leader of the young French state, Napoleon failed to win over the Belgians. In 1815, when he was finally defeated by the allies (Britain, Prussia, Austria and Russia) at **Waterloo**, just south of Brussels, the majority of Belgians celebrated his downfall too. They thought their hour had come.

A 19th-century Tourist

It can no longer boast of being the emporium of the trade of all nations, and of having consuls from every kingdom of Europe...

The East India trade no longer comes through the Red Sea, by Alexandria to Genoa and Venice, and the cities of London and Amsterdam have gained the trade of the wood, the tallow, the hemp, the tar, and the iron of Scandinavia. Such as it is, Bruges is still a great and respectable city...

The numerous nobles and opulent merchants retired from trade, who are domiciliated in it, impart an elegance and dignity to the manners of the people. The streets, though narrow, are clean, and the houses are lofty and spacious.

Tour Through Belgium, James Mitchell (1816)

The United Kingdom of the Netherlands (1815–31) and the 1830 Revolution

It hadn't. The **Congress of Vienna** in 1815 decided instead to create the United Kingdom of the Netherlands, tacking Belgium on to the Netherlands and entrusting it to the care of **William of Orange** (called William I).

It was an insensitive decision: all the historic resentments about big-power carve-ups and about rule by a Protestant Netherlands, combined with the aspirations to Belgian nationhood, gave William I an impossible task. He was not exactly a master of diplomacy: he tried to impose Dutch as the national language of the whole country, and he failed to grant Belgium fair representation in the States General (the Netherlands parliament). Above all, he was Protestant.

All the while, the economy of Belgium was beginning to stir with the **Industrial Revolution**. Ghent became the centre of a vibrant textile industry, but Bruges slumbered. However, it was appointed the capital of the province of West Flanders, and maintained a certain dignity in its repose, now witnessed by the new trail of tourists from Britain who passed through the city on the way to visit the battlefield of Waterloo.

In 1830 the July Revolution in France removed the revisionist **King Charles X** (*r.* 1824–30) and put the more egalitarian **Louis Philippe** (*r.* 1830–48) in his place. In Belgium, too, revolt was in the air. On 25 August a new opera called *La Muette de Portici* (The Dumb Girl of Portici) by the contemporary French composer Daniel-François-Esprit Auber was performed at the Théâtre de la Monnaie in Brussels. The story concerns a revolutionary called Masaniello who led an uprising in Naples against the Spanish in 1647.

Such sentiments as, 'Far better to die than to live a wretched life in slavery and shame! Away with the yoke before which we tremble; away with the foreigner who laughs at our torment!' incited the audience to a ferment. They ran out to join a workers' demonstration already taking place in the Place de la Monnaie, stormed the Palais de Justice, drove out the Dutch garrison and raised the flag of Brabant over the Hôtel de Ville. Barricades were erected and uprisings spread throughout the provinces. William of Orange responded by sending in the troops, which defeated the rebels at Hasselt.

On 23 September the Dutch troops advanced on Brussels and four days of street fighting ensued. Gradually the Dutch were confined to what is now the Parc de Bruxelles, surrounded by revolutionaries. From there, during the night of 27 September, the Dutch simply melted away. Brussels was free. On 4 October the Provisional Government declared Belgium independent, but the fighting was not quite over yet. In the northeast of the country volunteers (dressed in their distinctive indigo-blue tunics) took on Dutch troops and battled to free Ghent and Antwerp, which finally fell to them in 1832, with the support of the French.

The New Nation Flourishes

Largely because Belgium's revolution was widely supported by the nobility and was not simply the work of an unruly rabble, independence was accepted by the international community at the London Conference of 1831. The European powers also insisted on Belgian neutrality.

Since constitutional monarchy was in vogue, the Belgians then looked for a king, and Prince Leopold of Saxe-Coburg, an uncle of Queen Victoria, agreed to take the throne as **King Leopold I** (r. 1831–65). He was given a rousing welcome by the people of Bruges as he passed through on his way from London to Brussels. In 1832 Leopold married Louise-Marie, daughter of King Louis Philippe of France, thus sealing the friendship between the two nations.

Belgium's 1830 constitution embodied many jealously guarded liberties, such as freedom of speech, of the press, and of association. As a result it became a refuge for numerous writers and intellectuals, such as **Karl Marx** and **Victor Hugo**, and something of a cultural and artistic melting pot. This also helped to fuel a constant fear of subversion on the part of the authorities: in the late 1840s Bruges came close to revolution as the city swelled with refugees from the crisis in farming, and as the price of linen—now one of its staple industries—collapsed. The poorer quarters of the city were crammed with inadequate one-room slums, where unemployment, alcoholism, typhoid and cholera were rife. In 1847 starving rioters attacked the bakeries in a desperate search for food. But Belgium weathered the European-wide spirit of revolt.

Leopold I was succeeded by his son **Leopold II** (*r.* 1865–1909), a man with great ambitions for his nation. During his reign Belgium was transformed into a modern industrial state, drawing on its great reserves of coal to fuel its new factories, producing iron and steel, textiles and pottery. Leopold II may be seen as Belgium's equivalent of Queen Victoria: both presided over what in retrospect appears to be an age of rapid progress and modernization accompanied by a sense of national pride and dignity, and a growing empire. In Leopold's case this was the **Belgian Congo**, which he ruled with cruel tyranny as a personal fiefdom until 1908. But again Bruges missed the boat of economic development.

Fanny Trollope (mother of the novelist Anthony), wrote in her *Belgium and Western Germany* (1833):

> *When the monopoly was transferred to Antwerp, both the splendour and activity of Bruges declined; and I was very gravely assured, that its principal trade at present is in beer and manure… In fact, there is no appearance of commerce in any part of the city… Many of the houses are extremely handsome, and almost all appear comfortable, and scrupulously clean. I never saw a city in which so little appearance of poverty met the eye…I was told that sixteen thousand of the inhabitants (the whole number being thirty-seven thousand) receive aid from public charities.*

Much of this charity was supplied by the almshouses, still an invaluable feature of the city, and an essential contributor to its survival.

This was a period in which the French-speaking south prospered at the expense of the Flemish north. The Walloons tended to be the pit-owners, the industrialists, the magnates. French, formerly the language of the nobility and the educated, was the language of success; indeed Flemish was not recognized as an official language of equal value until 1898. For many of the Flemish, cast as the workforce of the nation, life was a Dickensian nightmare of drudgery and squalor. Women and children worked in the mines until the 1890s, half a century after this practice had been outlawed in Britain. This transparent inequality was expressed in a growing Flemish movement, initially linguistic and literary, but later political.

Undisturbed by the industrial revolution, trapped in the past and gently mouldering, Bruges appealed to the Romantics—from those who revelled in fantasies about the Middle Ages, as evoked by writers such as Sir Walter Scott, to those of the dark and Gothic bent.

The French poet **Charles Baudelaire**, never a great fan of things Belgian, came to Bruges during his exile from France (1864–6) and wrote: 'Ghostly town, mummified town, more or less preserved. One great work attributed to Michelangelo. It smells of death, the Middle Ages, Venice, the jack-o'-lanterns, the tombs.— *Béguinage*. Carillons. Yet Bruges itself is also decaying.' From his pen, this was almost praise.

British neo-medievalists fell in love with the city, and helped to initiate a programme of renovation and (sometimes heavy-handed) restoration. But just as this work was putting a fresh face on many of the delapidated vestiges of the medieval past, Bruges' reputation for decay was sealed by a novella called *Bruges-la-Morte* (Bruges the Dead) by the Belgian symbolist writer **Georges Rodenbach** (1855–98). The pronouncement of death was premature. In 1907 the Boudewijn Canal was built to link Bruges with a new port at Zeebrugge. Completed in 1907, it encouraged the beginnings of an industrial base.

The Two World Wars

By the early 20th century the European nations were again jostling dangerously with each other for pre-eminence, both within Europe and across the continents that they had carved up between them. In June 1914 the assassination in Sarajevo of the **Archduke Ferdinand**, heir to the Austro-Hungarian throne, triggered off a complicated system of alliances that dragged all the great powers of Europe into war. Germany invaded Belgium, breaching its neutrality, and came to a grinding halt close to the Belgian border with France. Three years of devastatingly costly trench warfare ensued. The beautiful medieval and Renaissance trading city of Ypres (Ieper) found itself at the heart of the conflict, and was flattened. The nearby region around **Passchendaele** was the scene of further carnage (1917–18), in which 245,000 British troops died.

The German occupying powers treated the Belgians harshly, brutally suppressing opposition, confiscating property and commandeering labour to work in Germany. Meanwhile the King of Belgium, **Albert I** (*r.* 1909–34), nephew of Leopold II, led the Belgian army in a spirited defence from the polders (reclaimed land) around the River Yser in northwest Belgium, causing havoc to the Germans by opening the sluice gates to flood the land. His persistence and fortitude endeared this 'Soldier King' to his nation.

After the First World War Belgium was left to pick up the pieces. Like the rest of Europe it faced the huge task of reconstruction against the background of **the Depression**. Many of Bruges' canal and port facilities had been destroyed in the war, setting back its agenda of prospective development.

The 1930s was a bleak decade, economically and politically. Albert I died when rock-climbing near Namur in 1934. He was succeeded by his son, **Leopold III** (*r.* 1934–51), but fortune soon struck a second cruel blow when the new king's wife, the beautiful Princess Astrid of Sweden, was killed in a motoring accident in

Switzerland in 1935. Belgium had renounced its neutrality after the war, but in the early 1930s the rise of **Adolf Hitler** in Germany began to send shudders through the nation. Belgium reasserted its neutrality in 1936, but to little avail. On 10 May 1940 Germany invaded the Netherlands and Belgium, and Leopold III surrendered.

The Belgian government found exile in England, but Leopold III stayed on. The German army of occupation gradually turned the screws on the Belgian people, transporting workers to factories in Germany, rounding up the Jews (25,000 Belgian Jews died in the war), meeting any activity of the Belgian Resistance movement with harsh reprisals. It was a time of immense bravery: Jews were concealed by non-Jewish families for years, and downed Allied pilots were spirited back across the Channel by clandestine Resistance networks at incalculable personal risk. Belgium also had its share of Nazi sympathizers and home-grown Fascists, particularly—but by no means exclusively—among the Flemish population, who were already disenchanted with Belgian nationhood and the traditional dominance of the French-speaking south. The Nazis were happy to exploit these tensions, and accorded Flanders a special status. There were even two Flemish units of the SS (the dreaded German security forces), which helped to run Belgium's own concentration camp at Breendonk.

Belgium was liberated in September 1944, but Allied progress very nearly came unstuck in December. As the nation settled down to enjoy its first Christmas in freedom for five years, German tank divisions under Field Marshal von Rundstedt launched a last-ditch counteroffensive across the Ardennes (the **Battle of the Bulge**), and bombed Antwerp and Liège. But eventually the Germans were pushed back. The offensive had cost them a total of 120,000 men and contributed to the rapid conclusion of the war.

Post-War Prosperity and Federalization

Belgium was free again, but immediately encountered a constitutional crisis about the controversial role of Leopold III during the war. Some argued that he had spared the nation a calamity by surrendering; and that he had suffered as an effective prisoner of the Germans, who had confined him to his palace at Laeken, then deported him to Germany in 1944. Many British military analysts argue that, by holding out against massive odds for 18 days, Leopold's 60,000 troops had permitted the Allied evacuation at Dunkirk. (Churchill had deliberately avoided informing Leopold of the evacuation, and sent a cable to Lord Gort, commander in chief of the British Expeditionary forces, saying: 'We are asking the Belgians to sacrifice themselves for us.' His vilification of Leopold after the war was considered quite shameful by many, including George VI.) In Belgium, however, Leopold's performance was compared unfavourably with that of his father, Albert I, in the

First World War, and many hinted darkly at collaboration. His wartime marriage to a commoner, Mary Lilian Baels, in 1941 didn't help.

Leopold's brother Charles stood in as regent from 1944 to 1950, and during this period Socialists and Communists (mainly from Wallonia) campaigned actively to form a republic. While Leopold III remained in self-imposed exile in Switzerland, a referendum showed that 57 per cent of the nation favoured his return—but the fact that 58 per cent of Walloons voted against it was effectively a thumbs down. He returned to Belgium nonetheless, but the mood soon turned ugly. Violent clashes resulted in three deaths, and Belgium seemed on the brink of civil war. In 1951, under pressure from Walloon socialists, Leopold III abdicated in favour of his son (by Queen Astrid), **Baudouin I** (*r.* 1951–93), hoping thereby to restore unity. These hopes were justified: Baudouin, although only 21 years old, demonstrated an exceptional ability to heal the rifts in the nation.

Since the war Belgium has once again found its historic form as a major industrial and trading nation. Like other European countries, it had to give up its colonial economy, and it granted independence to the **Congo** (later Zaire) in 1960—although it was much criticized for its haste. It also had to go through the painful transition from heavy industry towards the light and service industries. This effectively removed the trump cards from the hands of the French-speaking south in favour of the Flemish north. Bruges took a part in this. Its link to the sea was restored during the 1950s, laying the foundations for a thriving industrial sector (set well away from the historic city) producing glass, electrical goods and chemicals.

The language divide, exploited successfully by politicians from both communities, has resulted in an increasingly devolved, federal system of government, with an undercurrent of tension. Under the '**St-Michel Accords**' of 1993, Belgian federalization was further reinforced, with the result that Belgium is now effectively ruled by three regional governments (Wallonia, Flanders and Brussels), overseen by a national government.

In its post-war history, the **European Community/Union** has proved a godsend to Belgium in two ways. Belgium was a founder member of the EEC, and Brussels, geographically at the heart, became its headquarters in the 1960s, with all the attention, status and income that that entails. Bruges became the seat of **Europa College**, founded in 1949, a respected postgraduate centre for European studies, which maintains the city's long cosmopolitan tradition.

In addition, Belgium's view of itself within the political framework of Europe—a Europe seen as a confederation of nations—has allowed it to accommodate a confederation within its own boundaries. By defining itself in terms of Europe, there is less pressure to define itself as a nation. But this has still not been enough to dampen the ardour of many Flemish people who want nothing to do with their Walloon counterparts, and see the French-speaking south virtually as a foreign country. Meanwhile Flanders has developed into one of the most prosperous regions of the European Union.

Throughout so much of its history Belgium has stood between competing nations, earning itself the sobriquet 'the cockpit of Europe'. History has taught it to be flexible and agile, and given it the ability to accept with grace what has become respectfully known as the 'Belgian Compromise'. It remains to be seen whether this essential characteristic of the nation is strong enough to prevent the country falling apart in the new millennium. But Bruges has always had an independent spirit, and traditionally regards itself as an autonomous entity rather than a bit part in the game of regional politics. Its true status in the new millennium will be on universal display when it becomes a Cultural Capital of Europe in 2002—also the 700th anniversary of the Battle of the Golden Spurs.

The Swans of Bruges

The coat of arms of Pieter Lanchals includes a swan—a play on words on his name, from the Dutch *lang* (long) and *hals* (neck). Archduke Maximilian bitterly resented the execution of Lanchals, his treasurer, by the Bruges rebels in 1488. The story goes that he made the citizens of Bruges pay penance by commanding them to keep swans on their canals in perpetuity, as a constant reminder of their misdeed. Even today the municipality keeps a controlled flock of swans, identified by a Gothic b inscribed on the side of the beak. It is clearly a myth that Maximilian was responsible for their introduction to the canals: they were here well before his time. But the myth carries with it the haunting memory of a historical truth.

Art and Architecture

Belgium has an enviable artistic heritage. It can lay claim to a host of exceptional painters who have become household names: Bruegel, Rubens, Van Dyck, Magritte. But Bruges is celebrated above all for its set of supreme artists who emerged in the late Middle Ages, and—thriving on the rich patronage of this great trading city— showed what the new medium of oil painting could achieve. Jan van Eyck, Rogier van der Weyden and Hans Memling all lived and worked in these streets, and although their work now hangs in galleries around the world, Bruges has managed to hold on to a rich collection, seen above all in the Groeningemuseum.

But as the Groeningemuseum vividly demonstrates, Belgian art is a bigger story than the work of these so-called 'primitives', and so what follows is a canter through its entire history to the present day, with notes about the architecture that evolved in parallel.

The Middle Ages

For over 700 years, until the Renaissance, the main inspiration for European art and architecture was the Church. When Charlemagne set up his court in Aachen in the late 8th century, it attracted some of the leading manuscript illustrators of the day; illuminated books remained one of the chief fields of artistic endeavour in the Low Countries for five centuries. One of the best-known series of illuminations, the *Très Riches Heures du Duc de Berry*, was produced by friars from the province of Limburg in around 1411.

The achievements of architecture during the Middle Ages were likewise principally ecclesiastical. The chief influences came from France, and for about 150 years after the 11th century the **Romanesque** style (called Norman in Britain) predominated. Romanesque churches were robust and solid, with massive supporting columns and semicircular arches. (They were supposedly influenced by Roman architecture, hence the name.)

If you look at the cross section of two intersecting rounded arches, you will see a pointed arch. This became the leading motif of the next phase of architecture, which evolved in the mid 12th century and was later dubbed **Gothic** by Renaissance architects, who considered it a barbarian perversion of the classical ideal. Architects now attempted to create magical illusions of space and light, filling walls with huge, elongated windows held in place by delicate columns and supported by external buttresses.

Flanders developed its own distinctive form of **Scheldt** (or Scaldian) **Gothic**: robust and sturdy, clinging on to Romanesque solidity with the tendency to fill in corners with towers, or by the use of polygonal ground plans. Because of the scarcity of stone, brick was often used, seen most strikingly in the towering spire of the Onze-Lieve-Vrouwekerk in Bruges. However, in the 14th century an increasingly frothy and flamboyant Gothic style was adopted, applied not just to churches, but also to civic architecture. The Stadhuis of Bruges (1376–1420) was a pioneer in this trend, setting a standard in exuberant self-confidence that was soon mirrored in other Flemish city halls.

Manuscript illuminations were highly detailed, brightly coloured and demonstrated great technical skills in portraiture and the depiction of textiles and artefacts. These same talents were put to work when oil painting was developed in the 15th century. Previously, any large-scale paintings had had to be done on the walls, but although fresco painting might have been appropriate in Italy, where it had been used since Roman times, it was not a suitable technique for the damp conditions of northern Europe. Oil paints, however, provided the ideal solution: a broad range of rich colours could be manufactured and applied to wooden panels with great control to give the kind of detail and intense coloration that were achieved in illuminated manuscripts. Furthermore, the paintings were now easily portable, which helped to create a new kind of art market.

Jan van Eyck (1390–1441) was the first artist to demonstrate the full potential of oil painting, and he produced some of the most dazzling work of the late medieval period. *The Adoration of the Mystic Lamb* (1426–32; painted with his brother Hubert) in Ghent cathedral is one of the supreme masterpieces of European art, full of saintliness and sensuality and luminescent detail. His second greatest work is the most prized possession of the Groeningemuseum: the *Madonna with Canon van der Paele* (1436).

Born in Ghent, but based in Bruges after 1430, Jan van Eyck was official painter to Philip the Good, Duke of Burgundy, who presided over an economic boom in the Low Countries. He is one of the earliest Flemish painters known to us by name, as he signed his work. At that time painters worked in guilds, usually remaining anonymous, hence speculative titles such as the Master of the St Lucy Legend. But as van Eyck was in the duke's employ, he was not subject to the restrictions imposed by the painter's guild.

As in Florence, the painters' guild in Bruges went by the name of St Luke's, patron saint of painters. Almost all the leading artists were members of the guild, which negotiated terms of contracts, the payments, the dimensions of the work commissioned, use of colour and so on. They worked for wealthy patrons, such as the nobility, merchants and city officials, who by and large commissioned them to paint sacred subjects—often church altarpieces before which prayers could be said for their souls after death. But increasingly in this era painters were called upon to do straightforward portraits, thus freeing art from the constraints of sacred subject matter. Jan van Eyck's *Arnolfini Marriage* (1434; in the National Gallery, London) is one of the most remarkable examples of this. Giovanni Arnolfini was a wealthy merchant from Lucca who settled in Bruges in 1420, and married here in 1434. Like many paintings of this era—secular or religious—it offers a fascinating insight into the quality of life of the well-to-do of the time, from the sumptuous textiles and furs, to the upholstery and ornately carved furnishings.

Petrus Christus (*c.* 1420–72), who came to Bruges from Ghent in 1444, may have studied under van Eyck; certainly he was strongly influenced by him, and he evokes a similar mood of silent wonder and spirituality with the same infinitely patient attention to detail. The Groeningemuseum has a number of his works (all panels of larger works), including *Isabella of Portugal and St Elizabeth* (*c.* 1458), portraying the wife of Philip the Good in her embroidered finery.

Van Eyck's place at Philip the Good's court was later taken by his pupil, **Rogier van der Weyden** (*c.* 1400–64), whose religious paintings are emotionally charged and full of stress, as in his great triptych, *The Seven Sacraments* (in the Koninklijk Museum voor Schone Kunsten, Antwerp). He spent much of his career in Brussels, but a contemporary copy of his *Philip the Good* is in the Groeningemuseum.

Other major names of this late medieval period include **Dirk Bouts** (1415–75) and **Hugo van der Goes** (?1435–82) who, although gifted artists in their own right, worked together on the painfully lurid *Triptych with the Martyrdom of St Hippolytus* (*c.* 1468) in the Groeningemuseum.

But in Bruges the only figure who really matches van Eyck in stature is **Hans Memling** (1435–94): the rich collection of his work commissioned by the Sint-Jansshospitaal is still normally housed in its chapel over 500 years on. Born near Frankfurt in Germany, Memling came to Bruges in the 1460s, and soon became one of the most successful and the wealthiest painters of the Burgundian era. His work is like an illuminated manuscript writ large, often filled with an exquisite tenderness, found in the gesture and portraiture. His most extraordinary piece is the *St Ursula Shrine*, an ornate casket with 14 jewel-like painted panels.

Gerard David (*c.* 1460–1523) carried these traditions into the 16th century, bringing a new richness and density of composition to works such as *The Judgement of Cambyses* (1498).

A distinctive mark of the work of these artists, however, was a limited understanding of space: perspective is either not rendered with complete confidence, or shows overmuch concern; landscapes are naïve, and groups of people are often packed slightly too close together. These problems were addressed by the next great phase of painting in the Low Countries.

The Renaissance

The Renaissance was a watershed between the medieval and the modern world, a long and gradual phenomenon that began in Italy in the 13th century and lasted for some 300 years. It was triggered by the rediscovery of classical learning and literature, and the gradual realization that not only had the Greeks and Romans achieved rather more than the medieval world in terms of science, medicine, architecture and philosophy, but that they had done so without the assistance of Christianity. The Renaissance, therefore, effectively freed people from the straitjacket of purely Christian teaching and encouraged them to approach all questions with an open mind.

Italian art and architecture were the leaders of fashion during the Renaissance, and accomplished artists from northern Europe travelled to Italy to admire and learn from the likes of Leonardo da Vinci, Michelangelo, Titian and Tintoretto. The Italian Renaissance, however, was only partially assimilated in the Low Countries. Although architects were happy to borrow Renaissance motifs, such as classical columns and garlands of flowers, their application of these was mainly cosmetic: their Renaissance façades were essentially adaptations of the traditional step gable (which had been around since the 11th century) tacked on to traditional Flemish houses. Bruges proved particularly resistant: Renaissance influence can be seen, for example, in the façade of the Oude Griffie in the Burg, but this is more the exception than the rule; the Gothic style remained popular even into the 17th century.

The heyday of the **North European Renaissance** was the 16th century, but this coincided with the decline of Bruges as a trading centre—and the rise of Antwerp. Art followed the money, and Antwerp became the main artistic centre in the southern Low Countries, while Brussels became the centre of power.

Flemish painting now followed two main tendencies. One set of artists was directly influenced by Italian painting: **Quentin Metsys** (1466–1530) represents the link between the medieval world and the Renaissance; his *The Lineage of St Anne* (c. 1508; in the Musea voor Schone Kunsten, Brussels) shows a real understanding of architectural perspective, and also uses the kind of hazy, distant blue landscape so beloved of Leonardo da Vinci. **Jan Provoost** (1465–1529) studied at Metsys' studio in Antwerp before coming to Bruges in 1494; his *Crucifixion* in the Groeningemuseum clearly shows the influence of the Italian Renaissance.

Bernard van Orley (c. 1499–1541) brought the Renaissance to Brussels, both in painting and in his designs for tapestry and stained glass. Other 'Romanists' include van Orley's pupil **Michiel Coxie** (1499–1592), who lived in Rome in the 1530s, and **Jan Gossaert of Mauberge** (1478–1532) (also known as Mabuse), who painted the first classically inspired nudes in Flemish art.

The most overtly classically inspired artist working in Bruges was **Lancelot Blondeel** (1498–1531), the painter, sculptor and architect responsible for the triumphant monumental chimney piece in the Renaissancezaal van het Brugse Vrije (1528–31) in the Burg. He also had a line in highly individualistic religious paintings, in which elaborate and fantastical architectural decoration takes precedence over the main subjects.

Meanwhile, followers of the second tendency developed a more independent Flemish style of painting, reflecting the distinctive outlook and heritage of the Low Countries. Supreme among them was **Pieter Bruegel the Elder** (c. 1525–69), who trained in Antwerp and whose trip to Italy in about 1551 appears to have left him unmoved. His interest lay in the people and landscape of his homeland: even when painting a classical subject such as his famous *Fall of Icarus* (1567; in the Musea voor Schone Kunsten, Brussels) his main focus is rural life, leaving poor Icarus' plight as virtually incidental. Bruegel was particularly successful in translating religious scenes into Flemish village life, breathing into them a new poignancy and relevance. Another line of work took him into the realms of bizarre fantasy associated with the Dutch painter Hieronymus Bosch (1450–1516)—as in *The Fall of Rebel Angels* (1562).

In 1563 Pieter Bruegel moved to Brussels and married. He had two sons late in life, both of whom became painters in their own right well after their father's death. **Pieter Bruegel the Younger** (1564–1638) painted numerous versions of his father's work, using a more polished style that somehow lacks the naïve spontaneity of his father's paintings (of which only some 40 examples have survived). His younger brother **Jan 'Velvet' Bruegel** (1568–1625) is celebrated for his landscapes and his delicate flower paintings.

Bruges and the rest of the Low Countries went through a traumatic period of religious strife at the end of the 16th century, during which many of the churches were destroyed by Protestant iconoclasts. In addition, Bruges was now in terminal commercial decline. This sombre period is reflected in the work of the last notable Bruges artist of the early era, **Pieter Pourbus** (c. 1523–84), who is celebrated more for his portraits than for his rather heavy-handed religious works, influenced by the Italian mannerists. He married Lancelot Blondeel's daughter and founded a dynasty of distinguished painters (Frans the Older and Frans the Younger).

Antwerp's Golden Age

A measure of stability returned during the 17th century, and now the Counter-Reformation brought its own flourish in both art and architecture.

Antwerp remained a cultural centre in the Low Countries during the 17th century largely because of one remarkable genius: **Pieter Paul Rubens** (1577–1640). In his twenties, he lived and worked in Italy for eight years, where he was strongly influenced by the work of Michelangelo, Titian and his contemporary Caravaggio, returning to Antwerp in 1608 with a glittering reputation; the following year he became court painter to Archduke Albert and the Infanta Isabella. His *Raising of the Cross* (1610) and *Descent from the Cross* (1612) for Antwerp Cathedral caused a sensation.

Rubens' ability to handle vast paintings on dramatic subjects was unsurpassed. His compositions carry the eye through the paintings with a unique vigour, assisted by his deft, virtuoso touch, often applied in thin, almost sketchy layers of paint. Throughout almost all his work there is a lusty, life-enhancing quality, very Flemish in nature.

After his first wife died in 1625, Rubens entered the diplomatic service. He travelled to Spain and England in an effort to broker peace, and he was rewarded for his services in England by a knighthood. He also won several major commissions in both countries (including the ceilings of the Banqueting House in Whitehall, London). He maintained a flow of work right up to the end of his life, bringing his total oeuvre to over 2000 major paintings.

The other two great Antwerp painters of this era were both closely associated with Rubens. **Antoon (Anthony) van Dyck** (1599–1641) was celebrated for his sedate portraits, which capture the solemnity and dignity of the affluent—notably after he became court artist to Charles I of England in 1632. **Jacob Jordaens** (1593–1678) painted in a vigorous, expressive style in the manner of Rubens, and specialized in joyous, bacchanalian scenes.

During this period Flemish 'genre' painting also thrived—portraits of ordinary rural and town life in inns, markets and kitchens, often spiced with gentle humour. Two of the leading genre painters of the period were **David Teniers the Younger** (1610–90) and **Adriaen Brouwer** (1605–38).

The fecund, flowing style of Rubens and his followers is typical of the **Baroque** period, which can be most readily identified in architecture. Baroque architecture was essentially a lavish, curvaceous interpretation of the classical style: pediments became broken pediments, columns became barley-sugar twists, façades became embellished with *oeil-de-boeuf* windows. Baroque can become overbearing, but with the right balance it is joyous and delicate, elegant and swanky, befitting the ostentatious lifestyles of the wealthy merchant classes of the 17th century.

It is a measure of the decline of Bruges that it partook in these developments only at second hand. It has no artists who came anywhere near the calibre of Rubens,

Van Dyck and Jordaens, although **Jacob van Oost the Elder** (1601–71) produced memorable and highly competent pictures of 17th-century society, which—without the Antwerp swagger—probably better reflected the mood in Bruges. His pupil **Jan Baptist van Meuninckxhove** (*c.* 1620–1703) was a gifted landscape artist whose work included beautifully observed views of Bruges.

As elsewhere, the damage wrought by the iconoclasts in Bruges was usually repaired with baroque flourishes. The Sint-Walburgakerk (1619–41), however, is pure baroque, and delicately judged by its Bruges-born architect, **Pieter Huyssens** (1577–1637). This was also the era of fantastically elaborate wooden pulpits: **Artus Quellinus the Younger** (1625–1700), from an Antwerp family of sculptors, excelled in this specialist art, and supplied the pulpit in the Sint-Walburgakerk. Bruges produced its own home-grown pulpit-maker in the next century, **Hendrik Pulinx** (1698–1781).

Classical Revival

During the 18th century fashions imitated the French once more, and in particular the styles associated with Louis XV. During this period architects reassessed the lessons of classical architecture and pressed for more stringent, sober adherence to these models, with emphasis on well-modulated proportions and symmetry. Both churches and mansions took on the outward appearance of Greek temples: in Bruges the greatest example of this was built on the Markt in the 1790s, to replace the medieval Waterhalle, but it survived only a century. Bruges also acquired its own Academy of Art, founded in 1717 and housed in the medieval Poortersloge. One of its directors was the prolific Rococo artist **Jan Garemijn** (1712–99), who painted the Bruges social set with a kind of Hogarthian crudeness.

The end of the 18th century was marked by the turbulence of the Brabançon Revolt and the French occupation. The prevailing style was again **neoclassical**. The French neoclassical painter Jacques-Louis David (1748–1825) spent the last years of his life in Brussels and had a number of disciples in Belgium but, with one or two possible exceptions, they lacked David's ability to inject a sense of noble drama into their classical scenes. A glance at work by **Frans J. Kinsoen** (1771–1838) and **Jozef Odevaere** (1775–1830) in the Groeningemuseum will show just how difficult it was to achieve this aggrandizing effect without drifting into the absurd.

Truly Belgian Art

Belgian independence in 1830 gave fresh impetus to artists, sculptors and architects. The new nation needed to make its own statements about its role in the world and to glamorize its heritage. Sculptors were called in to evoke the Belgian past through historical sculptures, often to rather leaden effect; **Paul de Vigne of Ghent** (1843–1901) and **Henry Pickery** (1828–94) of Bruges contributed such statues to Bruges' public places. In painting, a wave of **Romanticism**—passionate, vigorous and poetic—swept neoclassicism before it.

Then, after the 1850s, a **realist** school evolved in the fashion of the French painter Gustave Courbet (1819–77), in which ordinary scenes such as peasants at work and cow byres were depicted with the Romantics' eye, but unprettified and (in principle) devoid of interpretation; in Belgium **Hippolyte Boulenger** (1837–74), **Jan Stobbaerts** (1838–1914) and **Henri de Braekeleer** (1840–88) are the best-known exponents of this trend. The social implications of Realism were taken up with greater vigour by the painter and sculptor **Constantin Meunier** (1831–1905), who focused on both the misery and the dignity of industrial labour.

In the latter part of the century, architecture took on all shapes and forms, ranging from the neogothic to the neoclassical, which were seen as complementary rather than contradictory. In Bruges, however, neogothic was considered the only appropriate style. Promoted vigorously by a British contingent of antiquarians, collectors and restorers such as John Steinmetz, William Brangwyn, James Weale and Robert Chantrell, it was adopted enthusiastically by a number of artists and architects.

Notable among them was Bruges' municipal architect **Louis Delacenserie** (1838–1909), who restored the Gruuthuse mansion, the Tolhuis, the Poorterloge, the Heilig-Bloedbasiliek, and designed the new Provinciaal Hof in the Markt.

Belgium was also noted as a liberal country, a refuge for artists from more repressive regimes, particularly France, and this fuelled a taste for the avant-garde. In Brussels various societies were formed to discuss and promote contemporary work. One of these was **Le Cercle des Vingt** (Les XX), founded by Octave Maus in 1883, which held controversial exhibitions of invited artists, many of whom were unknown at the time. Paul Cézanne, for example—later dubbed the 'father of modern art'—was exhibited by Les XX long before he was recognized in his own country.

Late 19th Century

Despite the influence of innovative groups such as these, Belgian art essentially followed the patterns of French painting during the late 19th century. Artists such as **Théo van Rysselberghe** (1862–1926) adopted a form of pointillist Impressionism; **Emile Claus** (1849–1924) created a kind of late Impressionism that he called 'Luminism', depicting rural scenes with famously fetching charm; there is a fine example, *River Lys at Astene* (1885), in the Groeningemuseum.

Belgium also produced more individualistic talents, notably the decidedly bizarre **James Ensor** (1860–1949). He began his painting career with well-made post-impressionist paintings of interiors and portraits, however in the mid-1880s his palette suddenly became charged with intense, clashing colours, which he applied with aggressive vigour to increasingly oddball subject matter, such as dead fish, animated skeletons and Punch-and-Judy-like caricatures. His great masterpiece is the carnival-like *Entry of Christ into Brussels* (1888).

At the same time a very loosely defined group of painters called the **Symbolists** began to explore the world of suggestion, mystery and dreams. Many of their works are fascinating for their sheer idiosyncrasy, such as the visionary fantasy world of **Jean Delville** (1867–1953). By contrast **Léon Frédéric** (1856–1940) painted large triptychs of social realism infused with the kind of saintly clarity found in the works of the medieval Flemish masters.

But perhaps the most haunting Symbolist of them all is **Fernand Khnopff** (1858–1921), who used a soft, polished style to bring a dreamlike quality to his work. He spent six years of his childhood in Bruges, and created two memorable works set in the city: *Secret-Reflet* (1902; in the Groeningemuseum) and *La Ville Abandonnée* (1904).

Another highly individual painter associated with Symbolism is **Léon Spilliaert** (1881–1946), a self-taught artist who brought a strong sense of design to his stylized interiors and unmistakable landscapes—often brooding silhouettes set against empty twilight coastlines around his native Ostend, filled with the abstract shapes of cloud and reflected patches of water.

Yet another kind of Symbolism can be seen in the work of artists influenced by the Pre-Raphaelite Brotherhood in England, such as **Théophile M. F. Lybaert** (1848–1927) of Ghent, and **Edmond Van Hove** (1853–1913) of Bruges. Their mystical, highly polished and detailed work reflected the paintings of the 'primitives' and fitted the neogothic mood in turn-of-the-century Bruges.

Les XX were superseded by **La Libre Esthétique** (1894–1914) as Brussels' leading artistic circle. This group encouraged cooperation between artists, architects and craftsmen, creating an atmosphere that fostered the emerging decorative style, **Art Nouveau**, a style that chimed well with Symbolism. Belgium was at the forefront of Art Nouveau, with leading figures such as **Victor Horta** (1861–1947), and **Henri van de Velde** (1863–1957), who became director of the Art and Crafts School in Weimar in 1901, which in 1919 evolved into the Bauhaus. Art Nouveau remained fashionable until the First World War in most major cities in Belgium, but is seen in Bruges only in a few isolated places.

The 20th Century

Out of Impressionism and postimpressionism grew **Fauvism**, whose name was based on a term of abuse meaning 'wild beast', applied by a critic, and reflecting their unbridled use of colour. Belgium's most successful exponent was **Rik Wouters** (1882–1916)—also a gifted sculptor—who used bright but carefully modulated colours to produce work of great charm and subtlety, usually featuring his wife Nel.

Meanwhile a school of painters developed in the village of Sint-Martens-Latem, near Ghent. The first wave, founded in around 1904, included mystic, symbolist-style painters such as **Valerius de Saedeleer** (1867–1941) and **Albert Servaes** (1883–1966). The second wave developed in around 1909, and in the post-war period was centred upon **Constant Permeke** (1886–1952), who painted emotionally charged, blocky portraits with thick dingy colours, a unique combination of social realism, Cubism and Expressionism.

Two of Belgium's best-known 20th-century painters are **Surrealists**. Surrealism developed in Paris in the 1920s as an effort to unveil a reality in the subconscious through spontaneous, automatic behaviour and events, usually of a highly unconventional nature. By extension, the term was applied to the dreamworld evoked by painters such as Salvador Dali. **René Magritte** (1898–1967) lived in Paris in the 1920s then returned to Belgium to begin producing his inimitable small-scale paintings of witty absurdities and visual puns, such as floating men in bowler hats, paintings within paintings, trains emerging from fireplaces and nude female torsos which become faces.

Meanwhile, **Paul Delvaux** (1897–1994) painted countless versions of his primary obsessions over his long lifetime: trams and stations by night, peopled by sleepwalkers, skeletons and reclining nudes, all suffused with a haunting, dreamlike quality and latent eroticism.

During most of the 20th century Belgian art has tended to reflect movements elsewhere in the world. In the immediate post-war years, a group called **La Jeune Peinture Belge** (1945–48) attempted to gather together the various strains of contemporary art. Its members produced primarily abstract work, influenced particularly by the mechanistic abstractions of **Victor Sevranckx** (1897–1965); **Anne Bonnet** (1908–60), **Louis van Lint** (1909–89) and **Gaston Bertrand** (b. 1910) are probably the best known of these today.

In 1948 an international group called **Cobra** (an acronym from Copenhagen, Brussels, Amsterdam) formed around a common interest in children's painting and primitive art, free of the encumbrance of Western painting traditions; Belgium's most famous participant is **Pierre Alechinsky** (b. 1927), whose poetic, semi-figurative works (particularly in inks) have reached the international stage.

Now, with growing prosperity and self-confidence, as well as new, pace-setting collections of contemporary art in both Antwerp and Ghent, Flanders is once again generating its own artistic impetus. Could it possibly be on the threshold of a new Golden Age?

The Seven Wonders of Bruges

A poster hangs in the tourist office in the Burg, showing a painting of about 1550, attributed to the Bruges artist Pieter Claeissens the Elder. It depicts, in a kind of collage form, the *Septem Admirationes Civitatis Brugensis*, the Seven Wonders of Bruges. It is a slightly odd selection (the Stadhuis is omitted, for instance), but shows what was most universally admired at the time:

The **Huis de Zeven Torens** (now a shell; *see* Walk III)

The **Belfort** (*see* Main Attractions)

The **Poortersloge** (*see* Walk II)

The **Oosterlingenhuis** (all but disappeared; *see* Walk II)

The **Onze-Lieve-Vrouwekerk** (*see* Main Attractions)

The **Waterhuis** (the pumphouse, since demolished; *see* Walk IV)

The **Waterhalle** (replaced by the Provinciaal Hof; *see* Walk I)

The Main Attractions

Dijver 16.

Open April–Sept daily 9.30–5; Oct–March daily 9.30–12.30 and 2–5, closed Tues; adm 80 BF.

This rewarding little museum, housed in an 18th-century neoclassical mansion, contains a stunning collection of European lace, much of it assembled by the historian Baron **Jean-Amédée Liedts,** and illustrated by paintings showing lace being worn (abundantly).

Upstairs is an extensive collection of paintings, prints, drawings, furniture and carpets donated to Bruges in 1936 by **Frank Brangwyn** (1867–1956). This British artist was born in Bruges where his father, William Curtis Brangwyn, worked as a neogothic architect and muralist (he was involved in the remodelling of the Heilig-Bloedbasiliek). Frank Brangwyn left Bruges aged eight, but always held a deep affection for the city of his birth.

Brangwyn later trained in William Morris' workshop and was associated with Siegfried Bing in Paris at the outset of the Art Nouveau movement, a connection clearly visible in, for example, his carpet called *The Vine* (1896–7). His furniture shows how his later work evolved towards Art Deco. His large and curious *British Empire Panel* (1925–30) was commissioned for the House of Lords in London, but its rich, almost psychedelic collage effect was clearly too racy for their Lordships. He was a powerful, expressionistic draughtsman, with a deft touch in all he turned his hand to. It is remarkable that he is not better known.

Begijnhof

Wijngaardstraat.

Open in daylight hours; gate closes at sunset.

The Begijnhof (in French *béguinage*) is one of Bruges' most beguiling backwaters, celebrated for the infectious tranquillity of its spirit of place. *Béguinages* were founded originally as refuges for the large numbers of single women at the time of the Crusades. The *béguines* lived pious lives, doing charity work, but they were not nuns, and could leave the community to marry (*see* p.107).

Bruges' *béguinage* has occupied this same site since 1244, since its foundation by Margaret of Constantinople, Countess of Flanders. Its full name is the **Prinselijk Begijnhof ten Wijngaarden** (Princely *Béguinage* of the Vineyard), because Philip the Fair, King of France, placed it under royal protection in 1299 (although no one can explain the vineyard bit).

Today it appears like an island, accessed by a bridge and a gatehouse (dated 1776). Within, low, white-painted gabled houses (mostly dating from the 17th and 18th centuries) are set around cobbled walkways shaded by tall trees and a spacious patch of grass which is awash with daffodils in spring.

The last of the *béguines* died in 1928; the nuns seen in the Begijnhof today are Benedictine sisters, whose order took over the site in 1930; they have, however, adopted the habits once worn by the *béguines*. The **Begijnhof church** (*open daily 7–12.15 and 3–6*) was built in 1602 to replace an earlier one that was burnt down; it has a simple wood-panelled interior and a contrasting baroque altarpiece.

There is also a small museum on the site, the **Beguinhuisje** (*open Mar–Nov daily 10–12 and 1.45–5, till 5.30 on weekends; Dec–Feb Mon, Tues and Fri 11–12, Wed and Thurs 2–4; adm 60 BF*), which contains mementoes of the Begijnhof, and presents a powerful evocation of how the interiors of the modest dwellings once looked.

Belfort

Markt 7.

Open April–Sept daily 9.30–5; Oct–Mar daily 9.30–12.30 and 1.30–5; adm 100 BF; family ticket 200 BF. Even though only 70 people are allowed into the Belfry at a time, it's worth coming early to avoid the crush.

The Belfort, or belfry, is the city's most prominent and striking landmark, and also provides one of its most exhilarating attractions—if you have the stamina to mount its 366 stairs. Over seven centuries it has served as a watchtower, a clocktower and as the symbol of Bruges' independent spirit. The city aldermen used to meet in the building below the belfry, and important announcements were formerly proclaimed to the public from its balcony. The belfry has always been at the very heart of civic life.

The **tower** is a remarkable hybrid building, with three main tiers rising to 83m (272ft) through a series of architectural styles. The lower part dates from 1282–96, the four corner towers from 1396, and the octagonal belltower from 1482–87. There used to be an additional tiered, knobbly spire which somehow made architectural sense of what lay beneath it, but this was destroyed by lightning in 1741 and never replaced. The result is that the tower now looks strangely top-heavy and architecturally unresolved.

You have to be fit to climb the steep and narrow staircase to the top. A strongroom called the **Schatkamer** (Treasury) near the base (after 55 steps) is where the burghers of Bruges kept under numerous locks and keys the precious documents guaranteeing the privileges granted to them by the Counts of Flanders. Look out also for the carillon keyboard (see below), and the iron fire-trumpet, which was used up to the 19th century as the city fire alarm. Two-thirds of the way up the tower is the lonely looking 'Victory Bell', with a diameter of over 2m (6½ft). It was brought here from the Onze-Lieve-Vrouwekerk in 1680, and is rung only on special occasions.

Close to the top is the splendid automatic **clock carillon**, installed in 1748, which rings 47 bronze bells on the quarter-hour like a giant musical box, and the room where the *beiaardier* (carillon player) has his keyboard to play the carillon bells directly (see p.97) From the summit there are unrivalled views over the waterways and rooftops of the city to the port and flat surrounding countryside. The noise from the wondrous Heath Robinson configuration of bells (weighing a total of 27 tons), wires and pulleys is all enveloping; having made it all the way to the top, it is definitely worth waiting to hear it chime at least the quarter-hour.

The Belfort rises up from a massive complex of buildings set around an austere courtyard. This is the *Halle*, an old covered market originally built in 1239, but added to over the next three centuries. In the 14th century this was a bustling marketplace for cloth, carpets, gloves, wooden clogs, saddles, clerical hats, exotic fruits and spices traded through Venice. There is a set of arches (1561–6) at the rear, spanning the pavement of the Oude Burg, where money-changers used to set out their stalls.

Burg

This small square is the historic heart of the city, and contains the most impressive and beautiful concentration of public buildings. Three are open to visitors, and are described below: the **Heilig-Bloedbasiliek**, the **Renaissancezaal van het Brugse Vrije**, and the **Stadhuis**. For a general description of the Burg, see pp.99–100.

Groeningemuseum

Dijver 12.

Open April–Sept daily 9.30–5; Oct–Mar daily 9.30–12.30 and 2–5, closed Tues; adm 200 BF. (While the Memlingmuseum remains closed for renovation, its collection will be at the Groeningemuseum.)

Entered through an archway and a series of courtyards from Dijver, the low-rise modern building housing this municipal museum comes as something of a surprise. Even greater is the surprise of the treasures within—one of Europe's most dazzling collections of medieval art. The museum is actually too small to exhibit its entire collection at the same time, so paintings are shown in rotation. Almost everything in it is of outstanding quality. It's a delight—provided that you can stomach the subject matter of so many of the exhibits: gruesome martyrdoms painted with loving attention to every horrific detail.

The great star of the collection is **Jan van Eyck**'s *Madonna with Canon van der Paele* (1436), a large work filled with stunning detail. The Madonna sits enthroned with Christ on her knee, while Canon van der Paele (who commissioned the work) kneels to her left, spectacles in hand. Behind him is St George, his patron saint, kitted out in a full set of ceremonial armour, and opposite him is St Donatian dressed in sumptuous vestments. (St Donatian was a Roman who in 390 became Bishop of Reims; his relics were brought to Bruges during the 9th century.)

This is not simply a religious work, but a portrait of living people, surrounded by the kind of luxurious setting that existed in Burgundian Bruges. Note the oriental carpet, and the African parrot held by Christ—evidence of the scope of Bruges' trade. In terms of technique, and of the sophistication of detail, this painting out-strips anything that was produced in Italy by at least three decades.

St Luke Drawing a Portrait of Our Lady, by van Eyck's pupil **Roger van der Weyden**, is another snapshot of contemporary life, in which the Virgin gives her breast to a rather starved-looking baby Jesus, surrounded by Renaissance textiles and architecture. **Dirk Bouts** is represented by a triptych featuring the *Martyrdom of St Hippolytus*, in which the saint is being pulled asunder by four horses, with ropes attached to each limb.

This is upstaged only by *The Judgement of Cambyses* (1498) by **Gerard David** (?1460–1523), who lived and died in Bruges and was the last great artist of the Bruges school. It depicts the corrupt judge Sisamnes being flayed alive with surgical precision by knaves in boots and cloaks; Cambyses, king of Persia in the 6th century BC, and other surrounding figures—including a mangy dog—are painted in great detail and look entirely unconcerned. The painting was commissioned for the Stadhuis by the contrite magistrates of Bruges following the disastrous events of 1488, when the Bruges authorities ill-advisedly put the unpopular governor of the Low Countries, Maximilian, under house arrest and executed his treasurer Pieter Lanchals in the Markt.

A series of panels depicting the legends of St Ursula, by the **Master of the Legends of St Ursula** and dated to before 1482, tells the story of the saint and the fate of her 11,000 virgins. According to the legend, St Ursula, the daughter of a king of Britain, escaped to Rome to avoid being married against her will, accompanied by a retinue of virgins. They then went to Cologne in Germany, where they were murdered simply because they were Christian. All this is based on a small inscription in Cologne, but it clearly caught the imagination of the medieval mind and snowballed into a legend in which an original contingent of 11 virgins became 11,000, plus a few bishops thrown in for good measure.

This is a subject taken up more famously by **Hans Memling** (1435–94) in his *St Ursula Shrine* (normally kept in the Memlingmuseum). The Groeningemuseum is guardian of his large and impressive *Moreel triptych* (1484), named after the donor Willem Moreel, burgomaster of Bruges who is depicted in the left-hand panel, his wife in the right-hand panel. The saints in the central panel are Christopher, Maurus and Giles. The painting shows the greater confidence in figure work, and in the use of perspective and scale, that Memling brought to Bruges painting.

Other highlights include a nightmarish *Last Judgement* by **Hieronymus Bosch**; the *Allegory of the Peace of the Netherlands* (1577) by **Pieter Claeissens the Younger**, one of a distinguished family of Bruges painters; and the startling portraits of Archduke Albert and Isabella the Infanta by **Frans Pourbus the Younger** (1569–1622).

The collection peters out somewhat in the period between the 17th and late 19th century, but it is worth looking out for a few of the notable Bruges artists of this era. There are fine, evocative pieces by **Jacob van Oost the Elder** (1601–71), portraying the world of the well-to-do around the time when Charles II of England and his desperate band of supporters loitered around Bruges. They reflect a sombre, dignified and self-effacing world, very different from the self-confidence and bravura of Bruges at its medieval zenith. Especially good is his *Portrait of a Bruges Family* (1645). *Afternoon Tea* (1778), by **Jan Antoon Garemijn** (1712–99), in French Rococo style, shows a very different social atmosphere a century later.

The collection picks up again in the late 19th century. There are some finely detailed pieces by **Edmond van Hove** (1853–1913), in Pre-Raphaelite Brotherhood style, echoing the work of the neo-medievalists in Bruges at the time; his self portrait, aged 26, is particularly strong. Other names to seek out are the postimpressionist 'Luminist' **Emile Claus**, the Symbolists **Fernand Khnopff**, **Léon Frédéric** and **Jean Delville**; the Sint-Martens-Latem School painters **Gustave de Smet**, **Constant Permeke** and **Gustave van de Woestijne**; and one-offs such as **Edgar Tytgat**, **Rik Wouters** and **Magritte**.

If you are intrigued by the Bruges-la-Morte myth, look out for Khnopff's *Secret-Reflet* (1902), which includes a drawing of the back of the Sint-Janshospitaal—a classic of dreamy Symbolist reverie.

Dijver 17.

Open April–Sept daily 9.30–5; Oct–Mar daily 9.30–12.30 and 2–5, closed Tues; adm 130 BF.

This 15th-century mansion owes its name to a herbal flavouring for beer called *gruut*, an alternative to hops. A tax on *gruut*, and later on beer, was the perk of an honorific title, 'Lord of Gruuthuse'.

The old Gruuthuse mansion, much restored, now contains a splendid collection of all the kinds of things that enriched the lives of the merchant classes of Bruges. Most of the objects are solid and utilitarian, but beautifully crafted and often charmingly decorated. Follow the room numbers to pursue a serpentine course through the museum past weapons, kitchen implements, Delftware, linenfold cupboards, leather trunks, clocks, scales, spinets and hurdy-gurdies, textiles and lace—and criminals' shackles, and a guillotine with a genuine French Revolutionary pedigree. One of the most treasured possessions is a polychrome terracotta and wood bust portraying **Emperor Charles V** aged about 20, carved in about 1520 and attributed to the celebrated German sculptor Konrad Meit (*c.* 1480–1551). Note the chain and emblem of the Order of the Golden Fleece around his neck.

There are a number of mementoes of **Charles II of England**, who stayed in Bruges during his exile from 1657 to 1658. They include an impressive memorial bust in black and white marble (1660–1) by François Dieussart, a copy of the one in the Schuttersgilde Sint-Sebastian, and made for the fellow archers, the Schuttersgilde Sint-Joris. A most unusual feature of the building is the little wooden gallery, erected in 1472, that leads across a bridge to the balcony-like oratory overlooking the interior of the Onze-Lieve-Vrouwekerk.

Heilig-Bloedbasiliek

Burg 10.

Open April–Sept daily 9.30–11.45 and 2–5.45; Oct–Mar daily 10–11.45 and 2–3.45, closed Wed afternoon; Schatkamer adm 40 BF.

The Heilig-Bloedbasiliek (Basilica of the Holy Blood) is a curious double act, with two quite distinct parts, one on top of the other. It is squeezed rather awkwardly into a corner of the Burg and surmounted by a strange trio of turrets, like fancy headdresses improvised from the Venetian doge's mitre.

The lower church is known as **St Basil's Chapel** after the relic (four vertebrae) of St Basil the Great that was brought back from Caesarea in the Holy Land in 1099. The chapel (entrance through the brown door to the left of the archway, marked *Basiliek*, beneath the array of neo-medieval gilded statues) is effectively a kind of undercroft, a robust piece of 12th-century architecture with massive pillars of raw, rough-hewn stone rising to Romanesque arches. The tone is bleak and thoroughly medieval: you could imagine crusaders clanking around here, haunted by distant memories of Jerusalem. To the right of the choir is a wooden polychrome statue of the Virgin and Child dating (1300), and there is a primitive stone sculpture depicting the baptism of Christ over the arch leading back from the side aisle to the nave.

Upstairs, reached by a splendid, broad staircase, is the **Chapel of the Holy Blood**, a 15th–16th-century addition, destroyed by the French in the 1790s but rebuilt, and richly decorated by the neo-medievalists in the 19th century. The relic of the Holy Blood—apparently blood washed from the body of Christ by Joseph of Arimathea—was, according to tradition, given by Baldwin III of Anjou, King of Jerusalem, to Derick of Alsace, Count of Flanders, in 1148, for his heroic deeds during the Second Crusade. In fact, it is rather more likely that the relic was acquired by Baldwin IX, Count of Flanders, when during the rapacious Fourth Crusade he was elected First Latin Emperor of Constantinople.

According to the legend, when it arrived in Bruges in 1150 the blood in its rock-crystal phial appeared to be dry, but it miraculously suddenly became liquid again, and would repeat this phenomenon every Friday. The relic of the Holy Blood became the focus of fervent devotion, and miraculous healings took place among the worshippers who assembled before it on Fridays.

This tradition is still maintained: the relic is displayed for veneration in the chapel on Fridays—but it hasn't turned liquid since 1325. The chapel is appealing in its own bespangled, multicoloured way, enhanced by the ingenious pulpit in the form of a complete globe, designed by Hendrick Pulinx and carved from a single piece of oak in around 1728.

Next to the chapel entrance upstairs is a tiny museum called the **Schatkamer**, or Treasure Chamber, the focus of which is an elaborate gold reliquary made by Jan Crabbe in 1617. This is used in the Heilig-Bloedprocessie, when the Holy Blood relic is paraded around the city on Ascension Day (*see* p.20). Among the precious stones decorating it is a large diamond said to have belonged to Mary Stuart. There are also two fine paintings by Pieter Pourbus (1524–84), actually the wings of a triptych, dated 1556, portraying the very sanctimonious-looking Members of the Brotherhood of the Precious Blood.

Mariastraat 38.

Closed for restoration until at least late 2000. Opening times to be announced. During this time, the Memling paintings will be on display at the Groeningemuseum.

The **Memlingmuseum** is a cultural jewel, a collection of exceptional paintings exhibited in the chapel of the very institution—the Sint-Janshospitaal, or Hospital of St John—which commissioned them over 500 years ago. According to tradition, the German-born painter **Hans Memling** (1435–94) came to the hospital as a wounded and dangerously sick mercenary in 1477, after the Battle of Nancy in which Charles the Bold, Duke of Burgundy, was defeated and killed. Memling was nursed back to health, and undertook to paint a series of works at low cost to express his gratitude (1479–80). It's an attractive theory, but a myth: Memling was already an established figure in Bruges 12 years before this.

Memling was probably a pupil of Roger van der Weyden in Brussels before he settled in Bruges during the last years of the reign of Philip the Good, one of Bruges' most splendid periods. He became a leading figure in the city, and one of its wealthiest citizens. Celebrated particularly in the 19th century as one of the masters of Flemish art, Memling's prodigious output is now scattered around many of the world's great galleries.

The most celebrated work in the collection is the *St Ursula Shrine*. Just one metre long, made of gilt wood, it contains a dozen or so small painted panels that tell in vivid and beautifully rendered detail the story of St Ursula and her 11,000 virgins. *The Mystic Marriage of St Catherine* (1479) also demonstrates Memling's sparkling attention to detail. The painting shows baby Jesus sliding a ring on to the finger of St Catherine (with the broken wheel on which the Romans attempted to martyr her), while St Barbara reads a book beside her. St Catherine is believed to symbolize Mary of Burgundy (daughter of Charles the Bold), and St Barbara her mother, Margaret of York. This polyptych was commissioned for this chapel, and the wings show the two St Johns (patrons of the hospital), with John the Baptist spurting blood after decapitation, and John the Divine (the Evangelist) on the island of Patmos, to which he was exiled. John the Divine can also be seen being boiled in a vat in Rome, which he is supposed to have survived—but the story is apocryphal. Other works include the *Adoration of the Magi* (1479), a *Pietà* (1480) and a striking portrait of a patron, *Maarten van Nieuwenhove* (1487). The museum also has a large number of polychrome wooden statues, mainly of religious subjects dating from the 14th to the 19th centuries.

The venerable old **Sint-Janshospitaal** was founded in about 1150, with three large parallel wards; the earliest one was built in the early 13th century, and the others were added to the north and south about 100 years later. The adjacent convent buildings were built in the 16th century. The total area covers 4 hectares, making this one of the most extensive institutions in the city—a measure of the civic pride and orderliness of Bruges in its heyday.

Operated by the city council and run for most of its history by nuns, the Sint-Janshospitaal maintained a long and devoted tradition of caring for the sick, wounded, homeless and deranged and indigent—following the old definitions of a hospital's role. It only ceased to be an operational (medical) hospital in 1976, when it moved to modern premises in the parish of Sint-Pieters. Since then it has become a museum where it is possible to glimpse what it was like through the centuries. As you leave the enclave, go through the door to the left of the exit. This leads to a 15th-century *Apotheek* (pharmacy), complete with glass jars, ceramic pots and box-drawers. It remained in use until 1971.

Museum voor Volkskunde (Folklore Museum)

Rolweg 40.

Open April–Sept daily 9.30–5; Oct–Mar daily 9.30–12.30 and 2–5, closed Tues; adm 80 BF.

Part of the charm of this rich and interesting folk museum is its location, in the former almshouses of the Shoemakers' Guild, in the quiet streets east of the city centre. It contains all kinds of furniture, tools, domestic implements, toys, lace, paintings and clothes, as well as replicas of a hatter's and a cobbler's workshop, an old grocery, an Empire-style pharmacy, a schoolchildren, and so on—all evoking strong impressions of craft techniques and daily life in the past (labels in Dutch). The museum also has its own pub, **De Zwarte Kat**, created in 1894 by a Bruges social and cultural society to emulate the Parisian cabaret bar called '*Le Chat Noir*', made famous by the singer Aristide Bruant.

Onze-Lieve-Vrouwekerk (Church of Our Lady)

Mariastraat.

Open Mon–Fri 9–11.30 and 2.30–5, Sat 9–11.30 and 2.30–4, Sun 2.30–5; free; museum open from 10am; adm 60 BF.

This is Bruges' most imposing and endearing church. Built over some 200 years from 1220, it has a stark, medieval feel to it. Its soaring, pinnacle-like tower, completed in 1350, rises to 122m (400ft) and is one of the highest in Belgium. The cream-painted interior has a bold simplicity, with hefty columns and black and white flagstones spread across three parallel aisles. This austerity is offset by outbursts of massive baroque ornament in the side chapels, and in the exuberant pulpit (1743) designed by Jan Garemijn, decked with cherubs and a depiction of Wisdom sitting on a globe. At the head of the southern aisle, protected by a glass screen, is one of Bruges' great treasures: the *Madonna and Child* (1504–5) by **Michelangelo**, one of the very few Michelangelo sculptures outside Italy, and the only one to leave Italy during his lifetime. Originally intended for the cathedral of Siena, it was acquired by Jan van Moscroen, a wealthy merchant and municipal treasurer, who donated it to this church in 1514. In this deeply and delicately sculpted work, Michelangelo has succeeded in turning stone into an image of great tenderness: it puts to shame virtually every other sculpture in Belgium. It has twice been carried off as war booty, once during the Napoleonic Wars, and once by the Nazis.

On the north side of the tower is the **Paradijsportaal** (Paradise gate), a baptistry originally built in 1465 to provide a grand entrance to the church away from the busy main road that abutted the western façade, but which was later closed off and converted into a chapel.

The main altar sits oddly in the middle of the church, and the choir behind it is fenced off as a **museum**. The main exhibits are the elaborate tombs of Charles the Bold and his daughter, Mary of Burgundy, who married Maximilian of Austria, but died after a fall from a horse in 1482 at the age of 25. Her fine tomb was constructed between 1495 and 1502, surmounted by a gilt-brass effigy of her in contemporary costume; her feet rest on a pair of dogs, the symbol of fidelity. Her father, Charles the Bold, was the son of Philip the Good, Duke of Burgundy, whom he succeeded in 1467. He reigned for 10 years before waging a disastrous war against France, and was killed at the Battle of Nancy in 1477, where his body was buried after, apparently, being half eaten by wolves. It was Charles V who ordered that the body should be brought to Bruges in 1550, a move fiercely resisted by the people of Nancy, who may have substituted the body of a knight instead. It eventually reached Bruges and was placed in a tomb similar to that of his daughter, made between 1559 and 1562; his feet rest on a lion, the symbol of strength.

In the **crypt**, visible through glass panels, you can see simple mural paintings of crucifixions dating from the 13th and 14th centuries, as well as the coffins of three canons. Crouch down, and beyond these you can see the coffin of Mary of Burgundy (it's not in her tomb), and on top of it an urn containing the heart of her son, Philip the Handsome (father of Charles V), who died in 1506.

The **choir** stalls bear the coats of arms of the knights of the Golden Fleece, mementoes of the chapter meeting called here by Charles the Bold in 1468, the year of his marriage to Margaret of York. The choir also contains a fine altarpiece by Bernard van Orley (1499–1541), and there are several paintings by Pieter Pourbus, including a *Last Supper* (1562), and the wings of a triptych (1573). Pieter Lanchals, the treasurer executed in 1488, is commemorated in a chapel off the south ambulatory, which also contains medieval coffins excavated from the crypt. Note the swan in Lanchals' coats of arms, which gave rise to the legend of Bruges' swans (*see* p.64). In the wall of the north ambulatory of the choir is a wooden gallery, which overlooks the altar. Built in 1472, it belonged to the Lords of Gruuthuse, whose mansion was next door (*see* the Gruuthusemuseum, above).

Renaissancezaal van het Brugse Vrije

Burg 11A.

Open April–Sept daily 10–12.30 and 1.15–5; Oct–Mar daily 9.30–12.30 and 2–5; adm 100 BF, ticket also valid for the Stadhuis.

Throughout much of the medieval period, the city of Bruges was virtually an autonomous state. The region surrounding it, and stretching as far west as Dunkirk, was run separately, under another authority called the **Brugse Vrije** (Bruges Liberty). Ruled by four burgomasters and 24 aldermen, it had control of its own administrative, legal and financial affairs, but was finally abolished by the French in 1795.

The aldermen of the Brugse Vrije used to meet in the 'Renaissance Hall', in part of the old palace of the Brugse Vrije, which now also houses the Bruges archives (there is a display of ancient manuscripts and books in the main hall). It has just one principal exhibit: its huge oak and black marble **chimneypiece** (1529–33), a robust and sensuous installation designed by Lancelot Blondeel (1496–?1561) and sculpted by Guyot de Beaugrant (d. 1551). This is effectively a monument to the ruler of the day, **Charles V**, whose oak statue appears in the centre, flanked by his two pairs of grandparents, Maximilian of Austria and Mary of Burgundy (left; parents of his father, Philip the Handsome), and Ferdinand of Aragon and Isabella of Castile (right; parents of his mother, Joanna of Navarre).

Charles V played a critical role in the history of Flanders by defeating the French king, Francis I, at the Battle of Pavia (1526), and forcing the French to give up their feudal power over Flanders in the Treaty of Cambrai (1529). Charles' prominent codpiece in this sculpture makes it plain enough that this is a work about fertility and lineage, but most remarkable of all is the pristine condition of the whole chimneypiece after over 450 years.

Note also the brass handles beneath the upper rim of the fireplace, designed so that the aldermen could lean safely over the fire to keep themselves warm on cold days. The fire basket on wheels could also be filled with embers and drawn into the room.

Steenstraat.

Open Mon 2–5.45, Tues–Fri 8.30–11.45 and 2–5.45, Sat 8.30–11.45 and 2–5.30, Sun 9–10.15 and 3–5.45.

Squat and built of yellow brick, this massive church is not quite the dominant building that its title would suggest, but then it only acquired the status of cathedral when Bruges became a bishopric in 1834. It then suffered a fire in 1839, which destroyed its roof and tower—subsequently rebuilt to a curious neo-Romanesque design by a British architect, Robert Chantrell.

The first church on this site was probably erected in the 9th century—although, according to an unlikely tradition, an even earlier church was founded here by Saint Eloi in about 640. A Romanesque church followed in 1127, and a Gothic one superseded this after 1275. Today the oldest part is the **choir**, which contains original medieval choir stalls and carved misericords, above which are the painted coats of arms of the knights of the Order of the Golden Fleece, originating from a chapter meeting called by Maximilian of Austria in 1478; Edward IV of England was one of the knights in attendance. Above these, unusually, hangs a series of Brussels tapestries (*c.* 1731), depicting religious scenes such as the Nativity and the Adoration.

The Shoemakers had a guildhouse in Steenstraat, just outside the church; their chapel in the north transept dates from 1372, although it was remodelled a century later. You can see their emblem, a crowned boot, beneath the barley-sugar columns on the baroque altar (1667). The carved oak doors date from the mid 15th century.

In the body of the cathedral there is an impressive pulpit (1778–85) by Hendrick Pulinx, as well as some large religious paintings by the Antwerp painter Erasmus Quellinus (1607–78), a pupil of and assistant to Rubens, who had considerable success after his master's death. The most arresting feature, however, is the remarkable baroque **organ** (1682) at the base of the nave, a mighty confection topped by angels and cherubs playing celestial music. The central statue, of the **Creator**, is by Artus Quellinus the Younger (1625–1700). Some medieval painted stone tombs have been opened to view in the porch (under the organ).

The cathedral has its own **museum** just off the north transept (*open Mon–Fri 2–5, Sun 3–5; closed Sat; adm 60 BF*), a mixed bag of treasures, paintings, relics and other curiosities, set in a series of splendidly dingy neo-Gothic ecclesiastical back-rooms around a cloister. Its most important works of art—many of which were brought here after the church of St Donatian's in the Burg was destroyed in 1799—are currently in the Groeningemuseum, including paintings by Dirk Bouts, Hugo van der Goes and Lancelot Blondeel.

Burg 12.

Open April–Sept daily 9.30–12.30 and 1.15–5; Oct–Mar daily 9.30–12.30 and 2–5; adm 100 BF, ticket also valid for the Renaissancezaal van het Brugse Vrije.

The town hall dates originally from 1376–1420, making it the oldest in Belgium; it is also one of the finest. The building has been heavily restored over the centuries, with the result that it is part medieval, part 19th-century medieval fantasy, part modern renovation. The statues of the counts and countess of Flanders in the niches between the windows were originally medieval, but were pulled down by French Revolutionaries in 1792, and replaced in modern times

The **Gothic Hall** on the upper floor still has its original vaulted wooden ceiling, dating from 1385. It has been beautifully restored, so that the decorated vault keys (illustrating scenes from the New Testament) and consoles next to the walls (illustrating the twelve months of the year and the four elements) can be seen in their full splendour. The walls have been decorated with rich and well-executed murals depicting scenes from Bruges' history, painted in 1895 by Albert and Julien Devriendt—a visually stunning monument to neo-medievalism. A neighbouring room contains a selection of prints relating to Bruges' canal system.

The best way to see Bruges is on foot. In fact, because traffic is so restricted, it is just about the only way to see Bruges. Besides, Bruges is very compact. It takes only fifteen or twenty minutes to walk from the centre to the farthest-flung sight, such as the windmills on the eastern perimeter, or the Begijnhof and Minnewater in the south.

In any case, the attraction of Bruges is not simply its key museums and churches, but the city landscape, with its streets winding along their medieval paths, criss-crossing the canals, providing ever-changing views of the distinctive spires and towers that pierce the skyline. Along the way there are tree-shaded squares, step-gabled houses overlooking the canals, stone benches on the bridges, clusters of whitewashed almshouses, enticing shop windows—countless details that invite you to take your time as you wander the city, and settle into its gentle pace of life.

Four suggested walks are presented here. It may seem a shame that the greatest riches of Bruges are not spread out more democratically across all four of them. But this is not geographically practical; nor

The Walks

would it suit the many visitors who come to Bruges for a brief visit. So all the 'essential' sights have been shoehorned into Walk I, a very rich and rewarding tour which makes a circuit from the centre to the south of the city. Visitors who do this walk in its entirety can justifiably claim to have seen the best of Bruges. It includes the Markt and the Burg (the two squares at the heart of the city), some of the most famous canal views, and Bruges' two largest churches, the Onze-Lieve-Vrouwekerk and the Sint-Salvatorskathedraal. It also passes the through the Begijnhof, the convent-like settlement for women, founded in the Middle Ages, which remains today a memorable sanctuary of calm.

The key to Bruges' medieval fortunes was its role as an international trading city. Walk II follows a path through the centre of the old mercantile district, where the trading houses of the Venetians, Genoese, English, Germans and many others were concentrated around the canals, customs posts and weigh houses. Here you can see the site of the world's first stock exchange, the turreted mansions of the well-to-do, and their richly endowed churches.

Walk III heads east into a less-visited area of Bruges. Religion has played a key role in Bruges' history: the city was home to dozens of religious institutions, notably after the religious strife of the 16th century. The ubiquitous and largely benign presence of piety can be witnessed in this walk in several remarkable churches and chapels, the convents, the huge seminary, the almshouses, and in the work of Bruges' famous 19th-century poet-priest, Guido Gezelle. The walk also leads down the towpath of the outer ring of canals, beneath the sails of four historic windmills which line the embankment where the mighty city walls once stood.

Walk IV takes you beyond the busy 't Zand square in the west of the city to a pretty grid of cobbled streets, next to the wooded banks of the canal. This quiet corner of Bruges contains a remarkably rich concentration of almshouses and chapels, and gives a strong impression of how Bruges was in the centuries after its medieval heyday. The walk then heads back across 't Zand, to the site of the Prinsenhof, once the grand palace complex of the medieval Dukes of Burgundy, before traversing several of the best shopping streets of the city.

Walk I: Essential Bruges

Start: *the Markt.*

Walking time: *less than an hour (the total distance is about 4km), but visiting all the monuments, museums and churches could easily consume a whole day.*

This walk gathers in Bruges' most famous sights, and includes all the 'must-see' attractions, which are clustered conveniently in the historic—and almost traffic-free—city centre and to its south. There's a bit of everything here: a panoramic view over the city from the dizzying height of the Belfort, the stately splendour of the Burg, the brilliant early Flemish paintings of the Groeningemuseum, the domestic treasures of the Gruuthusemuseum, a Michelangelo sculpture. Even if you're happy not to rush, you'll still need to be selective. But none of these attractions is far from the centre, so you can always come back another time.

Besides, this walk is more than a checklist of key sights. It also passes along some of the most beautiful canals and streets of the city, affording changing views of the spires, gables and bridges reflected in the waterways.

Note that in winter the Groeningemuseum is closed on Wednesday: and in winter both the Gruuthusemuseum and the Branwynmuseum are closed on Tuesday.

lunch/cafés

1. **Frituur Peter**, Markt. Green-painted kiosks under the Belfort selling Belgian chips with a dollop of mayonnaise. The chips with *stoofvlees* (beef stew) is surprisingly good.

2. **De Garre**, De Garre 1. Cosy *staminee* (pub), in a passageway off Breidelstraat. Good beer and light snacks.

3. **Breydel–De Coninc**, Breidelstraat 24. *Closed Wed.* Hearty portions of mussels and seafood, easy-going, modern ambience.

4. **Straffe Hendrik–De Halve Maan**, Walplein 26. The brewery tavern. Snacks include beer soup (*see* p.163).

5. **De Bron**, Katelijnestraat 82. *Open 12–2 only; closed Mon.* Agreeable vegetarian restaurant in an old town house built in 1647.

6. **Marieke van Brugghe**, Mariastraat 17. The galley of a Spanish galleon, with a modern designer twist. The *vlaamse stoverij met kasteelbier*, a succulent stew, comes with soft-fried chips, perfect for soaking up the juices.

7. **De Serre–Eetcaf 'De Vuyst'**, Simon Stevinplein 15. *Closed Tues.* Friendly and bright. Quick lunch menu 525 BF.

8. **'t Keteltje**, Oude Burg 20. *Closed Sun.* Fresh linen, fresh flowers and an unfussy atmosphere; inventive French-style cuisine. Lunch menu at 490 BF.

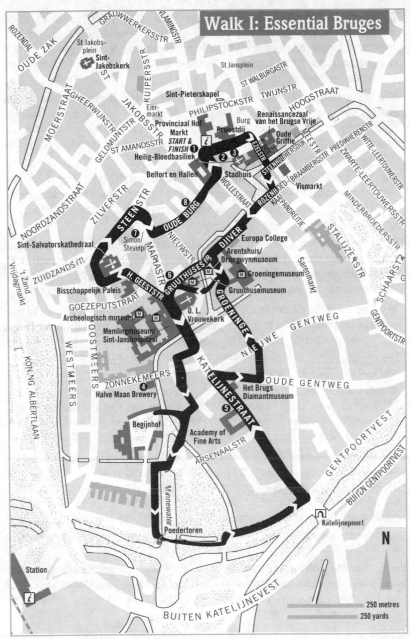

Walk I: Essential Bruges

GRAUWWERKERSSTR
VLAMINGSTR
ROZENDAL
OUDE ZAK
St Jakobs-plein
Sint-Jakobskerk
JAST
GHEERWIJNSTR
JAKOBSSTR
MOERSTRAAT
KUIPERSSTR
St Jansplein
St WALBURGASTR
Sint-Pieterskapel
TWIJNSTR
Eiermarkt
PHILIPSTOCKSTR
HOOGSTRAAT
GELDMUNTSTR
Provinciaal Hof
Markt
Renaissancezaal
van het Brugse Vrije
ST AMANDSSTR
Burg
Proostdij
Oude
Griffie
START & FINISH
Heilig-Bloedbasiliek
PREDIKHERENSTR
WITTE-LEERTOUWERSSTR
ZWARTE-LEERTOUWERSSTR
Belfort en Hallen
Stadhuis
Vismarkt
NOORDZANDSTRAAT
ZILVERSTR
OUDE BURG
WOLLESTRAAT
KAAI
PANDREITJE
MINDERBROEDERSSTR
STEENSTR
Sint-Salvatorskathedraal
Simon/
Stevinpl
MARIASTR
NIEUWSTR
DIJVER
Europa College
Arentshuis/
Brangwynmuseum
Groeningemuseum
Sareemarkt
STALIJZERSTR
SCHAARST
ZUIDZANDS
't Zand
Vrijdaemarkt
H. GEESTSTR
GRUUTHUSESTR
Gruuthusemuseum
Bisschoppelijk Paleis
GOEZEPUTSTRAAT
Archeologisch museum
O. L.
Vrouwekerk
GROENINGE
NIEUWE GENTWEG
GENTPOORTSTR
Memlingmuseum/
Sint-Janshospitaal
WESTMEERS
OOSTMEERS
KONING ALBERTLAAN
ZONNEKEMEERS
Halve Maan Brewery
KATELIJNESTRAAT
OUDE GENTWEG
Het Brugs
Diamantmuseum
Begijnhof
Academy of
Fine Arts
ARSENAALSTR
BUITEN GENTPOORTVEST
GENTPOORTVEST
Mannewater
Katelijnepoort
Poedertoren
Station
BUITEN KATELIJNEVEST

N

250 metres
250 yards

95

The **Markt**, the old marketplace, is at the very heart of the city. This was the scene of great trade fairs, of grand medieval jousts and public executions. Given this pedigree, it is architecturally somewhat disappointing and workaday, especially if compared with the gilded brilliance of some of the central squares of other Belgian towns, such as Antwerp and Brussels.

The 17th-century gabled houses on its north and western flanks have been much altered, and now house banks, souvenir shops and the kinds of restaurants that offer menus in four languages. Yet, the Markt has an invigorating sense of space, underlined by the soaring tower of the Belfort, and much enhanced since the removal of the carpark in 1996.

It is still a working **market square**. For a thousand years it was the scene of a regular Saturday market, a tradition interrupted in 1993 when the market was shifted to 't Zand in the west of the city. This was soon regretted, and the market was reinstated, but now takes place on Wednesdays (*7am–1pm*).

By far the most impressive feature of the Markt is the **Belfort** (belfry), a gawky but endearing giant dominating the southern flank. (The English author and wit G. K. Chesterton compared it to a giraffe.) You can climb to the top for a remarkable view across the city from under the bells (*see* pp. 79–80).

In the centre of the eastern (lower) side is the **Provinciaal Hof**, the provincial government building (Bruges is the capital of the province of West Flanders). It was built in neogothic style between 1881 and 1921—dainty with its crocheted spires and finials, tracery balustrades, dormer windows and arches; but its neat and unweathered finish betrays it as a johnny-come-lately.

It stands on the site of the remarkable old **Waterhalle**, built between 1285 and 1294, which was a central feature of Bruges' trading life. Vast and handsome with Gothic detail, it ranked as one of the 'Seven Marvels of Bruges' in the 16th century. As its name suggests, it was a covered hall over the Kraanrei canal, where cargoes of trade goods were unloaded from flat-bottomed barges.

The Kraanrei, a canalized section of the River Reie, used to run down this side of the Markt, connecting the Spiegelrei to the present set of canals to the south. By the late 18th century the crumbling Waterhalle was deemed to have outlived its function. It was pulled down between 1787 and 1789, the canal was filled in, and a large neoclassical building rose in its place—elegant, but out of keeping with medieval Bruges.

When this was destroyed by arson in 1878, the ardent neo-medievalists insisted on a new building reflecting Bruges' Gothic heritage. The Bruges-born municipal architect **Louis Delacenserie** (1838–1909) came up with this scheme, reflecting

Carillons

The happy jingle of carillon bells has been a familiar feature of the Low Countries since the 1500s. They have won many admirers, from Peter the Great of Russia to John D. Rockefeller; they have also exerted a fascination on writers. The American poet, Henry Wadsworth Longfellow, an admirer of Bruges, wrote of the carillon in his poem 'The Belfry of Bruges' (1845). Georges Rodenbach's sequel to *Bruges-la-Morte* was called *Le Carillonneur* (1897).

At their simplest, carillons consist of a set of bells, usually mounted in the town's clock tower, which play a ditty to alert the public that the hour is about to strike. The mechanism, attached to the clock, is like a giant musical box. Metal pegs, fixed to a revolving drum in a carefully planned order, trigger keys that pull wires attached to the clappers in the bells to sound out a tune. The one at the top of Bruges' Belfort is a particularly fine specimen, dating from 1748 and operating 47 bells.

Like many of the great carillons, this one can also be played manually, from a keyboard. This operates rather like a piano, but instead of triggering hammers to hit strings, the carillon keyboard pulls wires attached to the bells. It is not easy to play: a *carillonneur* (*beiaardier* in Dutch), has to undergo years of training, such as the six-year diploma course at the famous Royal Carillon School at Mechelen. It's also hard work: playing a carillon keyboard and controlling up to 40 tons of bells requires physical strength.

Carillon-playing nearly became an extinct art in the 19th century, when it was dismissed as unsophisticated and folksy, but it was saved by the work of various practitioners who improved the responsiveness of the keyboard to provide a more controlled and expressive sound.

Bruges' *stadsbeiaardier* (town *carillonneur*) **Aimé Lombaert**, follows in a long line of respected predecessors, and has a treasured role in the community. His keyboard is in a cramped office at the top of the Belfort (prompting the quip that he is Bruges' 'highest paid official'). From here his music rings forth across the city in regular concerts throughout the year, performed to a published schedule, with increased frequency during the summer. (*Usually open winter Sun, Wed and Sat 2.15–3; summer Mon, Wed and Sat 9–10pm, Sun 2.15–3.*)

his own neo-Gothic passions which he brought to bear in many restorations and rebuildings throughout the city. He is best known for the magnificent Renaissance-style railway station that he designed for Antwerp 20 years later.

In the centre of the square is a statue (1887) by Paul de Vigne of the weaver **Pieter de Coninck** (c. 1250–1333) and the butcher **Jan Breydel** (c. 1264–c. 1331), leading figures of the 1301–2 Flemish rebellion against the French (see p.45). They helped organize the massacre of the French at the notorious Bruges Matins in 1302, which was followed by the resounding victory of the Flemish over the French at the **Battle of the Golden Spurs** later that year—from which time Coninck and Breydel became potent symbols of Flemish independence and pride.

This was never clearer than during the debacle surrounding the inauguration of the statue in 1887. The local Breydel Committee celebrated the completion of the statue on the anniversary of the battle, 11 July, but the city authorities had arranged for the official unveiling by King Leopold II to take place on 15 August, which happened to be the anniversary of the Battle of Pevelenberg (1304)—the battle that dealt the first serious blow to the Flemish revolt. Furthermore, Leopold and the Bruges burgomaster made their speeches entirely in French, inflaming Flemish sensitivities.

On the west side of the Markt, at No.16 on the corner of Sint-Amandstraat, is the step-gabled **Craenenburg**, now a café, with a neogothic façade dating from 1955. This was once a grand private house where **Archduke Maximilian of Austria**, the governor of Flanders, was held prisoner for three weeks in 1488 (see p.50).

On the opposite corner is the **Huis Bouchotte**, with the oldest genuine façade in the Markt, dating from the late 15th century, and restored in the 1850s. The mighty **Charles V** (1500–58) is said to have stayed here during his infrequent visits to the city. The dial on the façade is not a clock; marked NOZW (noord, oost, zuid and west), it is part of a weathervane erected in 1682. With its needle connected to a weathervane on the roof, it indicated the wind direction to the city traders—critical information in the days of the sail.

The plot on the northwest flank (between Sint-Jakobsstraat and Geernaartstraat) used to be occupied by a church—the medieval church of St Christopher, seen in topographical prints as a prominent feature of the Markt—but it fell into disrepair, and was destroyed in 1786 as part of the Austrian programme of modernization. Many of the buildings lining the Markt to either side of this were once guild houses, the headquarters of the powerful organizations that controlled the trades: No.28, with the conical basket on its step-gable, was the guild house of the Tilers (1622); No.33 was the guild house of the Free Fishmongers (1621).

Leave the Markt by Breidelstraat, named after Jan Breydel, a street of lace shops that leads to the **Burg***. Note the picturesque, miniscule alleyway on the right-hand side, called Die Garre.*

If the Markt is the centre of Bruges, the Burg is its historical heart, once the site of the castle around which Bruges grew. Here you will find a cluster of the city's most impressive civic buildings, as well as its most atmospheric church.

On the east flank, in the centre, is the **Stadhuis** (town hall; *see* p.90), with its tall Gothic windows and pepperpot ornamental towers. This was not only the centre of the city's administration after its construction from 1376 to 1420; it was also a symbol of Bruges' prestige, setting a new standard for flamboyant civic architecture. It was later emulated (and exceeded) by Leuven's celebrated town hall, built between 1448 and 1478.

To its right (occupying the corner site) is the **Heilig-Bloedbasiliek** (*see* pp.83–4), a two-layered church built of grey stone with ornate ogive arches. This was the custodian of Bruges' most treasured sacred relic, drops of Christ's blood. The church stood next to the old castle, the '*Steen*', built originally in the 11th century and used by the Counts of Flanders until 1400. It then became a prison, but was damaged in a fire in 1689 and finally demolished in 1784. Running through the site is a modern shopping arcade called **Ter Steeghere** (after the staircase to the upper level of the Heilig-Bloedbasiliek), which joins the Burg to Wollestraat.

To the left of the Stadhuis is the **Oude Griffie** (Old Recorder's House), pierced by the arched entrance to an alleyway, and surmounted by a statue of blind Justice. An ornate Renaissance building dating from 1534–7, it acted as an annexe to the law courts next door between 1883 and 1984. Beside this, and crammed into the corner, is the oldest surviving part of the palace of the Brugse Vrije, whose aldermen used to meet in the **Renaissancezaal van het Brugse Vrije** (*see* p.88), warmed by the fire beneath its remarkable chimney piece.

While the city of Bruges was administered from the Stadhuis, the surrounding region—a large and virtually autonomous subdivision of the county of Flanders called the Brugse Vrije (the Bruges Liberty)—was ruled by its own set of administrators from this end of the Burg. Their palace, the **Landshuis van het Brugse Vrije**, built in 1525, occupied the entire eastern flank. But only the original façade overlooking the canal has survived; the rest was replaced in 1722–7 by the present stolid, neoclassical building around a courtyard. After the Brugse Vrije was abolished by the French in 1795, the building became the Gerechtshof (law courts), where justice was dispensed until 1984. It now contains city administrative offices, as well as the main tourist information office.

The north side of the Burg is a leafy open space. This was not part of the original plan. On this site, squaring off the Burg, was the city's central church, a mighty Romanesque hulk with a squat lantern tower, built on the site of a 9th-century chapel dedicated to the 4th-century Roman bishop of Reims, Saint Donatian. The **Sint-Donaaskerk** was a major landmark, filled with numerous treasures. Jan van Eyck was buried here in 1441, and here Charles the Good, Count of Flanders, was murdered at prayer by a nephew of the provost in 1127, the victim of bitter clan warfare. This was the trigger for a bout of vicious slaughter, after which the streets of the Burg are said to have run with blood.

It became the city's cathedral in 1559, but this heritage meant nothing to the zealous French administrators charged with running Belgium after 1795, and anxious to rid it of the symbols of the *ancien régime*. The Sint-Donaaskathedraal was duly closed, then in 1799 they sent in a team of demolition experts, well experienced in flattening redundant church property. Their technique was to jack up the roof a little, replace stones in the columns with wooden blocks, and then set fire to them. The building then simply collapsed on itself. For years this site was piled high with rubble; now all that remains of the church fabric are some foundations that were excavated during building work on the adjacent Holiday Inn Hotel (where you can still ask to see them). There is also a small stone model of the church, as it may have looked in AD 900, in the square.

Another feature of this open space is a modern statue entitled *The Lovers*, featuring a couple on their way to their marriage in the Stadhuis. It is a self portrait by the local artists **Stefaan Depuyt** (b. 1937) and (Italian-born) **Livia Canestraro** (b. 1936), also the creators of the remarkable set of statues on 't Zand (*see* p.144), along with numerous other sculptural works in the city.

Filling in the rest of this north flank of the Burg is the **Proostdij** (Provost's House), a finely orchestrated Flemish-Baroque building dating from 1662, and crowned by blind Justice. It used to belong to the provost of the Sint-Donaaskerk. The 18th-century neo-classical building tucked away behind it (Burg 3) served as the bishop's residence until the French occupation. It has had a curious guest list since, including Napoleon and Empress Marie Louise on a state visit in 1810; King Leopold III agonizing over the capitulation of Belgium in 1940; and the German Field Marshal Erwin Rommel, the 'Desert Fox', sent to shore up North Sea defences, prior to his enforced suicide over the bomb plot that failed to kill Hitler in July 1944.

> *Leave the Burg by the vaulted passage between the Stadhuis and the Oude Griffie. This is **Blinde Ezelstraat**.*

There is great speculation as to where Blinde Ezelstraat (Blind Donkey Street) got its name. One theory is that donkeys had to be blindfolded to negotiate the narrow alley when fully loaded, however, it is probably a reference to a nearby tavern,

The Almshouses of Bruges

Almshouses (*Godshuizen*) have been an integral part of the Bruges landscape since late medieval times. They were set up and endowed by the guilds for former members and their widows, and by wealthy merchants as sheltered accommodation for the deserving poor and aged. Many still bear the name of their original sponsors. *Godshuizen* usually consist of clusters of about six similar houses, perhaps sharing a communal garden and a chapel, where residents could pray for the founder's salvation. After Bruges went into decline in the 16th century, the need became even greater, and more and more almshouses were built. By the 18th century there were some 300 almshouses in the city; 42 of them still survive.

Since the French occupation from 1795 to 1814 they have been owned and operated by the municipality, and most are still used as homes for the elderly. Their charm lies in their small scale and their cottage-like intimacy, their whitewashed walls, trim gardens and windowboxes. Being house-proud is, of course, a deeply ingrained tradition among the Belgians, but the *Godshuizen* also manage to exude a timeless air of piety, charity and gratitude.

perhaps so-called because it sold the cheapest beer in town, with the result that its clients became as drunk as 'blind donkeys'.

*Cross the canal to reach **Steenhouwersdijk** (Stonemasons' Embankment). You are now in one of the most picturesque parts of Bruges.*

At the **Vismarkt** (Fishmarket), fish—mainly from the port of Zeebrugge—is still sold from the stone slabs set out beneath covered colonnades (*Tues–Sat until 1pm*). Erected in 1826, this elegant neoclassical construction and its monumental water pump are among the very few architectural mementoes from the era when Belgium was ruled by the Netherlands.

A bronze bust on Steenhouwersdijk celebrates **Frank van Acker**, an influential socialist mayor of Bruges from 1977 to 1992.

*The street that follows the canal to the left leads to **Groenerei** (green canal), which offers some of the most famous views of the Burg, the Belfort, and the fetchingly crooked houses that overlook the canal.*

The bridges here, Meebrug and Peerdenbrug, are among the oldest and prettiest in the city. On the south side of Groenerei (Nos.8–12) is an old almshouse called De Pelikaan, dated 1714. The pelican is a symbol of Christian charity because females were thought to peck at their own breasts to draw blood to feed their chicks.

Return to the bridge at the Blinde Ezelstraat, and follow the road round to the left, into **Huidenvettersplein**.

This charming square is named after the tanners (*huidenvetters*), whose guild house (1630) was located here on the right. The statue in the middle (1925) depicts two lions, the emblems of the guild.

Exit the square from the other end, and turn right along **Rozenhoedkaai**. *This offers one of the classic viewpoints of Bruges, with the Belfort in one direction and the Onze-Lieve-Vrouwekerk in the other.*

Rozenhoedkaai means 'rosary quay'. Bruges' craftsmen were famed for their deft skills in the Middle Ages, and among their best-known products were rosaries—those made from amber (from the Baltic region) and ivory (from Africa) were a speciality. This picturesque quay has caught the imagination of a number of writers and poets, including the German Rainer Maria Rilke (1875–1965), who wrote a poem called 'Quai du Rosaire'. More prosaically, until the 16th century the quay was called Zoutdijk (salt embankment), because this was where traders brought shipments of salt, mainly from Germany and France. In medieval times salt was a valuable commodity—essential for preserving meat and fish.

The bridge at the end of Rozenhoedkaai is called the **Nepomucenusbrug**, and bears a statue to St John Nepomuk (1767, erected 1811) by the Bruges-born sculptor Pieter Pepers (1730–85). This St John was confessor to the queen of Bohemia and, when in 1393 he refused to pass on the contents of her confessions, King Wenceslas IV had him thrown to his death in the River Moldau from a bridge in Prague, hence his role as patron saint of bridges.

At the bottom end of Wollestraat (Wool Street), at No.53, is the ornate **De Malvenda** house, built in late-Gothic style in around 1500. It was the house of Juan Perez Malvenda, a Spanish magistrate, who hid the relic of the Holy Blood here during the period of Protestant iconoclasm (1578–84).

Continue westwards along the canal, which opens up into a pretty tree-lined section called **Dijver**.

No.9 is the headquarters of the **Europa College**, or College of Europe, a respected centre for postgraduate European studies, founded in 1949, which each year invites a European head of state to inaugurate its academic year. The British prime minister Margaret Thatcher came to Bruges on 20 September 1988 and made a famous speech in which she pronounced her deep reservations about European integration. 'Working more closely together does not require power to be centralized in Brussels,' she declared. 'Europe will be stronger precisely because it has France as France, Spain as Spain, Britain as Britain, each with its own customs, traditions and identity.'

This inspired the foundation of the Conservative Euro-sceptic 'Bruges Group'—not a tag that Bruges is particularly grateful for.

At No.12 Dijver is the entrance to the **Groeningemuseum**, Bruges' premier collection of art (see pp.80–82). No introduction to Bruges is complete without seeing this, for the paintings of Jan van Eyck, Dirk Bouts, Hans Memling, Frans Pourbus and others provide the best evidence of quite how magnificent the city was in its heyday. Bruges itself features in many of the pictures, as in the background to *St Nicholas*, by the Master of the St Lucy Legend (1486–93). The museum occupies part of the extensive grounds of **Eekhout Abbey**, once one of Bruges' great religious institutions, until it became another victim of the French occupation— razed to the ground in 1795. The name of the museum comes from the street that flanks it to the west: Groeninge has a special significance in Flemish history as the plain near Kortrijk (Courtrai) where the Battle of the Golden Spurs was fought.

> *Leave the Greoeningemuseum by the exit on to the street called Groeninge, and cross the street to a small park dotted with bronze sculptures. This is the **Arentshof**, or Arentspark*

The sculptures, depicting the *Knights of the Apocalypse* (1987), are by the contemporary neoexpressionist sculptor **Rik Poot**. Note also the pillars standing in the park—the last surviving remnants of the Waterhalle.

At the top end of the park is the **Arentshuis**, a museum containing an important collection of antique lace, and the work of Frank Brangwyn (see p.78). A splendid array of historic carriages and sleighs is on view behind the glass in the building opposite the musuem.

> *From the Arentshof, cross the little footbridge that leads over the River Reie towards the huge church spire of the **Onze-Lieve-Vrouwekerk**.*

This is the **Bonifaciusbrug**, one of Bruges' most charming spots; but despite its weathered features, the bridge dates only from 1910. It was named after St Boniface of Crediton (c. 675–755), a much-loved Anglo-Saxon missionary sent to evangelize the Germans, who later became Bishop of Mainz. To help in his work he engaged a number of English missionaries from Wessex, including St Walburga, who has a church in Bruges named after her (see pp.119–120). Aged 70, St Boniface set off to convert the pagans of Friesland in the northern Netherlands, and met his death at their hands. Relics of the martyred saint later found their way to the Onze-Lieve-Vrouwekerk.

Close to the bridge is a modern bust of **Juan Luis Vivés** (1492–1540), a Spanish humanist of Jewish origin who fled the Inquisition in Spain aged 17, and later settled in Bruges. He studied in Paris and then taught at Leuven, before joining the court of Henry VIII of England. He refused to accept Henry's divorce from

Catherine of Aragon in 1527 and, after a spell in prison, returned to the Low Countries. Resident in Bruges, he was visited by both Erasmus, his former teacher, and Thomas More.

Vivés is best remembered for his radical proposals for education, which included using the vernacular instead of Latin, studying nature, broadening the education of women, and opening schools for the poor. This last idea was put into practice by the pioneering Bogaarden schools for poor children (*see* below p.109).

> *The Onze-Lieve-Vrouwekerk has the peculiar habit of closing for a three-hour lunch break (open Mon–Fri 9–11.30 and 2.30–5, Sat 9–11.30 and 2.30–4, Sun 2.30–5), so it might suit your timing to visit it now. Otherwise we will come back to it after the Gruuthusemuseum.*

> *Take the path beneath the arches to the right of the church, and turn right into* **Gruuthusestraat**. *The Gruuthusemuseum is immediately on your right.*

The **Gruuthusemuseum** is a celebration of bourgeois comforts (*see* p.83)—offering an excellent way to get a feel for how the well-to-do used to live in Bruges, through the objects that surrounded them in their homes.

Its building is one of the city's great historic mansions, although it was the victim of rather over-zealous restoration in the 1870s. In medieval times the lucky Lord of Gruuthuse had the monopoly on *gruut*, a special mixture of herbs and flowers which was used to flavour beer. Since beer was the drink of the age—boiled in manufacture so safer than water—the Lord of Gruuthuse was a wealthy man. When, in the 14th century through German influence, hops became the preferred flavouring for beer, the Lord of Gruuthuse was given the privilege of collecting a tax on beer instead.

The Lords of Gruuthuse were powerful figures in Bruges, and none more so than **Lodewijk van Gruuthuse** (or Louis of Bruges, *c.* 1427–92), son of Jan IV van Gruuthuse, who originally built this house in 1425. In 1449 Lodewijk was appointed cupbearer to Philip the Good, Duke of Burgundy—a great honour conferred by feudal lords only to their most trusted associates. He became governor of Bruges in 1452, and was made a Knight of the Golden Fleece in 1461.

This high office continued with Philip's successor, Charles the Bold, under whom Lodewijk became commander in chief of the army and navy. Charles was married to Margaret of York, whose brother, Edward IV of England, fled to Bruges (1470–1) with 800 followers. Lodewijk was appointed to act as his host, and Edward IV, stayed for six months at this house along with his brother, the notorious Richard 'Crookback', the future Richard III. Edward so appreciated the services and financial assistance of Lodewijk van Gruuthuse that, on his restoration, he made him Earl of Winchester.

When Charles the Bold died in battle in 1477, leaving his 20-year-old daughter Mary to inherit the Duchy, Lodewijk assisted her mother in finding a husband for her, to ward off the predations of the French king. They selected Maximilian of Austria but, after Mary's early and tragic death, Lodewijk—like most of Bruges—fell from favour. He was even imprisoned for three years after 1485, being released only to help negotiate the release of Maximilian, who was under house arrest in the Markt. Lodewijk died at the Gruuthuse in 1492. Part of his legacy was a massive collection of illuminated manuscripts, but his son took these with him as he transferred his allegiance and relocated to France, and they ended up in the *Bibliothèque Nationale de Paris*.

The Gruuthuse mansion lay redundant and increasingly derelict for a century, until in 1628 it was taken over by the **Berg van Barmhartigheid**, a charitable bank founded by Archduchess Isabella and based on the Italian institution *Mons Pietas*. It lent money at low or no interest to those who had fallen on hard times: in the 17th century, as Bruges suffered bouts of economic depression, this bank came to the rescue of many who would otherwise have had to resort to exorbitant loans from the commercial banks.

In the late 19th century the house caught the attention of the new breed of antiquarians and enthusiasts, William Brangwyn among them. The architect **Louis Delacenserie** (he of the Provinciaal Hof in the Markt) restored it as a museum to house their collections, but the work, carried out from 1873 to 1900, unfortunately involved almost as much neogothic fantasy as careful restoration, thus stripping it of much of its authenticity. It became a municipal museum in 1894.

> *Turn left when exiting the Gruuthusemuseum, and left again into* **Mariastraat**. *If you have the energy, you could pop into the Archeologisch Museum (see p.154) at Mariastraat 36A. Otherwise walk southward down Mariastraat, beneath the huge and dynamic brick spire of the Onze-Lieve-Vrouwekerk. The entrance to the church is on the south side, opposite Onze-Lieve-Vrouwekerkhof Zuid.*

Bruges has a historic affection for the Virgin Mary, as witnessed by the 300 or so Madonnas that appear on street corners and niches throughout the city. It is appropriate, therefore, that its greatest church, the **Onze-Lieve-Vrouwekerk** (*see* pp.86–8), should be dedicated to her. Within its walls is one of Bruges' outstanding treasures: the *Madonna and Child* by **Michelangelo**.

Opposite the church, note the rare intrusion of Art Nouveau in the façades of Nos. 6–8 Onze-Lieve-Vrouwekerkhof Zuid. Art Nouveau (here called *Jugendstil*) first emerged as an architectural style in Brussels in 1893, and rapidly became all the rage for new buildings in Brussels, Antwerp, Ghent and across Europe. Bruges, by contrast, remained unmoved, and Art Nouveau appears only in one or two isolated places, such as these houses, completed in 1904.

Facing the Onze-Lieve-Vrouwekerk, on the other side of Mariastraat, is the Sint-Janshospitaal, and its chapel, which houses the Memlingmuseum (see pp.85–6).

The **Sint-Janshospitaal** is a monument to the traditions of civilized, humanitarian behaviour, which have run like a thread through Bruges' history from early medieval times. This was evident still in the 1830s when the English traveller and writer Fanny Trollope was invited to visit the hospital, where she witnessed the work of the *Soeurs de la Charité*, the unpaid nuns who ran the hospital and were its only nurses.

The rest of the party declined from joining us, from a fear of encountering disagreeable objects; but they were wrong.
The pain, which the sight, or even the idea of human suffering must ever occasion, was a thousand times overbalanced by the pleasure of witnessing the tender care, the sedulous attention, the effective usefulness of those heavenly-minded beings,
Les Soeurs de la Charité.

The **Memlingmuseum** gives a rare opportunity to see medieval religious paintings in their proper context, a chapel, and surrounded by a complex that still breathes piety and charity.

Continue southwards along Mariastraat, taking a moment to look at the view from the bridge, Mariabrug, where the Sint-Janshospitaal lines the canal—the view that Fernand Khnopff used in his evocative pastel Secret-Reflet, in the Groeningemuseum.

*Continue down Katelijnestraat, but take the first right, Stoofstraat, which leads into the leafy **Walplein** (Rampart Square).*

The old **Halve Mann Brewery**, at Walplein 26, is now the source of Bruges' powerful Straffe Hendrik beer. For details, and information about visits to the brewery, *see* p.163.

*Continue southwards to Wijngaardstraat. Almost opposite the junction is **Noordstraat**.*

At the end of Noordstraat (Nos.4–14) is one of the prettiest set of almshouses, called **De Vos**, set around a garden. It was founded in 1683 by Christiaan de Vos.

Continue westwards along Wijngaardstraat and cross the bridge over the Reie to the arched entrance, emblazoned 1776.

This is the gateway to the **Begijnhof** (*see* pp.78–9), a charmed and restful enclave.

The History of *Béguinages*

Béguinages were communities of single women which developed during the 13th century, mainly in response to the imbalance caused by the Crusades: for several centuries there just weren't enough men to go round. Rather than living in isolation or with married relatives, many unmarried women preferred to join a *béguinage* until a suitable partner turned up. Widows (themselves often young) could also stay in a *béguinage*. By and large the women came from fairly well-off families as they had to pay an entry fee and maintenance.

These were pious communities, usually closely connected to a church, but the *béguines* were not nuns. They made simple vows of chastity and obedience to their elected superiors, applicable for the duration of their stay, and they led modest but comfortable lives, assisted by servants and estate workers, spending their time in prayer, in making lace, biscuits and sweets, in looking after the sick in their infirmary, and in distributing gifts to the poor.

The origin of the word *béguinage/begijnhof* remains obscure. One legend refers to **St Begga**, a 7th-century noblewoman who founded a convent and seven churches near Namur after her son found a hen shielding seven chicks from his hounds. A more plausible derivation recalls a priest from Liège, **Lambert le Bègue** ('the Stutterer'), who in about 1189 encouraged crusaders' widows to form communities, an idea that was revived by Margaret and Joanna of Constantinople, themselves orphaned by the Crusades. Their father was Baldwin IX, Count of Flanders, a leader of the Fourth Crusade (and the first Latin Emperor of Constantinople), who was captured by the Belgians and died in captivity in 1205.

Margaret and Joanna founded many of Belgium's most famous *béguinages*, at Antwerp, Ghent, Leuven and Bruges. The idea quickly spread throughout the Netherlands and Germany, and *béguinages* remained a widespread feature of society in the Low Countries—the larger ones had over a thousand members—until the 18th century. Even when deserted, they have a unique atmosphere of care, moderation and tranquillity.

Leaving the Begijnhof, continue south along Wijngaardstraat to the large rectangular lake called the **Minnewater**.

The Minnewater—a broad stretch of water, the River Reie, connected to the canals, and eventually the sea—was once a hive of activity as dozens of ships and barges jockeyed for position along the quays. The sluicegate had the important task of controlling the flow of water through the city. Today it is a quiet backwater, enjoyed by strollers and swans, perhaps now more atune to its popular name the 'Lake of Love'. Kenneth Hare alludes to this in his *Guide to Bruges* (1928), as well as to the unhealthy state of Bruges' canal water—a problem frequently referred to by visitors until a cleanup in the 1970s:

> *It is common knowledge that the water is charmed, and that the lover who drinks of it proves irresistible to the lady of his choice. The twentieth-century lover who first sterilizes the draught may go one better than his fourteenth-century ancestor. He may live to supervise the upbringing of children.*

Minne means 'love' in Dutch, but apparently in this case it was a mistranslation; Minnewater originally meant something like 'common water', or 'inner water'. It is a stretch of protected water off the outlying canals where the River Reie enters the city, which has served as a harbour since the 13th century, when the **Brugse Vesten**—the last, and largest, defensive ring of ramparts—was thrown up around the city and rimmed with a canal. This outer waterway became significantly busier after 1622, when it formed part of the Ghent–Bruges–Ostend canal.

Near the sluicegate house (*sashuis*) at the top end of the Minnewater is a bust of **Maurits Sabbe** (1873–1938), the Bruges-born academic and novelist who wrote several popular works set in the city, including *De Filosoof van het Sashuis* and *Aan 't Minnewater*. His vision of Bruges is upbeat and engaging, in contrast to the gloomy melancholy of Georges Rodenbach. It stands to reason that Sabbe gets a statue and Rodenbach doesn't.

At the southern end of the Minnewater is the old **Poedertoren** (gunpowder tower), built in 1398. Formerly an arsenal, it was once part of the Brugse Vesten, and it used to form one of a pair guarding the entrance to the harbour. Its twin was dismantled in 1621 and until the First World War served as an icehouse, where winter ice from the Minnewater was stored for summer use.

> *Continue round the southern end of the lake (there is a good view of the spires of Bruges across the water from the bridge at the base of the Minnewater), and along Katelijnevest. As the term 'vest' suggests, you are following the line of the old city ramparts, destroyed under the modernizing Emperor Joseph II in 1782–4.*

*Turn left up **Katelijnestraat**, to start heading back to the town centre.*

The **Bogaarden Convent** once stood on a site just beyond the corner with Arsenaalstraat. This was originally a settlement for *beghards*, the male equivalent of *béguines*, who spent their quiet lives mainly working with textiles. But the movement did not have the longevity of its female counterpart and died out in the early 16th century.

In 1513 the city fathers used the site to found the first Bogaarden school for poor children—a movement which went on to have a significant social impact across the Low Countries in the 16th and 17th centuries. The site is now occupied by Bruges' **Stedelijke Academie voor Schone Kunsten** (Academy of Fine Arts).

There are more almshouses here, on the eastern side of Katelijnestraat. The **Godshuis Hertsberge** (1683) is at Nos.87–101; the **Godshuis de Generaliteit** (1572) at Nos.79–83.

*A little further north along Katelijnestraat, at the junction with Oude Gentweg (the Old Ghent Road), is the **Bruges Diamond Museum**.*

Het Brugs Diamantmuseum (*43 Katelijnestraat, ✆ 33 64 33, open daily 10.30–5.30; diamond polishing demonstration daily at 12.15; adm 200 BF*) was opened in 1999. It offers a well-presented insight not only into the world of diamonds—mining, cutting, polishing, setting—but also into the role that luxury goods played in Bruges' past. It also has a section devoted to the general history of medieval Bruges, to set diamonds in their context, and translates details of jewellery from contemporary paintings into reaity.

Bruges has a historic connection with diamonds, developing as a centre for diamonds before Antwerp and Amsterdam. In 1476 the goldsmith **Lodewijk van Berquem** is said to have invented the technique of cutting and polishing diamonds by using diamond powder on a rotating disk.

*From Katelijnestraat, turn east along Oude Gentweg, then first left up **Driekroezenstraat**.*

There are three more almshouses here. In Driekroezenstraat is the **Godshuis Onze-Lieve-Vrouw der Zeven Weeën** (Almshouse of Our Lady of the Seven Sorrows), founded in 1654, a set of seven houses said to symbolize the 'Seven Sorrows of Mary'—the seven trials of her life from the Flight into Egypt to the Crucifixion.

In Nieuwe Gentweg are the **Godshuis Sint-Josef** (Nos.24–32), founded in 1634, and the **Godhuis de Meulenare** (Nos.8–22), founded in 1613.

Cross over the Nieuwe Gentweg and walk up the street called Groeninge, back to the Dijver canal, then turn left along the Gruuthusestraat—back in front of the Gruuthusemuseum again.

The north side of the street opens up as the **Guido Gezelleplein**, dedicated to Guido Gezelle (1830–99), Bruges' best-loved poet (*see* pp.31–3). The statue of the poet, by Jules Lagae (1862–1931), was inaugurated in 1930 by King Albert I and Queen Elisabeth to mark the centenary of his birth.

*Take the second right, the **Heilige-Geestraat** (Holy Ghost Street).*

At the end of the street is the Sint-Salvatorskathedraal, which has been Bruges' cathedral since 1834. Before that, after the corner with Goezeputstraat, is the former episcopal palace. This neoclassical mansion was built in 1740 on the site of the 16th-century Hof van Pittem, by the flamboyant bishop Hendrik van Susteren (1716–42), whose grandiose tomb by Hendrik Pulinx can be seen in the cathedral.

Continue to the Sint-Salvatorskathedraal; follow the wall round to the entrance on Steenstraat.

The **Sint-Salvatorskathedraal** (*see* p.89) is a bit of a mixed bag. Its billing as Bruges' cathedral raises expectations too high, but it can be strangely atmospheric, particular on dark days. The cathedral museum has some historic curiosities, as well as notable treasures, for example an inscribed lead tablet found beneath the skull of Gunhilde in her tomb in the church of St Donatian. Gunhilde was the sister of Harold Godwinson, King of England. After he was slain by William the Conqueror at the Battle of Hastings in 1066, she fled to Bruges, where she spent the rest of her life doing good works. After her death in 1087, she was regarded as a saint and later canonized.

*Head east along **Steenstraat**, one of Bruges' main shopping streets.*

A number of guilds had their headquarters in this street, but these have now mostly been taken over by shops. The finest are at No.40 (with its boot-and-crown emblem), the Shoemakers' and No.25, the Masons' (1620).

*Retrace your steps to where the right-hand side of Steenstraat opens up into the tree-lined **Simon Stevinplein**.*

This was once the site of a huge butchers' hall, the **Westvleeshuis**, dating back to the 14th century. It is now dominated by a bronze statue of **Simon Stevin** (1548–1620), made by Louis-Eugène Simonis and erected in 1847. Stevin was a remarkable figure, with a truly Renaissance breadth of talents—one of the out-standing figures of the age—but he joined the 16th-century brain drain to the Protestant Netherlands, and as a result was disowned by Bruges for 250 years.

Simon Stevin

Born out of wedlock in Bruges in 1548, Simon Stevin was a tax inspector in his youth, before he went to the newly founded University of Leiden. He soon developed a reputation for mathematics and hydraulic engineering, but was also interested in astronomy, navigation, perspective and book-keeping.

He made a number of ground-breaking discoveries: in 1586, by dropping weights from a church tower in Delft, he disproved Aristotle's theory that weight determines the speed at which objects fall—three years before Galileo's experiment from the Leaning Tower of Pisa. He also discovered that the downward pressure of a liquid depends on its height and base, not on the shape of the container. He is credited by some as the inventor of the decimal point; if not the inventor, he certainly standardized its usage, and predicted that the future lay in the decimalization of units.

As adviser to Prince Maurits of Nassau, son of William of Orange, he undertook wide-ranging engineering projects, such as coastal flood protection, and canal systems with sluices that also had applications for military defence.

He taught at Leiden, and was instrumental in the creation of the world's first faculty of engineering. He was one of the first academics to publish scientific books in the vernacular, as opposed to Latin. He is also fondly remembered for his sand-yacht, a contraption with two sails that bowled along the seashore carrying 26 people.

When his memory was honoured in the early 19th century by dedicating this square to him, there were still opponents who did not want to give such recognition to a heretic.

> *Walk south, through Simon Stevinplein, and turn left at the bottom into* **Oude Burg**.

At No.27 is an old patrician's mansion, the **Hof van Watervliet**. It was formerly called the Hof van Sint-Joris and was owned by Jan de Baenst, a leading figure in Burgundian Bruges under Philip the Good and Charles the Bold. It then became the home of the ill-fated treasurer of Maximilian I, Pieter Lanchals, who was executed in 1488. The house later belonged to the humanist Mark Laurin, Lord of Watervliet and dean of the church of St Donatian. His home was a gathering place for some of the leading humanists of the day, including Erasmus and Thomas More, who were drawn to Bruges on special occasions, such as the State Entry (*Joyeuse Entrée/ Blijde Intreden*) for Charles V in 1515. It's now a centre for the social and health services.

At the entrance to Kartuizerinnenstraat (street of the Carthusian Nuns), further down Oude Burg on the right, is a large arch surmounted by a coat of arms—a **memorial** to the Bruges dead of the first World War. Their names are inscribed on plaques on the wall of the old church (1716; *not open to the public*) of the Carthusian convent, a short way down the street, to which have been added the victims of the Second World War. The crypt of the church also contains the ashes of victims of Dachau.

> *Walk to the end of the Oude Burg, beneath the arches at the back of the Halle, then turn left into Wollestraat to return to the Markt.*

Walk II: City of Trade

Start: *the Markt.*
Walking time: *allow at least 2 hours
(the total distance is about 4km).*

In the Middle Ages, Bruges was one of the wealthiest cities in the world, prospering from the vibrant activity of its traders. It was an international and cosmopolitan city, with a web of contacts stretching across Europe to the Baltic and Russia, the Mediterranean and the Middle East, and North Africa. The engine room of this business culture was the network of streets that lies to the north of the Markt. This is where the deals were struck, and where the barges came to unload their cargoes of wool, cloth, dyes, salted fish, wine, spices, silks, oriental carpets, jewellery and live exotic animals.

Our second walk will give you a glimpse of this world and the rewards that it generated. It is almost exclusively an exterior walk: the only buildings that you can normally go inside are the three churches (and even they have very restricted opening hours), but they are not essential to the walk. The Sint-Jakobskerk (the best of them) is open only in July and August, in the afternoon. Otherwise you cannot hope to get inside any of them, unless on the off chance.

The only day to avoid, therefore, is one when it is pouring with rain.

lunch/cafés

① **Lotus**, Wapenmakersstraat 5. Relaxed, elegant vegetarian restaurant, with inventive and well-priced dishes, including some fish.

② **Hermitage**, Ezelstraat 18. *Closed mid-July to mid-Aug.* Delightful 17th-century mansionserving light French favourites. Menus from 2,000 BF.

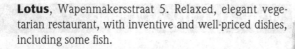

③ **'t stil Ende**, Scheepsdalelaan 12. *Closed Sat lunch, Mon, last 2 weeks of July.* Crisp modern interpretations of classic French dishes served in a stylish, modern setting. Menus from 950 BF (lunch).

④ **Boterhuis Brasserie**, Sint-Jakobsstraat 38. Warm welcome in a traditional brasserie setting, with steaks (400 BF), brochettes, pasta and snacks.

⑤ **'t Vorske Malpertus**, Eiermarkt 9. Solid Flemish food, including rabbit dishes and delicious *waterzooi*, in medieval cellars which once formed part of a monastery.

⑥ **Het Dagelijks Brood**, Philipstockstraat 21. *Open 7–6, Sun 8–6; closed Tues.* A branch of the successful *Pain Quotidien* chain. Bakery snacks and upmarket sandwiches. Seating around a big central table.

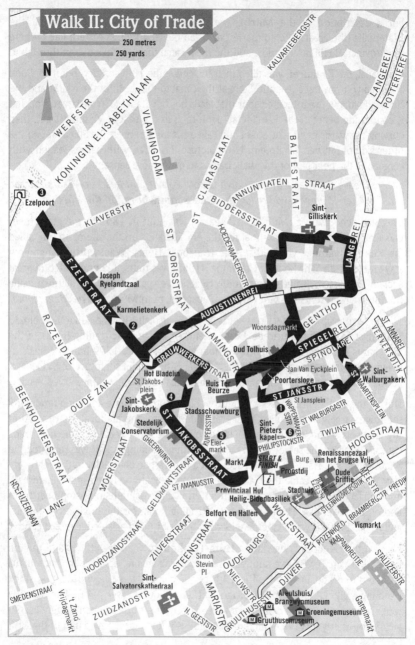

Walk II: City of Trade

250 metres
250 yards

N

③ Ezelpoort

ST CLARASTRAAT

KALVARIEBERGSTR

LANGEREI

POTTERIEREI

WERFSTR

KONINGIN ELISABETHLAAN

VLAMINGDAM

KLAVERSTR

ST JORISSTRAAT

BIDDERSSTRAAT

ANNUNTIATEN STRAAT

BALIESTRAAT

HOEDENMAKERSSTR

Sint-Gilliskerk

EZELSTRAAT

Joseph Ryelandtzaal

Karmelietenkerk

②

ROZENDAL

OUDE ZAK

AUGUSTIJNENREI

VLAMINGSTRAAT

LANGEREI

GENTHOF

SPIEGELREI

Woensdagmarkt

SPINOLAREI

ST ANNAREI

VERVERSDIJK

GRAUWWERKERSTRAAT

Oud Tolhuis

Jan Van Eyckplein

Poortersloge

Sint-Walburgakerk

BEENHOUWERSSTRAAT

Hof Bladelin
St Jakobs-plein

Huis Ter Beurze

ST MAARTENSPLEIN

Sint-Jakobskerk

④

Stadsschouwburg

ST JANSSTR

St Jansplein

WAPENMAKER SSTR

ST WALBURGASTR

Stedelijk Conservatorium

KUIPERSSTR

⑤
Eier-markt

Sint-Pieters kapel

⑥

PHILIPSTOCKSTR

TWIJNSTR

HOOGSTRAAT

MOERSTRAAT

GHEERWIJNSTR

ST JAKOBSSTRAAT

GELDMUNTSTRAAT

Markt

①

Renaissancezaal van het Brugse Vrije

HOEFIJZERLAAN

ST AMANUSSTR

START & FINISH

Burg

Proostdij

Oude Griffie

BRAAMBERGSTR

PREDIK

Provinciaal Hof
Heilig-Bloedbasiliek

i

Stadhuis

STEENHOUWERSDIJK

ROZENHOED-KAAI

Vismarkt

NOORDZANDSTRAAT

ZILVERSTRAAT

STEENSTRAAT

OUDE BURG

WOLLESTRAAT

ST ANDRIES

STALIZERSTR

Belfort en Hallen

Simon Stevin Pl

't Zand Vrijdagmarkt

SMEDENSTRAAT

ZUIDZANDSTR

Sint-Salvatorskathedraal

H. GEESTSTR

MARIASTR

NIEUWSTRAAT

GRUUTHUSESTR

DIJVER

Arents-huis/
Brangwynmuseum

Gruuthusemuseum

Groeningemuseum

Garenmarkt

For a description of the **Markt** *see* **Walk I**, pp.96–8. Remember that the Waterhalle (the great covered market hall) ran the length of its eastern flank where the Provinciaal Hof now stands, and the main canal through the city ran through it.

This canal, the **Kraanrei**, was filled in at the end of the 18th century, but if you look at a map you can trace its path. Start at the canal to the south of the Markt and the Burg, and follow the truncated spur that leads north, parallel to Wollestraat. Imagine it continuing beneath the Provinciaal Hof, then to the east of Vlamingstraat, then curving eastwards beside the street still called Kraanrei to meet the Spiegelrei on the other side of Jan van Eyckplein. Now picture this filled with barges loaded with cargo, and the next part of this walk begins to make more sense.

*Leave the Markt by the northeastern corner and head up Vlamingstraat. After 150m you will reach the **Stadsschouwburg**, on the lefthand side.*

The Stadsschouwburg (Municipal Theatre) was built in 1868 in the grand neo-classical style considered essential for the era. It stands on the site of an inn called De Koorneblomme, where the American poet Henry Wadsworth Longfellow stayed. His poem 'The Song of Hiawatha' (1855) was translated into Dutch to great acclaim in 1886 by Bruges' poet Guido Gezelle (*see* pp.31–33). The statue outside the theatre represents the bird-catcher, Papageno, from Mozart's *The Magic Flute*.

A little further up the street, in what is called Beursplein (Bourse Square), at No.33 Vlamingstraat, is the **Genuese Loge** (Genoese Lodge), the trading house of the merchants from the Italian city of Genoa. Not a lot of the 1399 building has survived, apart from the entrance (with a 19th-century relief sculpture of St George, patron saint of Genoa, slaying his dragon, a replica of the original, preserved inside).

During the 16th century, serge (a light woollen cloth) became a leading product of the town, largely as a result of concerted efforts to regenerate local industry. After the Genoans abandoned Bruges in 1516 to join the other traders in the new trade centre, Antwerp, the serge-weavers took over their building, and it was renamed the **Saaihalle** (Serge Hall). In 1720 it acquired a Dutch-style bell gable. In the 19th century the building became the Café Rosimont, with boarding house and billiard hall, and the façade was emblazoned with lettering advertising its non-stop beefsteaks and other provender. Then it became a Reading Room for the English community and in the 1920s it was a cinema. Now restored, it is used as an educational centre.

Next to the Genoese Lodge is the **Huis Ter Beurze**. This was the site of the inn run by the Van Ter Beurze family, where moneychangers, bankers and merchants gathered to do business from the 13th century on. It was the world's first stock exchange, giving rise to the international term 'bourse' (*see* p.44). The building looks very much as it did in the mid 15th century, but has been largely reconstructed. Latterly it was a branch of the Bank van Roeselare, now a part of the KBC

The Rules of the Trade

Foreign traders in Bruges during medieval times were allowed considerable freedoms, such as the right to purchase or rent property, and to carry arms unchallenged. The most important general restriction, however, was that they were not allowed to undertake retail trade, nor to resell within the city goods that they bought there: they were strictly import-and-export merchants and the main export was Flemish textiles. The trading houses—which became increasingly extravagant architecturally—offered their nationals a common meeting place, protection and representation, an information service for newcomers, and in some cases a chapel. They also took responsibility for policing their own compatriots, and laid down the etiquette of trade and general rules of behaviour, governing drinking, gambling and even bedtimes. Offenders were punished by fines or banishment. As a result, this trading environment tended to be orderly, businesslike and civilized, and any disputes were quickly settled by negotiation. (The common language was Latin.) By and large the atmosphere within the city was trusting and peaceable, even though the Flemish cities, the French and the English were often at war.

Bank. The building is currently being used as the organisational headquarters for Bruges' role in Euro 2000 (UEFA soccer) and Bruges 2002.

It was no accident that the Huis Ter Beurze became a centre for financial transactions: the entry point to the Kraanrei canal lay 200m away, and the Beursplein was flanked by the lodges of the Genoans, the Florentines and the Venetians, who won the privilege of constructing the first national lodge in 1322, at right angles to the Huis Ter Beurze. The crumbled remains of their house were removed in 1965. Next to that, separated by a narrow continuation of Vlamingstraat, was the Florentine lodge, described in 1926 as 'a beautiful building flanked by four graceful turrets, now entirely spoilt'. That too has gone, but a marble plaque on the side of No.1 Academiestraat, recalls it with a verse about Flemish dike-building from the *Inferno* by the Florentine poet Dante (1265–1321).

> *Turn right into Academiestraat, which broadens out into **Jan van Eyckplein**.*

At the end of the street, on the right, is the **Poortersloge**, built in the 14th century but much restored. It is one of the few buildings that has retained its tower (rebuilt after a fire in 1775), a common feature of prestige architecture in the medieval period. This was a meeting place for a select group of successful city burghers, and the Society of the White Bear, charged with organizing jousting tournaments, was also based here, hence the statue of a bear in one of the niches. According to legend, when Baldwin Iron-Arm first built his castle and founded Bruges, the only living creature on the site was a bear—the city's first inhabitant. In 1739 the building was bought by the city and was home to its Academy of Arts for 150 years (hence the street's name). The Poortersloge was cited as one of the 'Seven Marvels of Bruges' in the 16th century, when it appeared in prints very much as it does today. It can also be seen in contemporary paintings, such as Gerard David's *The Judgement of Cambyses* (1498) in the Groeningemuseum.

Diametrically opposite, overlooking Jan van Eyckplein, is the **Oud Tolhuis** (Old Customs House). Over the arched entrance is the coat of arms of Peter of Luxembourg, the receiver of the toll who ordered the reconstruction of the building in 1477. The extremely narrow building next to the Tolhuis is the Huis de Lastdragers (1470), the guildhouse of the Stevedores. Both have been heavily restored. The location of these buildings is significant, for they overlooked the Sint-Jansbrug where there was a weighhouse belonging to the Tolhuis, and where, after weighing, customs were levied on all incoming cargoes. However, the bridge has gone, and the canals were removed in the 18th century to be replaced by Jan van Eyckplein, with a statue (1878) of the great 15th-century painter by the Bruges sculptor Henry Pickery (1828–94). (For more on Jan van Eyck, *see* pp.67–8.)

The Spiegelrei canal now stops short of the Jan van Eyckplein (we shall come to this later), but it used to intersect the Jan van Eyckplein and the southern part has retained its old name, Biskajersplein, after the trading house of the Biscayan (or Basque) merchants at No.6a—built in 1494 and now much restored.

*We now trace the path of the old canal a short distance by taking the Kraanrei west from the top of Biskajersplein to the **Kraanplein**.*

Kraan means crane. The 'town crane' in question was a herculean contraption, pictured in 16th-century prints and maps. It was built like a wooden barn, but with a triangular projection rising from it—the crane arm. The pulleys were driven by a pair of human treadmills and the whole machine swivelled round to lift barrels, sacks and other heavy cargo from barges on to the quayside. The crane was run and maintained by a team of dedicated workers, who operated it from dawn to dusk.

*Turn left at Kraanplein into Sint-Jansstraat (St John's Street). You will soon come to **Sint-Jansplein**.*

The most striking feature of the square is the brick **Huis de Cone**, at the corner with Wijnzakstraat, a late-Gothic house, formerly a wine tavern, built in about 1500. The centre of Sint-Jansplein (now the site of a late 18th-century monumental water pump) used to be occupied by the Sint-Janskerk, a church used until the 16th century by English merchants who lived in this neighbourhood, but it was demolished in the 1780s.

Continue along Sint-Jansstraat to **Engelsestraat**.

Engelsestraat was so named because this was the heart of Bruges' English community. As purveyors of the high-quality wool on which the Flemish textile trade was based, they occupied a pivotal position in Bruges' business affairs. To facilitate business, the English were granted the privilege of having their own weighhouse, set up in this street in the 1330s, which meant that they could weigh their goods near their trading house without recourse to the public weighhouses. During the 15th century the English consular house was close to the corner with Sint-Jansstraat, before it was moved into Sint-Jansplein, and then to Spiegelrei.

Turn right into Engelsestraat, then first left into Korte Ridderstraat. The Bruges poet Guido Gezelle lived at No.5 from 1865 to 1872. The street brings you swiftly to **Sint-Maartensplein**.

Sint-Maartensplein used to be called Schottenplaats, after the Scottish contingent who had a consular house here. Today the dominant feature is the baroque façade of the **Sint-Walburgakerk**.

We are now looking at a later era, when Bruges had passed its medieval heyday, and most of the trauma of the religious wars. The Sint-Walburgakerk is a political statement, a triumphant beacon of the Counter-Reformation designed to put the puritanical modesty of the Protestants in the shade. Unfortunately it is not easy to get inside (*open Easter–Sept daily 8pm–10pm only, when it is evocatively lit and recorded church music is played*), but it has a glass door which usually allows you to peer into the interior. It is also sometimes used as a venue for concerts.

Among the leading forces in the Counter-Reformation were the Jesuits, members of the 'Society of Jesus' founded in the 1530s by the Spanish-born St Ignatius of Loyola. St Ignatius visited Bruges between 1528 and 1530, when studying in Paris, and stayed with Gonzalez d'Aguilera, a leading figure in the Basque community. The Jesuit movement had a strong following in Bruges, and this square became their focus, with a monastery and college. This was the monastery church, built between 1619 and 1643 to designs by the Bruges-born Jesuit lay-brother, Pieter Huyssens (architect also of the Sint-Carolus Borromeuskerk in Antwerp). It was the first church to be dedicated to St Francis Xavier, the great Jesuit missionary who died in China in 1552, and was canonized in 1622; his statue looks down from the façade. The Jesuits were suppressed under the Austrians in 1773, and this then became the parish church of St Walburga, taking over that role from another church nearby that was demolished in 1781.

St Walburga was an 8th-century English nun who accompanied St Boniface of Crediton on his missionary work to Germany. She was abbess of Heidenheim, but after her death her remains were transferred to Eichstätt on the eve of May Day— bad luck for the blameless Walburga, for this was a pagan festival associated with witchcraft, which subsequently became known as Walpurgisnacht.

During the French occupation the Sint-Walburgakerk had a spell as a Temple of Law. Despite this varied history, the Jesuit heritage remains very much in evidence—exuberant baroque decorations, swags, garlands, cherubs and broken pediments—but all elegantly modulated. The fine wooden pulpit (1667–69) was made by Artus Quellinus the Younger at about the time that his gifted pupil, Dutch-born Grinling Gibbons, went to England to start his career as one of the great master-carvers of all time. The high altar is an equally elaborate piece by Jacob Cocx, with a painting of the *Resurrection* (1783) by Bruges-born artist Joseph B. Suvée, who went on to become the director of the French Academy in Rome.

Guido Gezelle was a priest at the church for seven years from 1865, which is why he lived at Korte Riddersstraat (and later at 20 Verversdijk, on the canal).

> *Continue northwards from Sint-Maartensplein, following Koningstraat (King Street) to the canal. Cross the Koningbrug to Spiegelrei (good view of the Poortersloge).*

Spiegel means 'mirror', and now that this stretch of canal no longer has through traffic of boats and barges it often is mirror-still. Spinolarei (on the south side) was named after an Italian general serving with the Spanish army, who captured Ostend in 1604.

No.15 Spiegelrei is now a school, but in the 15th century it was the headquarters of the English Merchant Adventurers who ran English business in Bruges, dealing mainly in wool, hides and tin. In 1464 the governor of the Adventurers was William Caxton, the man who brought printing to England (*see* p.49). At No.17 is a rare surviving example of a spy mirror, projecting from the window frame. This allowed people inside the house to see what was going on in the street outside. The Bruges streets were once full of them, and visitors used to complain that it gave them the eerie feeling of being constantly watched.

> *Walk back westwards along the **Spiegelrei** to head back towards Jan van Eyckplein.*

The house on the corner with Genthof, called Roode Steen, used to bear a plaque commemorating Georges Rodenbach, author of *Bruges-la-Morte*. It was put up in 1948, 50 years after his death—at his family's expense. It has since been removed.

> *Turn right at the end of Spiegelrei into Genthof.*

At No.7 is one of the very few surviving wooden houses in Bruges, dating from the 16th century. During the medieval era most houses in the city were made of wood—hence the importance of the Scottish timber trade, but fire was an ever-present hazard. Thatch was progressively banned, and area by area after 1417 the town subsidized householders to replace thatch with tiles and slate, but the parallel restrictions on wooden houses were not introduced until the 1600s.

Continue to **Woensdagmarkt.**

Woensdagmarkt is the site of the old Wednesday market. The statue of the German-born painter Hans Memling (see p.68) is by Henry Pickery, completed four years before his Jan van Eyck to the south. The square is overlooked by a tall brick tower, typical of a late-medieval trader's mansion.

To the north Woensdagmarkt merges with **Oosterlingenplein.**

This is named after the *Oosterlingen*, 'easterners' (in other words the Germans), representatives of the powerful trading cities of the Hanseatic League. Formed during the 13th century, the Hanseatic League bound together German trading associations (*Hanse*) by treaties of mutual protection. It grew to include over 70 German cities—notably Bremen, Hamburg, Lübeck and Cologne—which traded across the Baltic and north Europe, and as far east as Novgorod in Russia, dealing in a huge range of goods that included iron ore, timber, grain, furs, salt, fish, beer, beeswax, honey and amber.

In fact the Hanseatic League was so powerful that it had a fractious relationship with the city, with continual disputes over import taxes. Although it was one of the first foreign groups to be established in Bruges, it was also one of the last to be granted the privilege of building a trading house. Late in the day, in 1470, as an inducement to keep it in Bruges, it was at last given property by the town, and between 1478 and 1481 built the finest lodge of them all, the Oosterlingenhuis, a massive late-Gothic enclave with a crenellated castle topped with a soaring tower. This was one of the 'Seven Marvels of Bruges', the list of the finest buildings selected in the 16th century. Nonetheless, the Germans were among the first to relocate to Antwerp. The Oosterlingenhuis fell into decay and was demolished in the 18th century; all that remains of this building is at No.1 Krom Genthof (brick house with flag).

A little further north Oosterlingenplein meets the canal. The street running westwards along the canal is the **Spaanse Loskaai.**

This part of town was effectively the Spanish quarter: the Spanish trading house was in Spanjaardstraat, just beyond Spaanse Loskaai. Their main trade was in wool, hides and fruit. After Bruges' decline in the 16th century, the Spanish remained the only foreign traders who maintained a large presence in the city, as part of the ruling elite; Flanders remained part of the Spanish Netherlands until 1713.

*Turn eastwards along the canal, following Gouden-Handrei. The canal here traces the path of the second set of city walls, built in about 1127. Turn left at the end, crossing Gouden-Handbrug, and head north along Langerei. The first street on the left is Gouden-Handstraat (Jan van Eyck lived at No.6). Take the next left, **Sint-Gilliskoorstraat**, to reach the church.*

The **Sint-Gilliskerk** (*open May–Sept Mon–Sat 10–12 and 2–5, Sun 11–12 and 2–5*) takes the typical Bruges form, with a hall-like interior formed by three robust parallel aisles. A single nave was built in around 1277, and two additional aisles were added in the second half of the 15th century. The remarkable wooden barrel vault is original.

The interior was devastated and stripped by Protestant iconoclasts in the 1570s, only to be restored with baroque flourishes in the Counter-Reformation, and in neogothic style in the 1880s. Its most interesting feature is the series of four paintings by the Bruges artist **Jan Garemijn** (1712–99) commemorating the work of the Bruges Trinitarian Brotherhood, founded in 1642, for whom this church served as headquarters. Following in the footsteps of the 12th-century Trinitarian movement, the Brotherhood collected money to raise the ransom for soldiers and travellers held captive in the Muslim Ottoman Empire, especially in North Africa where they were sold as slaves. Among those rescued was Francis van Mulder, the son of a Bruges potter; one of the paintings shows his happy return to Dunkirk in 1780. The Brotherhood was suppressed in 1786 by the Austrians.

Outside, to the left of the door, is a modern memorial stone to Hans Memling. He was a resi-dent of the parish, and was buried in the church in 1494, although no part of his tomb has survived. He had several properties in Sint-Jorisstraat and his studio was in Jan Miraelstraat, west of the church.

*Take Lange Raamstraat and then take the first left, Schottinnenstraat. Worm your way south by taking the first right (Sterstraat), and then the first left (Oost-Gistelstraat) to reach the Augustijnenrei (named after the Augustinian friars). Continue along Augustijnenrei to the next bridge, **Vlamingbrug**.*

Vlamingbrug has pretty views up and down the canal; the stone seats were used by traders to set out their wares. Just over the bridge, at No.2 Kortewinkel, is another of Bruges' rare wooden houses.

*Continue along the north side of the canal following **Pottermakkers-straat** (Potters Street).*

If you look south from here over the canal, you can see the last remnant of the 1127 city walls: part of a tower, now set in the garden wall of a house in Pieter Pourbusstraat. The canal here also used to serve as a moat.

The Discalced Carmelites

In 1630 a mendicant order of friars called the Discalced (barefooted) Carmelites came to Bruges. Because there was a large population of mendicant monks and nuns in a city already economically stretched, they were not made very welcome. However, the following year Bruges was struck by plague. The Discalced Carmelites acted with selfless charity and tended to the sick, and they were rewarded with the unenviable honour of being appointed the official plague priests, led by the 'Pest-Pater', who carried a red warning stick with a cross on top. The plague continued for seven years, but the Discalced Carmelites never shrank from their duty. As one caught the plague and died, another would volunteer to take over his task, even putting on the dead man's habit. The grateful city granted them property in Ezelstraat in 1633, where a new convent was built after 1680. The order continued to do good works through the hard decades that followed, but it was suppressed in 1798, and many of the friars were transported to western France. They were allowed to return after 1800; their numbers rapidly dwindled before a revival in the 1840s, and they are still there.

> At Ezelstraat (Donkey Street) you have a choice. You can either turn right along Ezelstraat and walk about 500m to the **Ezelpoort**, one of the four surviving city gates; or you can turn left across the Ezelbrug and start heading back to the centre of the city, in which case turn to p.124.
>
> Turning right along Ezelstraat, after 200m you reach a church on the righthand side, on the corner with Jan Boninstraat. This is the **Karmelietenkerk** (not open to the public).

The convent church of the Discalced Carmelite nuns is further up the road, on the right-hand side, on Achiel van Ackerplein. It became an Anglican church in 1820, a measure of the growing English community in the city. In 1983 it was converted into the **Joseph Ryelandtzaal**, a municipal concert hall named after a Bruges-born composer (1870–1965) who became a professor at the Conservatoire of Ghent and wrote various symphonic works and an opera called *Sainte Cécile*. The sculptures (1987) on the façade are by Stefaan Depuydt and Livia Canestraro, creators of the large sculpture on 't Zand.

Achiel van Acker (1898–1975) after whom the square is named, was a Bruges-born socialist politician who was prime minister between 1945 and 1946 and between 1954 and 1958, and who was instrumental in establishing the welfare state in post-war Belgium.

*Continue to the end of Ezelstraat, where the **Ezelpoort** lies on the other side of the Koningin Elisabethlaan.*

The Ezelpoort was one of eight city gates built in the late 14th century to reinforce the outer defences of the city (*see* p.135). With its weathered brick, a backdrop of trees and shallow arches spanning the canal—often dappled with swans—it is the prettiest of the four surviving gates, and also the latest, having been rebuilt in 1615. Note the bell on the roof, which announced when the gate was closing.

*Now walk back down Ezelstraat and cross the **Ezelbrug** to rejoin those who skipped the detour to Ezelpoort.*

*Turn left along Grauwwerkerstraat, then first right into **Naaldenstraat** (Needle Street).*

At No.19 is **Hof Bladelin**, one of the great private mansions of the Burgundian era, complete with a tower (*courtyard open April–Sept Mon–Sat 10–12 and 2–5, Sun 10.30–12; Oct–March Mon–Sat 10–12 and 2–4, Sun 10.30–12; ring the doorbell for access*). It was built in about 1450 by Pieter Bladelin (1410–72), municipal treasurer and councillor to Philip the Good, treasurer of the Order of the Golden Fleece, and one of the wealthiest men in the city. The sculpture (1892) over the main entrance depicting Pieter Bladelin kneeling before the Virgin is by the neogothic architect Louis Delacenserie, who also designed the Provinciaal Hof in the Markt.

In 1469 the house was bought by the Medici Bank of Florence, hence the terracotta medallions on the walls of the courtyard, depicting Lorenzo de' Medici ('The Magnificent') and his wife Clarissa Orsini. One of its representatives, Tommaso Portinari, lived here from 1473 to 1497, and exercised a powerful role in the city as the banker who could underwrite the extravagances of Charles the Bold's court. He was also a patron of Hans Memling and Hugo van de Goes (whose triptych featuring the Nativity, now in the Uffizi Museum in Florence, is called the *Portinari Triptych*). After Charles the Bold's death in 1477, on his ill-advised military adventure against France, the Medici Bank dismissed Portinari for financial recklessness. He stayed in Bruges and worked on his own account, until bankrupted in 1497—a sign of the failing economy of the city.

Opposite Hof Bladelin on the corner of Kuipersstraat (Coopers Street) is the site of the trading house of the Italian city of Lucca, built in 1394. Only the cellars remain. The tower at No.7 marks the site of the **Hof van Gistel**, a palace built in 1444 by Antoine de Bourbon, Duke of Vendôme, Lord of Gistel. It was later owned by the head of the Spanish community in Bruges, Jean de Matance of Burgos.

*Take the arched alley by No.9 Naaldenstraat, **Boterhuis**, so-called because it passes beneath the arch of the Boterhuis (Butter House), a market for dairy produce from the 16th century to the mid 19th century.*

The Wealth of Bruges

In 1438 a Spaniard called Pero Tafur visited Bruges and recorded his impressions:

> *In the whole of the west there is no other great mercantile centre except Bruges... and thither repair all nations of the world, and they say that at times the number of ships sailing from the harbour of Bruges exceeds seven hundred a day...The people of this part of the country are exceedingly fastidious in their apparel, very extravagant in their food, and much given to all kinds of luxury... Without doubt the goddess of luxury has great power there, but it is not a place for poor men, who would be badly received. But any one who has money and wishes to spend it, will find in this town alone everything which the whole world produces. I saw there oranges and lemons from Castile, which seemed only just to have been gathered from the trees, fruits and wine from Greece, as abundant as in that country. I saw also confections and spices from Alexandria and all the Levant just as if one were there; furs from the Black Sea, as if they had been produced in the district. Here was all Italy with its brocades, silks and armour, and everything which is made there; and indeed there is no part of the world whose products are not found here at their best.*

Opposite the end of Boterhuis, at No.41 Sint-Jakobsstraat, is the Hotel Navarra. In the 16th century this was the consulate of Navarre, a kingdom that straddled the Pyrenees between Spain and France, before being absorbed by those countries in 1515 an 1589 respectively.

> *Turn right at Sint-Jakobsstraat to reach **Sint-Jakobskerk** (St James's Church; open July and Aug Mon–Fri and Sun 2–5.30, Sat 2–4).*

Sint-Jakobskerk is the richest of the parish churches in Bruges, but unfortunately it has very limited opening hours. The first building on this site was a 13th-century chapel, but it was enlarged in the 15th and 16th centuries, and remodelled in baroque style in the 17th century in the wake of the destruction by the iconoclasts in 1580. It had an impressive range of benefactors in the Burgundian era, including Charles the Bold and Tommaso Portinari, as well as a dozen guilds, whose altars animated the side chapels and pillars. The church once contained paintings by Rogier van der Weyden, Hugo van de Goes and Hans Memling, but these were rescued from the iconoclasts and never returned.

The church still contains a good collection of some 80 paintings, including *The Legend of St Lucy* (*c.* 1480) by the Master of the St Lucy Legend, and work by Pieter Pourbus and Jacob van Oost the Elder. It also has one of the most ornate side chapels in Bruges to the right of the choir, with the polychrome tomb of Ferry de Gros, treasurer of the Order of the Golden Fleece, who died in 1544. This tomb is curious because it includes both his wives: a statue of his first wife, who died in 1521 after producing 16 children, lies beside his effigy; his second wife also died before him in 1530 (after just three children), so she has been slotted in on the level below.

> On leaving the church, head back down Sint-Jakobsstraat which opens up into **Eiermarkt** (Egg Market)—with its monumental water pump (1761) designed by Pieter Pepers—and leads you back to the Markt.

Walk III: Canals and Windmills

Start: *the Burg.*

Walking time: *about 1½ hours—the total distance is about 6km—but visiting the museums and churches could easily take 4 hours.*

Eastern Bruges is agreeably quiet, with spacious streets lined with cottages and terraced houses, and infrequent cars rumbling over the cobbles. It would be an exaggeration to say that this walk takes you off the beaten track, but you will be surprised how busy the centre of Bruges seems when you return to it at the end.

The walk takes in a number of small museums and churches, which all have a slight note of quaint eccentricity about them. The row of windmills lining the earth bank along the canal also lends a rustic air, freshened by breezes that drive in across the polders from the North Sea. When you've done all the big sites in the city centre, you deserve this walk, and will find here the relaxed mood that is the authentic beat of the city.

The Museum voor Volkskunde (Folklore Museum) is the best museum in the walk; note that it is closed on Tuesdays in winter (*Oct–Mar*). The church and museum of Onze-Lieve-Vrouw ter Potterie are closed on Wednesdays in winter. The Jeruzalemkerk is closed on Sundays.

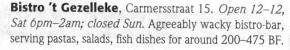

lunch/cafés

① **Bistro 't Gezelleke**, Carmersstraat 15. *Open 12–12, Sat 6pm–2am; closed Sun.* Agreeably wacky bistro-bar, serving pastas, salads, fish dishes for around 200–475 BF.

② **Café Vlissinghe**, Blekersstraat 2. *Open 11am–midnight; closed Tues.* Atmospheric, wood-panelled bar, with a cast-iron stove. Boules court in the garden. Soup, cheese, ham platters and pasta.

③ **De Windmolen**, Carmersstraat 135. *Open 10–9; closed Sat.* Charming, folksy, family-run bistro and bar, decorated with dried flowers and *bric-à-brac*, and serving pasta, sandwiches, *garnaalkroketten* for around 250 BF.

④ **Bistro De Schaar**, Hooistraat 2. *Open 12–2.30 and 6–11; closed Sun.* Agreeable little bistro: fish soup, stuffed mushrooms with snails.

⑤ **Toermalijn**, Coupure 29a. Organic vegetarian restaurant in the Hotel Dante, overlooking the canal. Excellent *Waterzooi* with tofu.

⑥ **L'Estaminet**, Gevangenisstraat 5. *Open from 11.30; closed Mon lunch and Sun.* Quaint pub with low beams: a trusty *drankhuis* since 1900.

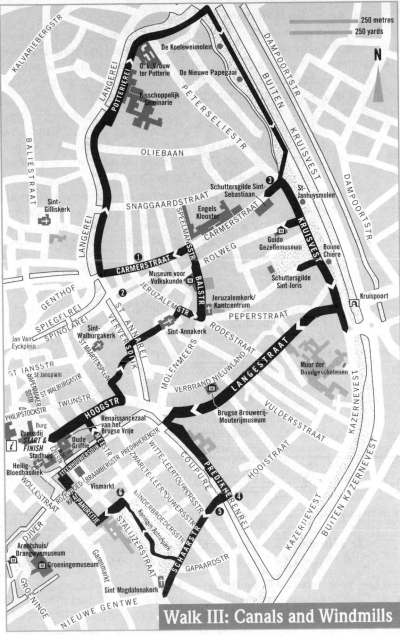

*Leave the Burg by **Hoogstraat** (High Street).*

It's hard to credit now, but the grimy brick frontage on the right, at No.6, was once part of one of the city's most spectacular medieval residences, the **Huis de Zeven Torens** (House of the Seven Towers). With its seven towers rising like jousters' lances from a huge Gothic hall, four storeys high, it ranked among the 'Seven Marvels of Bruges' in the 16th century, and is now semi-derelict.

It was built in about 1300, and known as the Domus Malleana, after its owners, the powerful de Male family. (Louis de Male was the last Count of Flanders (*r.* 1346–84), handing over power to the Dukes of Burgundy.) The future Charles II of England stayed here during his exile (1656–8). However, the towers were demolished in 1717, and the building slid into a long decline.

*Continue along Hoogstraat, and turn left up Boomgaardstraat (Orchard Street), then take the alley on the first right, Kandelaarstraat (Candlestick Street). This leads to the Verversdijk (Dyers' Embankment) on the canal. Turn left and cross the canal on the Sint-Annabrug. Continue along Sint-Annakerkstraat to **Sint-Annakerk** (open April–Sept Mon–Fri 10–12 and 2–4, Sat 10–12; closed Sun).*

This is a fine barrel-vaulted church, originally consecrated in 1497, but wrecked by the iconoclasts in 1581. It was completely refurbished after 1624, and has retained its authentic 17th- and 18th-century interior, complete with chandeliers, marble rood screen, and carved oak panelling, with statues and barley-sugar columns in sombre oak. It may not have many great treasures, but the Sint-Annakerk has a sense of decorative unity unmatched by any other church in Bruges.

It is easy to picture in your mind's eye the nave filled with the kind of well-to-do burghers portrayed in paintings by Jacob van Oost in the Groeningemuseum (also represented in the church), and perhaps members of Charles II's entourage swaggering in for a refreshing dose of confession and penitence. Guido Gezelle, the Bruges poet whom we shall meet later, was baptized and made his first communion here. The vast *Last Judgement* (over the entrance) by **Hendrik Herregouts** (1685) has the distinction of being Bruges' largest painting, measuring over 100 square metres.

*Continue eastwards through Sint-Annaplein, and turn right on to Jeruzalemstraat. On the corner of Balstraat and Peperstraat is the **Jeruzalemkerk** and **Kantcentrum** (Lace Centre; open Mon–Fri 10–12 and 2–6, Sat 10–12 and 2–5; closed Sun; adm 60 BF; demonstrations of lace-making every afternoon).*

The Jeruzalemkerk is an unusual church for several reasons, not least its polygonal tower surmounted by two tiers of wooden lanterns and crowned by a tin orb which heralds an even more eccentric and remarkable interior. It could be mistaken for a water tower, but in fact its influence is Byzantium.

This corner of Bruges was home to the distinguished **Adorno (or Adorni) family**, scions of one of the leading families of Genoa in Italy. Oppicino Adorno (d. 1307) joined the crusader forces of Guy de Dampierre, Count of Flanders, and settled in Bruges. In 1427 brothers **Pietro** and **Jacob** Adorno, returning from a visit to the Holy Land, refurbished the family chapel as a replica of the Church of the Holy Sepulchre in Jerusalem, including a reconstruction of Christ's tomb (with a life-size naked body of Christ) in the crypt. The crypt also contains a fragment of the Holy Cross in a gilded silver cross (behind the ornate grille). The altar reinforces the theme: it is dominated by a macabre carving of a skull-laden Golgotha, and three stark crosses.

Pietro was a leading figure in Bruges' political life and carried the torch for Renaissance humanism, but he was also deeply pious, and his intention was to recreate a slice of the Holy Land in Bruges which the public could share in.

His son **Anselmo** (often referred to as Anselm Adornes) maintained this tradition. He became treasurer of Bruges, and likewise visited the Holy Land, adding to the collection of holy relics in the church. In the service of Charles the Bold, Duke of Burgundy, he travelled on a number of diplomatic missions, including to Scotland.

In 1472 he was appointed governor of the guild of Scottish wool-traders, and became an adviser to King James III of Scotland. This led to an involvement in Scottish politics, which resulted in his murder in 1483 by armed assassins in North Berwick. His effigy appears next to his wife's (d. 1472) on their fine black-marble tomb in the church; it has a sword hilt in his ribs to indicate the foul means of his death, and the tomb in fact contains only his heart.

The church is still privately owned by the descendants of the family, and retains the distinctive atmosphere of a family chapel. Stained glass, dating from 1560 and commemorating the family, is among the earliest and best in Bruges.

The Adorno mansion, and some almshouses sponsored by the family, adjoined the church. These were taken over by a religious order in the 17th century, and the 14th-century almhouses have now been converted into the **Kantcentrum**.

Its small **museum** contains examples of Belgian lace—tablemats, handkerchiefs, collars, cuffs and borders—and underlines the important role that lace has played in fashion over time. But it's the afternoon demonstrations that bring this museum to life: a crowd of local practitioners sit chatting and laughing as they operate with lightning speed the numerous bobbins and pins on the cushions on their knees. (For more on lace, *see* pp.30–31.)

*Turn left into Balstraat. Occupying a set of almshouses on the lefthand side is the entertaining **Museum voor Volkskunde** (Folklore Museum; see p.86). The entrance is at 40 Rolweg, the next street on the left.*

*To continue the walk, cross Rolweg into **Korte Speelmansstraat**.*

The imposing building lining the north side of Carmersstraat (Carmelite Street), to the right, is the **Engels Klooster** (English Convent), distinguished by containing Bruges' only domed church. Religious strife in England during the 16th century caused many Roman Catholics to flee to Europe, and to the Spanish Netherlands in particular, where Catholicism was reasserted after 1585. English sisters had gathered at the Augustinian convent of St Ursula in Leuven, but in 1629 a number of them relocated to Bruges and founded their own order here in Carmersstraat, in a settlement they called 'Nazareth'.

The convent was well funded: Catherine of Braganza, wife of Charles II of England, took a particular interest in its welfare. In 1739 it was able to renovate its church (*entrance at No.85; sometimes open to the public*) in Baroque style, to designs by the distinguished Bruges-born architect Hendrik Pulinx (1698–1781), but when the French revolutionaries took over Bruges in 1795, the convent was closed down and the nuns fled. They returned in 1802, and the complex became a boarding school for English girls from wealthy Catholic families.

Guido Gezelle—who always maintained close ties with the English—became rector of the convent in 1899, and it was here that he died seven months later. It still serves as a convent.

*Turn left into **Carmersstraat** (we'll return to the eastern end of the street later).*

The Miracle of the Well

On the corner of Korte Speelmansstraat and Carmersstraat is a crucifix dating from 1760, one of the city's more elaborate and charming street-side shrines which commemorates a local miracle. On a cold winter's day, a girl called Anna went to fetch water for a sick neighbour. She was attacked by a pair of thugs and thrown into the well, and her mother, in despair, set off on her knees to appeal to the famous Madonna at the church of Onze-Lieve-Vrouw ter Potterie, a kilometre away. When she returned, she found that Anna had miraculously emerged from the well, safe and sound. Some cynics pointed out that the well was frozen over, but why allow a scientific explanation to get in the way of a good miracle?

The western end of Carmersstraat was once the site of the Carmelite monastery that gave the street its name. The monastery was demolished by the Protestants in the 1580s, rebuilt in the 17th century, then sold off under the French. An English seminary college was set up here in the next century, where Guido Gezelle taught in the 1860s; it later became the St-Leocollege (entrance at 3 Carmersstraat and 11 Potterierei).

> *Turn right at the Potterierei (Pottery Quay) and follow the canal north along a street with numerous step-gabled houses. After about 700m you will come to the **Duinenbrug**.*

Rebuilt in 1976, this is one of the few drawbridges left in the city, designed to lift up to allow tall barges to pass. It takes its name from the Cistercian Abbey called Ter Duinen (the Dunes) founded in the 12th century at Koksijde, near Veurne, to the west of Bruges. Following the religious turmoil of the 16th century, and unsustainable encroachment by the coastal dunes, the abbey moved to Bruges in 1629 to a site lying just beyond the bridge (at 72 Potterierei). They developed a massive new complex around a fine baroque church (not open to the public), and when Bruges became a bishopric again in 1833 (with Sint-Salvator as its cathedral), this became the **Bisschoppelijk Seminarie** (Episcopal Seminary).

> *A little further along the Potterierei, at No.79, is the **Onze-Lieve-Vrouw ter Potterie** (open April–Sept daily 9.30–12.30 and 1.15–5; Oct–Mar daily 9.30–12.30 and 2–5, closed Wed; adm 60 BF).*

This was the site of an old hospital, founded outside the city walls in 1276 as a refuge for the sick and poor, and for shelterless travellers and pilgrims. In 1359 it acquired its own church, possibly on the site of a chapel attached to the potters' guild, hence the name, Our Lady of the Pottery. From 1623 to 1625 it was revamped in lavish baroque style, and a Lady Chapel was added in the form of a second nave. The result is richly intense.

The most important possession of the **Lady Chapel** is a 14th-century stone statue, the *Madonna and Child*, which is believed to have miraculous powers. It is now surrounded by an extravagant baroque altar and silver ex-voto offerings A fine set of folksy 17th-century tapestries recording the miracles of Our Lady of the Pottery hangs between the columns of the nave. The remains of St Idesbald, abbot of Ter Duinen (d. 1167), were brought here in the 19th century and placed in a neogothic mausoleum on the south side of the Lady Chapel.

A small but agreeable **museum** contains furniture, paintings (including a number of fine triptych altarpieces) and various church treasures accumulated over the centuries—an interesting showpiece of Bruges craftsmanship. (Look out for the elegantly carved wooden leper's clapper by the reception desk.)

But the charm of this place is less the content and more the enclave as a whole, where the almshouses still serve as part of an extensive old people's home.

Continue along Potterierei. Just before the broad canal, turn right down the tree-lined tow path towards the windmill.

This waterway is part of the Ghent-Bruges-Ostend Canal, and the massive 100m-long barges that ply Europe's inland waterways can often be seen moored at the canalside. The canal was once the moat that surrounded the **Brugse Vesten**, the last set of city walls, built after 1297. Today virtually all that remains of the walls is an earth embankment, now the site of a series of four historic windmills.

There used to be over 20 windmills on the earth ramparts around the city, before they became redundant in the age of steam. Only one, the Sint-Janshuysmolen, still occupies the site on which it was originally built; the others have been moved here to form a kind of open-air museum. From north to south they are: **De Koeleweimolen** (a flour mill, brought here in the 1990s), **De Nieuwe Papegai** (an oil mill, brought here in 1970), **Sint-Janshuysmolen** (a flour mill, built here in 1770 and in use until 1914; restored in 1964), and **Bonne Chiere** (a flour mill, brought here from Olsene, East Flanders, in 1911).

Two of these are still operational and can be visited: De Koeleweimolen (*open June–Sept daily 9.30–12 and 1.15–5; adm 40 BF*), and Sint-Janshuysmolen (*open May–Sept daily 9.30–12 and 1.15–5; adm 40 BF*), with a nice view over Bruges.

Take the path to the right after the second windmill, De Nieuwe Papegai, cross Peterseliestraat (Parsley Street) and walk up Carmersstraat.

At No.174 is the **Schuttersgilde Sint-Sebastiaan** (literally, the 'Marksmen's Guild of St Sebastian'), a fine red-brick guildhouse dating from 1565 and still boasting its rocket-shaped tower. These marksmen were archers (long-bow archers to be precise) who formed a key element in the city's defences in medieval times and were also crusaders (their coat of arms includes the Cross of Jerusalem).

Founded in the 13th century, the guild far outlived the age of bows and arrows as military weapons, and continued its existence as a celebrated club. When Charles II, future king of England, was in Bruges between 1656 and 1658 he was awarded the title 'King of the Archers' by the guild, and he founded the Grenadier Guards here. Since he was penniless at the time, he pledged 1000 crowns as his entrance fee, payable on his death; in fact he paid it back after his restoration, with interest.

The royal connections have been maintained by the guild: all British sovereigns have been members since the days of Charles II; Queen Victoria and Prince Albert came here in 1843, and duly signed the register.

The City Ramparts

Bruges has had three sets of city ramparts, if you include the palisades that surrounded the fort built by Baldwin Iron-Arm in c. AD 865. The first set of proper city walls was constructed in about 1127, around what is now the city centre. The next set, built after 1297, threw a loop 7km long around the city, underlined by a double set of moats-cum-canals, with further fortifications on the intervening embankment. A hundred years later, the eight city gates were enlarged, not just as a defensive measure, but also to control and tax incoming trade.

These outer city walls, the **Brugse Vesten**, were reinforced with bastions during the 17th century. They would have been turned into earth and stone ravelins, to contend with the increased power of cannon, had Bruges adopted the plans drawn up by the energetic French fort-builder Marshal Vauban. But lack of funds was cited, and Bruges' fortifications had become totally obsolete by the time they were demolished by the Austrians in the 1780s, in the interests of modernity.

Four gates escaped demolition—the Kruispoort (1403), the Gentpoort (1401), the Smedenpoort (1367) and the Ezelpoort (1615)—and they only survived because in the late 18th century they still served a tax-raising function, levying the '*octrois*' paid by traders bringing goods into the city.

The small **museum** (*open April–Sept Mon, Wed, Fri and Sat 10–12 and 2–5; adm 40 BF*)—essentially its grand assembly hall or 'Kings' Room'—contains paintings, fine empire-style chandeliers, drums, cannons and various royal mementoes, including a marble bust of Charles II (1660–1) by François Dieussart.

The guild is still an active archery club. Beyond the covered shooting gallery parallel to the Kings' Room rises the white painted "standing perch"—a traditional archery game of ancient origin. The perch is lowered on a hinge, and the top is fitted with a frame holding fifty or so feather "birds", which are then raised as a target for archers below.

> *Return to Peterseliestraat and turn right, where it becomes Kruisvest. Then turn right into* **Rolweg**.

No.64 was the birthplace of **Guido Gezelle** (1830–99), a priest and also one of Flanders' most celebrated poets (*see* pp.31–3). The fetching brick house, where he also spent his childhood, is now a **museum** (*open April–Sept daily 9.30–12.30 and 1.15–5; Oct–Mar daily 9.30–12.30 and 2–5, closed Tues; adm 60 BF*).

Some of the house contains simple reconstructed rooms as Gezelle might have known it as a boy, leading a family life of thrift and piety, studying plants and flowers—and stuffing birds. But the collection, although admirably presented, consists primarily of documents and mementoes, and is of limited interest unless you know his work. The large garden is believed to have played a major role in shaping his abiding love of nature.

> *Return to the Kruisvest. Turn right, then second right, into **Stijn Streuvelsstraat**.*

Stijn Streuvels was the pen name of **Frank Lateur** (1871–1969), a nephew of Guido Gezelle and author of powerful novels of social deprivation. In his day he was considered a serious contender for the Nobel Prize.

On the right-hand side of Stijn Streuvelsstraat is a small park belonging to the **Schuttersgilde Sint-Joris**, the 'Marksmen's Guild of St George'—another archers' guild, this time for crossbowmen. The guild was disbanded in 1872, and the original building was demolished, to be re-established in this new building in the 1930s. What looks like a tall radio mast in the garden is in fact its "standing perch" target.

Charles II was also a member of this guild, and made a name for himself at the opening of a gala by hitting a 'bird' with his first shot. The Schuttersgilde Sint-Joris also has its own small **museum** of mementoes (*open Mon, Tues, Thurs and Fri 3–5*)—paintings, archives and a collection of crossbows.

> *Return once more to the Kruisvest and turn right. At the foot of the road is the mighty city gate, the **Kruispoort**.*

This hulk (1403) once protected the city with a drawbridge and portcullis, and is set apart from the other surviving gates by its composition: white brick. Its castellated city side looks far more benign than its altogether more daunting exterior, overlooking what was the moat. The scale of this gate gives an indication of the colossal size of the old city walls.

> *You can now make a small side trip to see a tragic memento of the First World War. Continue southwards some 200m, along **Kazernevest**, past the new courts of justice, formerly the barracks (kazerne). A turning to the right brings you to the Beluik der Gefusilleerden (Memorial to the Shot).*

Behind a pair of large iron gates is the **Muur der Doodgeschotenen** (Wall of the Executed Prisoners), where 11 Belgians, one Frenchman and one Englishman were shot by the Germans during the First World War. Bullet marks can still be seen in the wall.

The Execution of Captain Fryatt

The Englishman killed at the Muur der Doodgeschotenen was called Algernon Charles Fryatt, the captain of a merchant steamship called *The Brussels* that plied the North Sea. His death was a *cause célèbre*.

On 4 February 1915 the Germans unilaterally declared that the North Sea was a war zone, and that all enemy shipping would be vulnerable to attack. A month later, a German U-Boat stopped a British merchant ship called *The Falcon*, which slowed down to surrender. Perhaps due to a misunderstanding, the U-Boat nonetheless attacked *The Falcon*, and sank her, with the loss of 104 lives. This caused outrage in Britain.

When, three weeks later, on 28 March 1915, *The Brussels* was similarly stopped by a U-Boat, Captain Fryatt gave orders to ram it, and sank it, this being—he argued—the only form of self-defence available to him. Fryatt was congratulated by King George V and the Admiralty.

A year later *The Brussels* was captured on its way back to London from Holland, carrying Belgian refugees. The Germans discovered that the captain was Fryatt, who had sunk the U-Boat, and he was taken to Zeebrugge where he was tried in a court martial (even though he was not in the military).

He was sentenced to death. The commandant of occupied Bruges, Baron von Büttlar, arranged for the execution to take place at the barracks on 27 July 1916, determined to make an example of Fryatt, and even supplying a brass band to accompany the firing squad and prisoner to the place of execution. The German High Command, however, had grave misgivings about the legitimacy—let alone the political wisdom—of the execution, and despatched a telegram to von Büttlar to cancel it.

It arrived half an hour after the execution had taken place.

Return to the Kruispoort, and turn left into **Langestraat**. *After about 500m you reach the* **De Gouden Boom Brewery** *on the righthand side, at No.45.*

The brewery was founded in 1584. It also has a brewery museum, the **Brugse Brouwerij-Mouterijmuseum**, the entrance to which is on the other side of the block, at 10 Verbrand Nieuwland (*see* p.163 for more details about both of these.)

*Turn left at the end of Langestraat and head down the **Predikherenrei**.*

The canal here is the Coupure, the new link cut between 1751 and 1753 to relieve the city centre of canal traffic.

Just beyond the junction with Hooistraat, there is a statue to Marieke, a character created in a song by the most famous Belgian songwriter and singer of recent times, **Jacques Brel** (1929–78). *Marieke*, a song of long-lost love and yearning, with words in both French and Dutch (unusually), paints a vivid and impassioned picture of the flat, windswept lands stretching between Bruges and Ghent.

> *Cross the canal on the Coupurebrug and continue eastwards along Schaarstraat (Shears Street) to the foot of the **Koningin Astridpark**.*

The Koningin Astridpark was named after Queen Astrid (1905–35), wife of Leopold III, King of the Belgians. A Swedish princess, she was cherished by the Belgians for her elegant beauty, common touch and charitable works. Mother of two young children, Prince Baudouin and Prince Albert (the current king), she died tragically young when a car driven by her husband crashed near Lake Lucerne. Her funeral in Brussels attracted 1.5 million mourners; many have pointed to the similarities with the death of Princess Diana in 1997.

With its bandstand and pond and attractive landscaping, the Koningin Astridpark (known locally as the **Botanieken Hof**) is the prettiest park in Bruges, filling the site vacated by the destruction of a Franciscan monastery in the late 18th century.

Now the only reminder of its former religious role is the large **St-Magdalenakerk** (*open Easter holiday 15 June–15 Sept Mon–Sat 9–12 and 2.30–5.30; rest of year Mon–Sat 9–12; closed Sun*), built in neo-Gothic style between 1851 and 1853, to designs by the British architect Thomas Harper King. Although a pupil of Augustus Pugin, author of the sumptuous neogothic interiors of the Palace of Westminster in London, this church is restrained—austere even. But there is some fine Victorian stained glass, and relief polychrome sculptures of the stations of the cross, placed in a medieval setting.

> *Double back on your steps and enter the park next to the children's adventure playground. Cross the park to its northern exit, and turn left into **Gevangenisstraat** (Prison Street).*

The prison in question was on the southern side of the street (at the foot of Pandreitje), but most of it was demolished in 1992, leaving just the entrance gate. Back in the 15th century this was a covered market called the Pand, where the goldsmiths and jewellers would set out their wares during Bruges' great month-long annual fair.

'Venice of the North'

Canals have played an integral role in the life of Bruges since its very foundation. In the 9th century the River Reie was the most reliable means of transport across the marshlands, and was soon given the additional role of defensive moat.

The canals that were developed from this river effectively always served the dual purpose of transport and defence, and the shape of the canals today corresponds closely to the circles of the three successive sets of city walls.

The River Reie still flows through the city, from the Minnewater to the Dampoort (city gate) in the northeast. The canal to Damme, cut in 1180, was the main artery to the sea throughout the medieval period. After the silting of the Zwin, new lifelines were forged to Ghent (in 1613) and to Ostend (in 1622), and the linked Ghent–Bruges–Ostend canal looped almost all the way round the city, on the outer ring.

By the 18th century the small canals winding through the city proved inadequate for commercial traffic, and by 1753 a new canal called the Coupure (the Cut) had been forged across the southeastern quarter to improve the link to the centre.

Finally, in 1907, the Boudewijnkanaal was cut to the new port of Zeebrugge, linking Bruges' new and extensive docks, just to the north of the city, to the sea. Each set of canals had become in turn larger and more industrialized, with a proportionate loss of charm.

Despite this, it only takes one glance at a map of Bruges to see that the title 'Venice of the North' is ridiculous—if, that is, you are only referring to the canals. Bruges has nothing like the profusion of canals in Venice, nor in Amsterdam, the other 'Venice of the North', but in another sense the epithet was perfectly apt—in the magnitude of the city as a trading centre.

Let's leave the last word to Pero Tafur, a 15th-century Spanish traveller, writing in 1438:

> *It is said that two cities compete with each other for commercial supremacy, Bruges in Flanders in the west, and Venice in the east. It seems to me, however, and many agree with my opinion, that there is much more commercial activity in Bruges than in Venice.*

Then in 1671 it became a house of detention called a 'rasp-house'—a feature of the Low Countries and Germany where vagrants and beggars were forced to earn their keep by rasping wood, a hard and unpleasant job, the product of which was used to make paint. In 1827 the building was turned into a prison. The site is now being converted into a large underground car park and apartment block.

> *Turn right at the end of Gevangenisstraat and walk up Pandreitje, which, as the name suggests, followed the path of a small canal until it was filled in in 1768. At Rozenhoedkaai you start retracing part of Walk I (see pp.101–102). Cross over into Huidenvettersplein, continue along the canal on Steenhouwersdijk, then cross the second bridge (Meebrug), which gives a view of the back of the property where the Huis de Zeven Torens once stood. Rejoin Hoogstraat to return to the Burg.*

Walk IV: Rich Man, Poor Man

Start: *'t Zand.*

Walking time: *1½ hours should be ample—the walk is less than 4km long and there is not a great deal to visit.*

For a century until the 1940s, a slice of western Bruges was isolated from the rest of the city by the Ostend–Ghent railway line, which carved a path through the streets and stopped at a station on the 't Zand. The tracks followed the path now occupied by the main road through the district, the Koning Albertlaan/Hoefijzerlaan. Formerly this isolated segment had snuggled up to the old city walls and the Smedenpoort. Come the railway, and it found itself in bed with a very different partner: noisy, self-absorbed and with its back turned.

The railway line and station have since gone, replaced by a busy road—although the worst of the traffic passes under 't Zand in a tunnel—but this quarter still feels faintly cut off. It seems to suit it rather well. Mostly residential, it also contains a remarkable concentration of almshouses and an old abbey, all of which seem to slumber contentedly in their isolation. Here the poor and aged were sheltered by the charity of the rich, and had a handful of religious communities to tend to them until the recent past. Circumstances have changed, but that spirit of place lives on.

After a short walk along the tree-lined canal, we head back into town, but along quiet streets, not the main thoroughfares. This leads to the Prinsenhof, once the hub of court life during the glittering era of the Burgundian dukes, but now, too, something of a backwater.

This is a gentle amble, with just one sight to visit near the start—suitable perhaps for an evening stroll. Any day is a good day.

lunch/cafés

Pick up what you need for a picnic by the canal from: **Lamourette**, Zuidzandstraat 29, **Tout Paris**, Zuidzandstraat 31, or **Traiteur de Poularde**, Smedenstraat 14 (*open 8am–7pm*).

1. **'t Pallieterke**, 't Zand 28. *Closed Tues.* Friendly French restaurant and tea room.

2. **De Medici Sorbetière**, Geldmuntstraat 9. Good coffee, sorbets and tasty lunch dishes in Art-Nouveau setting.

3. **'t Brugs Beertje**, Kemelstraat 5. *Open 4pm–1am; closed Wed.* Mecca for beer-lovers; more than 300 brews. Pâté and cheese snacks.

4. **De Lotteburg**, Goezeputstraat 43. *Closed Mon and Thurs exc hols.* Regional specialities and fresh fish dishes. Lunch menu from 1,195 BF.

5. **De Watermolen**, Oostmeers 130. *Closed Wed.* Bistro with terrace.

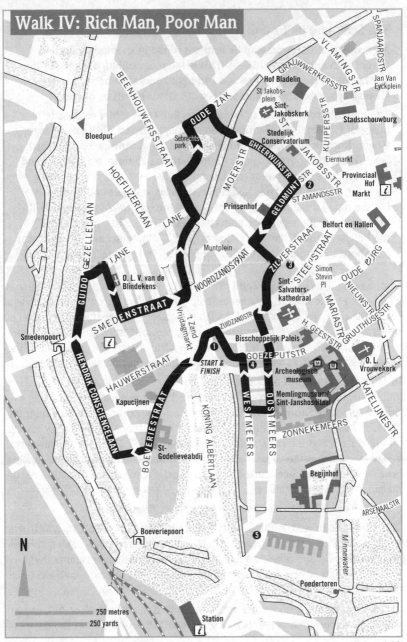

Walk IV: Rich Man, Poor Man

N

250 metres
250 yards

The Sculpture in 't Zand

A great part of the success of this square is due to its large modern statue, with fountains (1985–6). This is the most ambitious piece in the city by the local sculptors **Stefaan Depuydt** and Italian-born **Livia Canestraro**, whose work can be seen at various points in Bruges.

The four groups of figures in the composition represent a composite image of Flanders: the 'Bathing Women' symbolize the cities of Antwerp, Ghent, Kortrijk and Bruges; the 'Fishermen' represent life on the North Sea; 'Ducks flying over Flat Land' represent the Flemish sea polders; and the 'Cyclists' express youth and the future. (Indeed, this is a gathering place for throngs of schoolchildren on bicycles at either end of the day.) On the top of a column sits the sprightly figure of *Tijl Uilenspiegel* (Till Eulenspiegel), the legendary prankster made famous in a novel (1867) by the Belgian writer **Charles de Coster** (1827–79), who cast him as a local hero born in Damme and fighting for Flemish independence from Spain.

Once a sandy hillock called **'t Zand** (the Sand) lay outside the city walls, serving as a horse and cattle market, a gathering point and place of execution. It became a part of the city when the last set of city walls embraced it after 1297. The arrival of the railway in 1844 transformed the district, and properties around the square were rapidly converted into hotels and cafés. The station was upgraded in the 1880s, with a grandiose neogothic building supported on a framework of iron.

In 1948 the railway was rerouted around the outer rim of canals, leaving 't Zand without its *raison d'être*—except on Saturday mornings, when this is the scene of Bruges' sprawling **Saturday market** (*open 7am–1pm*), transferred here from the Markt in 1993. In fact from medieval times up until 1939 a regular Friday market was held here, and the eastern side of the square is still called the Vrijdagmarkt. Today the square is the lid on a giant bunker, with the main-road traffic running beneath it through a tunnel flanked by a vast underground carpark. This has freed up the ground level into an unusually large empty, and rather refreshing urban space.

Leave 't Zand by the southwestern corner, **Boeveriestraat**.

This road used to lead to the old city gate called the Boeveriepoort, which was finally demolished in 1863. It is now a quiet and pretty street, flanked by numerous **almshouses**, *Godshuizen*, and a handful of chapels. (For more on almshouses, *see* p.101.) There are several almshouses on the lefthand side, and more on the cobbled Gloribusstraat.

On the righthand side of Boeveriestraat, at No.4, is the chapel of the former convent of the Capuchin nuns (*Kapucijnen*); at No.18 is the 19th-century monastery of the Capuchin friars. The Capuchins were a reformist order of Franciscans, set up in 1525 to revive St Francis' traditions of frugality and austerity, who became a major force in the Counter-Refomation, noted for their self-sacrifice. Their original monastery (now the site of the Sofitel), was founded in 1592, but they had to make way for the expanding railway and moved here in 1869. No.34 has a wall shrine to **Onze-Lieve-Vrouw van Salette** (1866) and named after the pilgrimage site in eastern France where the Virgin Mary appeared to two young shepherds in 1846.

However, the main religious institution is at No.45, on the other side of the road: the **Sint-Godelieveabdij** (Abbey of St Godelieve; *church open in principle Mon–Sat 9–12 and 2.30–6.30; Sun 10.30–12 and 2.30–6.30*).

No.73 used to be the **Sint-Juliaanshospitaal**, founded in 1290 by the *Filles Dieu* (Daughters of God), from northern France, as a hospital and refuge for the homeless, assisted by monks of the Sint-Juliaan Brotherhood. After 1600 it served as a mental home and foundling hospital.

In 1480 the governor of the Sint-Juliaanshospitaal, Donaas de Moor, founded a set of almshouses at Nos.52–76 Boeveriestraat, for the use of former staff of the hospital and for members of the carpenters', masons' and coopers' guilds. Three years later, he was thanked by banishment from Bruges for siding with Archduke Maximilian in the growing crisis of the 1480s, and he died in exile on his estates outside the city limits.

St Godelieve

St Godelieve was born near Boulogne in about 1045, and at the age of 18 she was married to Bertulf, Lord of Gistel (to the west of Bruges). The ruffian promptly deserted her, leaving her in the hands of her cruel mother-in-law. Seeing her plight, Godelieve's father, assisted by the Bishop of Tournai, lent upon Bertulf to return to her, but Bertulf wasn't one to do another's bidding. He hatched a plan to rid himself of Godelieve by getting a couple of his retainers to strangle her and drown her in a well, making it look like an accident. It worked: Bertulf got off scot-free. But he hadn't counted on divine intercession. Locals were convinced that Godelieve was the victim of skulduggery; her story as an innocent victim of male oppression struck a chord, and she was elevated to sainthood, and a number of miracles were attributed to her. St Godelieve became the focus of a cult at Gistel, and a nunnery was founded.

During the Protestant rampages of 1578, the nuns fled to Bruges and settled here. In 1623 they were joined by Benedictines, and established this abbey. In 1723, to celebrate its centenary, its modest but appealing church was refitted in baroque style.

Retrace your steps to Van Voldenstraat.

On the corner with Van Voldenstraat is a bell, once the fire bell in the Belfort. It recalls the fact that there used to be an important bell foundry in Klokstraat (two streets back), run by the Dumery family, which produced, among many others, 26 bells which are still in the Belfort carillon.

*Walk up Van Voldenstraat to **Hendrik Consciencelaan**.*

This street commemorates **Hendrik Conscience** (1812–83), an Antwerp-born novelist, whose best-known work is *De Leeuw van Vlaanderen* ('The Lion of Flanders'), a stirring account of the Flemish revolt before the Battle of the Golden Spurs in 1302. The book did much to popularize a sense of pride in Flemish heritage and was a bestseller; however, the one place where it was not enthusiastically received was Bruges itself. In 1983 it was made into a film.

> *Cross the Hendrik Consciencelaan and enter the wooded park that lines the canal. Turn right to follow the canal.*

This path follows the course of the **Boverievest**, part of the Brugse Vesten (*see* p.135). Along the way you can see the last remnant of the city's old water system, devised to pump water into the pipes that fed the city. Bruges had an underground water distribution system as early as the 13th century. A waterwheel driven by horses was used at the old pumphouse (*oud waterhuis*) next to the path. Feeding the water pumps and fountains of the city, it was considered wondrous enough in its day to rank as one of the 'Seven Wonders of Bruges' (see p.76).

> *Continue along the path to the **Smedenpoort**.*

The Smedenpoort (Blacksmith's Gate) is the earliest surviving city gate, dating from 1367 (rebuilt in 1615). Picturesque it may be, but a bronze skull set into the wall on the city side is a reminder of its deadly serious role. The skull was put here in 1911 to replace the genuine skull of a man who was accused of betraying the city by trying to open the gate to the French forces of Louis XIV.

> *Continue along the canal-side park, which here becomes an arboretum with labelled species of a broad range of trees. After about 150m, turn right to reach the Guido Gezellelaan. Turn right into Greinschuurstraat, left into Lane, and second right into **Kreupelenstraat**. (Cripple Street).*

At No.8 is a chapel called the **Onze-Lieve-Vrouw van de Blindekens** (Our Lady of the Blind; *open only ½hour before services, Sat 6pm and Sun 9am, or by appointment with the rector, ✆ 050 34 12 03*), with attached almshouses. From the 14th century on, this settlement was a home for the blind, rebuilt in 1415, and again in 1651.

The Miracle of Our Lady

The Onze-Lieve-Vrouw van de Blindekens contains a number of curiosities, including the 14th-century wooden statue (with silver frame) of Our Lady, said to have miraculous powers.

During the Protestant era (1578–84), the chapel was desecrated by iconoclasts. By 1588 the city was suffering from famine, while the countryside was controlled by armed gangs. Starving parishioners pleaded for relief before the statue, and subsequently a ship, *St Michael*, broke through the blockade on the canals to bring grain. A model of the ship hanging from the vault commemorates this 'miracle'.

On 15 August each year parishioners take part in the **Blindekensprocessie**. The procession celebrates the safe return of Flemish soldiers after the Battle of Pevelenberg in 1304, following a pledge made by their womenfolk to carry a 36lb candle each year on that day to the chapel of Onze-Lieve-Vrouw ter Potterie.

There are more almshouses in Kammakersstraat (Combmakers Street).

> *At the end of Kreupelenstraat turn left into Smedenstraat. Continue along the northern side of 't Zand, and turn left into **Speelmansrei**, just before the canal.*

This street is named after the guildhouse of minstrels and actors, whose 15th-century chapel lies at the northern end (now desecrated).

> *Turn left at the first bridge, the Sleutelbrug (Key Bridge), and walk up Beenhouwersstraat (Bone Carvers' Street). Turn right through a gate into the **Sebrechtspark**.*

Like the Koningin Astridpark, this was formerly the site of a convent, destroyed by the French in the 1790s. Dedicated to St Elizabeth, it was run by the Grauwzusters (Grey Sisters) as a mental hospital. It was later bought by a Professor Sebrechts, and became a municipal park in 1981.

> *Cross the park to the street called Oude Zak (Old Sack), turn right into Leeuwstraat (Lion Street, after the Flemish emblem), and cross Leeuwbrug. Continue over Moerstraat into Gheerwijnstraat (to the left is the Sint-Jakobskerk, see Walk II, pp.125–6) which leads into **Muntplein**.*

This pretty square was once the site of the old city mint, which produced coins from 1300 to 1786. The bronze statue, *Flandria Nostra* (1901), by Jules Lagae, depicts Mary of Burgundy, wife of Charles the Bold.

*At the foot of Gheerwijnstraat, turn right into **Geldmuntstraat**.*

The frontage of the shop at No.9 (to your left), now the De Medici Sorbetière, is a rare example in Bruges of turn-of-the-century Art Nouveau/*Jugenstil* architecture.

*Continue along Geldmuntstraat, until it turns into Noordzandstraat, a quality shopping street. Turn right into **Prinsenhof** and walk down to the little square.*

For 60 years the Prinsenhof was the epicentre of Burgundian rule, a glamorous and extensive ducal palace that witnessed the great set pieces of the era. Built originally in about 1350, it became an enclave of power, set around a series of courtyards stretching from here to Gheerwijnstraat and the mint, and north to Moerstraat. There were fountains, flower gardens, tennis courts and heated bath houses. The palace itself was crowned by turrets and had an eight-storey donjon attached to it, with a parapet and minstrels' gallery. An engraving of 1641 still shows it in good condition, but by this time it was well past its heyday.

After the death of Mary of Burgundy in 1482, and the humiliation of her unpopular husband Maximilian in 1488, political power shifted elsewhere, and gradually parts of the complex were sold off. In 1662 the remaining buildings were turned into a boarding school for English girls run by Franciscan nuns, and in 1795 they were sold off as national property by the French. Part of the complex was rebuilt in neogothic style in the 1880s, when it was taken over by a French community of nuns from Boulogne. Today little remains of the original palace.

*Continue along Noordzandstraat, then turn left into the narrow Giststraat (Yeast Street), and right into **Zilverstraat** (Silver Street).*

No.38 (1468; now a restaurant) is called the **Vasquezhuis**, after the private secretary of Isabella of Portugal.

*At the end of Zilverstraat is the Sint-Salvatorskathedraal (see pp.89 and 110). Cross Zuidzandstraat, and take the little alley Lendestraat down the hill into Oranjeboomstraat (Orange Tree Street). Continue into **Oostmeers**.*

Meer means lake, or in this context, marsh. This low-lying district of picturesque little streets once formed a quiet hinterland to the Sint-Janshospitaal and the Sint-Salvatorskathedraal, but in the 1840s it was rudely awoken to the 19th century, when the railway was driven through the district just to the west of here. What is now the green space between the Westmeers and Koning Albertlaan once contained seven tracks of marshalling yards and the main line. Since the rerouting of the railway, this grid of streets has regained some of its former calm.

Turn right along Sint-Obrechtsstraat, right again into Westmeers, and then left along Hoogste van Brugge, which leads you back into 't Zand.

Apart from the canal that still connects it to Bruges, it is hard to believe that Damme was once a major port. Today it is surrounded by fields of grazing horses and sleepy dairy cows, and the polders stretch out for miles in all directions, divided only by roads and waterways lined with tall poplars.

However, throughout Bruges' heyday in medieval times, Damme (meaning a dam or dyke) was an integral part of the city's fortunes, created by Philip of Alsace, Count of Flanders, in about 1180, to serve as an entrepôt on the Zwin where trade goods were transferred to barges to be shipped up the canalized River Reie to Bruges.

Damme also became a wealthy enclave, with its own trading houses, a town hall and mansions. Although destroyed in 1213 by the forces of Philip II of France, it was quickly rebuilt, and the town's population grew to about 10,000. One of its most celebrated sons was the writer Jacob van Maerlant (or Maerlandt, c. 1225–92), who translated popular tales and fables from Latin into Flemish.

But all the while the Zwin was silting up and, despite desperate efforts to dredge it, by the end of the 15th century it was unusable. The merchants of Bruges extended the canal 10km beyond Damme to Sluis, but only won a temporary reprieve and Damme fell into terminal decline.

Damme

By the 1920s its population had sunk to just 800, but it had acquired a new mythology. The Belgian writer Charles de Coster (1827–79) claimed that this was the home of the trickster, Tijl Uilenspiegel. His picaresque tale of the fight for independence from Spain during the religious wars of the 16th century features three main characters: Tijl, his fiancée Nele and their loyal pal Lamme Goedzak, all very much a part of the Damme landscape today.

Getting There

Damme is just a 7km walk or cycle from the centre of Bruges along the road that follows the canal.

Alternatively, **Sightseeing Line/City Tour** buses leave from the Markt (*April–Sept departures daily at 2pm and 4pm; 660 BF; historical commentary included*). After about an hour you return by canal on the little paddle steamer *Lamme Goedzak*, and then by bus back to the Markt.

You can also journey from Bruges to Damme by canal aboard the ***Lamme Goedzak***, leaving from Noorweegse Kaai, just beyond Bruges' old city ramparts, at Dampoort (bus no.4 from the Markt, direction St-Jozef-Koolkerke; *Easter–Sept daily 10, 12, 4.20 and 6; 190 BF single, 230 BF return*).

Quasimodo (*see* p.22) organizes bicycle tours to Damme, leaving from the Burg (*June–Aug daily 5pm; 650 BF*).

lunch/cafés

De Lieve, Jacob van Maerlantstraat 10, ✆ 050 35 66 30. One of the most celebrated restaurants of West Flanders, with a relaxed, tastefully rustic setting, serving fine and inventive French cuisine, with seasonal notes. Menus 1100–2100 BF. *Closed 1–15 July, Mon evening and Tues.*

Gasthof Maerlant, Kerkstraat 21, ✆ 050 35 29 52. The 1920s are recalled in Art Deco style, as a backdrop for Belgian-style cuisine, and local produce. Terrace in summer. Menu *c.* 1250 BF. *Closed Tues evening and Wed.*

De Drie Zilveren Kannen, Markt 9, ✆ 050 35 56 77. Panelled interior richly adorned with antiques, and inspired French cooking. Also has a tea-room for light snacks. *Closed Mon.*

De Gulden Kogge, Damse Vaart Zuid 12, ✆ 050 35 42 17. Quiet, agreeable hotel-restaurant. Menus 1350–1975 BF. *Closed Wed eve and Thurs in winter.*

Bij Lamme Goedzak, Kerkstraat 13, ✆ 050 35 20 03. Flemish traditional décor for gastronomic regional food, as well as lighter meals and snacks. Has large garden terrace. Menus at 890–1650 BF.

Taverne 't Hemeltje, Kerkstraat 46, ✆ 050 36 07 07. Terrace in summer, open fire in winter. Specializes in eels. Menus from 350 BF. *Closed Wed.*

Eetcafé De Spiegel, Jacob van Maerlantstraat 1, ✆ 050 37 11 30. Snacks, tea and cakes, or a full meal. Terraces front and back. Menu of the day from 300 BF.

Tourist Office: Huyse de Grote Sterre, Jacob van Maerlantstraat 3, ✉ 8340 Damme, ✆ 050 35 33 19 (*open 16 April–15 Oct Mon–Fri 9–12 and 2–6, weekends 10–12 and 2–6; 16 Oct–15 April Mon–Fri 9–12 and 2–5, weekends 3–5*). Can arrange bicycle hire.

Visiting Damme

The **Stadhuis** (Marktplein; *open July–Sept daily 10–12 and 2–6; guided tours in winter, ask at the tourist office; adm 40 BF*) was built between 1464 and 1468, as a scaled-down version of Bruges' Gothic Stadhuis, replacing a much larger hall built in 1241. During rather over-zealous restoration work in the 19th century, the exterior was furnished with statues of the Counts of Flanders; on the far right Charles the Bold can be seen offering his marriage ring to a coy-looking Margaret of York. The two stones hanging from the façade are known as the 'stones of justice'—to be hung around the neck or feet of adulterous women or scolds. The interior contains some atmospheric rooms where the aldermen met and worked. The building also served as a trading hall, and the shutters of the trading booths can still be seen.

In the Marktplein outside is a statue (1860) of **Jacob van Maerlant** by the Bruges sculptor Henry Pickery, who was also responsible for the statues of Jan van Eyck and Hans Memling in Bruges.

Huyse De Grote Sterre (Jacob van Maerlantstraat 3) is a fine 15th-century building, which also served as the residence of the Spanish military governor during the 17th century. It contains not only the tourist office but also a small **museum** dedicated to Tijl Uilenspiegel (*open 16 April–15 Oct daily 9–12 and 2–6; 16 Oct–15 April daily 9–12 and 2–5; adm 100 BF*).

The **monument to Tijl Uilenspiegel** (1979) by Jef Claerhout on Daamse Vaart-Zuid was erected on the centenary of Charles de Coster's death. It shows Tijl with various allegorical animals representing aspects of human nature.

Huis Saint-Jean-d'Angély (Huis Sint-Jan; Jacob van Maerlantstraat 11) is a 15th-century house built by the town of Saint-Jean-d'Angély in southwest France, one of 19 wine-trading enterprises located in Damme. It was in this house that Charles the Bold, Duke of Burgundy, and Margaret of York were married in 1468, before entering Bruges for their grand *Blijde Intreden* (Joyous Entry).

The **Sint-Janshospitaal** (Kerkstraat 33; *open April–Sept daily 11–12 and 2–6; closed Mon and Fri; Oct–Mar Sat and Sun only 2–6.30; adm 40 BF*)—according to tradition—was founded in 1249 by Margaret of Constantinople, who also founded the Begijnhof in Bruges. Some of the buildings date from the 13th century, while the chapel is largely baroque. Its museum contains a mixed collection of church treasures, paintings and medieval and Renaissance furniture and ceramics.

The **Onze-Lieve-Vrouwekerk** (*open May–Sept daily 10–12 and 2.30–5.30; adm 20 BF*) has been left in a semi-ruined state since partial collapse in 1725, when the parishioners could not afford to repair it. It still has its 13th-century triple aisle in the style called Scheldt Gothic, with 16th- and 17th-century furnishings. The statues of the apostles date from the 14th century. Jacob van Maerlant lies buried beneath the tower, which now stands separate from the body of the church. There are fine views across the polders from the summit of the tower (43m/140ft); from here it is possible to detect traces of buildings long since gone, indicating how the town has shrunk over the past 500 years.

The **Haringmarkt** (Herring Market) was once a key centre for the herring trade, which, at its height in the 15th century, was shifting 28 million salted or smoked (and barrelled) herrings a year. Damme is twinned with Damme-Oldenburg in Germany, and this is celebrated in a statue by Jef Claerhout depicting the emblems of the two towns, a dog and St Victor respectively. Damme's dog comes from a legend about the town's beginnings. When Friesian workers hired by Philip of Alsace were building the first dyke, they found they could not close it off because the place was haunted by a dog. Their solution was to sacrifice another dog and throw it into the hole. For this reason the town took the name Hondsdamme (Dog's Dyke); the dog was dropped from the name, but remained in the coat of arms.

The white painted **Schellemolen windmill** (*open July–Aug daily 10.30–12.30 and 2–5*) dates from 1867, but a windmill has operated on this site since 1267.

Museums and Monuments

This is a glossary of Bruges' key attractions—designed for readers who prefer to pick a few sights *à la carte*, and then amble, rather than follow one of the itineraries in the Walks section.

Note that a *Combinatieticket* (Combination ticket) is available at the tourist office in the Burg for 400 BF, which gives you access to four sights: the Arentshuis, Groeningemuseum, Gruuthusemuseum, and the Belfort or Stadhuis.

Archeologisch Museum, Mariastraat 36a. *Open Tues, Thurs, Sat, Sun 9.30–12.30 and 1.15–5; adm 60 BF.* Small, well presented, if a bit specialist, occupying part of the old Sint-Janshospitaal: a collection of Roman glass, medieval pottery shards and painted tombs. Its exhibits of eating habits, WCs and garbage through the ages are fascinating. Labels in Dutch, but English cards give broader explanations.

Arentshuis (Brangwynmuseum), Dijver 16. *Open April–Sept daily 9.30–5; Oct–Mar daily 9.30–12.30 and 2–5; closed Tues; adm 80 BF.* A museum of two halves. The ground floor has a fine collection of antique lace. Upstairs contains the remarkable legacy of paintings, prints and furniture by the British artist Frank Brangwyn (1867–1956).

Begijnhof, Wijngaardstraat. *Open in daylight hours; adm free to the grounds.* The delightful *béguinage* is one of Bruges' prettiest and most memorable sights. It contains a small museum, the **Beguinhuisje**. *Open Mar–Nov daily 10–12 and 1.45–5, till 5.30 on weekends; Dec–Feb Mon, Tues, Fri 11–12, Wed and Thurs 2–4; adm 60 BF.*

Belfort, Markt 7. *Open April–Sept daily 9.30–5; Oct–Mar daily 9.30–12.30 and 1.30–5; adm 100 BF; family ticket 200 BF.* The towering Belfry, one of Bruges' main landmarks, offers views over the city from beneath the bells, at a height of 83m/272ft (reached by 366 steps).

Brugse Brouwerij-Mouterijmuseum (De Gouden Boom), Verbrand Nieuwlandstraat 10. *Open May–Sept Wed–Sun 2–6; adm 150 BF (including one free drink).* A brewery museum, housed in an old malthouse, belonging to De Gouden Boom, one of the city's leading breweries.

Groeningemuseum, Dijver 12. *Open April–Sept daily 9.30–5; Oct–Mar daily 9.30–12.30 and 2–5; closed Tues; adm 200 BF.* Bruges' premier art collection, famous above all for its late-medieval works by van Eyck, Memling and others.

Gruuthusemuseum, Dijver 17. *Open April–Sept daily 9.30–5; Oct–Mar daily 9.30–12.30 and 2–5; closed Tues; adm 130 BF.* Fine collection of antique furniture, weapons, kitchen implements, Delftware, musical instruments—the riches that filled the homes of the well-to-do in Bruges' past.

Guido Gezellemuseum, Rolweg 64. *Open April–Sept daily 9.30–12.30 and 1.15–5; Oct–Mar daily 9.30–12.30 and 2–5; closed Tues; adm 60 BF.* The birthplace of Flanders' best known 19th-century poet, Guido Gezelle (1830–99), with an exhibition of his manuscripts and work.

Kantcentrum (Lace Centre), Peperstraat 3a. *Open Mon–Fri 10–12 and 2–6, Sat 10–12 and 2–5; closed Sun; combined adm 60 BF with the Jeruzalemkerk next door.* A small museum, housed in former almshouses, showing examples of Belgian lace, with demonstrations by practitioners in the afternoons.

Memlingmuseum/Sint-Janshospitaal, Mariastraat 38. *Closed for restoration until at least late 2000, perhaps 2001; opening times to be announced.* The old medieval hospital served for 800 years; its historic main wards can be visited. In the late 15th century the hospital commissioned a number of exquisite paintings by Hans Memling, which are usually exhibited in its chapel. (During restoration, these have been transferred to the Groeningemuseum.)

Museum voor Volkskunde (Folklore Museum), Rolweg 40. *Open April–Sept daily 9.30–5; Oct–Mar 9.30–12.30 and 2–5; closed Tues; adm 80 BF.* A comprehensive collection of artefacts from the lives of ordinary people and craftworkers, mainly from the 19th century; well presented in a set of old almshouses.

Renaissancezaal van het Brugse Vrije, Burg 11A. *Open April–Sept daily 10–12.30 and 1.15–5; Oct–Mar daily 9.30–12.30 and 2–5; adm 100 BF, ticket also valid for the Stadhuis.* The assembly room for aldermen of the Brugse Vrije administrative zone. Its prime exhibit is an extraordinarily elaborate carved wooden chimney piece (1529–33), designed by Lancelot Blondeel.

Schuttersgilde Sint-Joris, Stijnstreuvelstraat 159. *Open Mon, Tues, Thurs and Fri 3–5; adm 60 BF.* Reconstructed 1930s guild house of the crossbow archers, with a collection of paintings, archives and crossbows.

Schuttersgilde Sint-Sebastiaan, Carmersstraat 174. *Open April–Sept Mon, Wed,* *Fri and Sat 10–12 and 2–5; adm 40 BF.* The fine 16th-century guildhouse of the longbow archers. The assembly room is crammed with paintings, while the old covered practice areas and traditional 'standing perch' target are still very much in use.

Stadhuis (Gothic Hall), Burg 12. *Open April–Sept daily 9.30–12.30 and 1.15–5; Oct–Mar daily 9.30–12.30 and 2–5; adm 100 BF, ticket also valid for the Renaissancezaal van het Brugse Vrije.* The first such splendid town hall in Belgium, heavily restored in the 19th century, with impressive neogothic murals in the vaulted Gothic Hall on the upper floor.

Huisbrouwerij De Halve Maan 'Straffe Hendrik', Walplein 16. *Guided tours April–Sept daily 10–5; Oct–Mar 11am and 3pm; adm 140 DF (including one free drink).* Tours of the brewery best known for its beer called 'Straffe Hendrik' (Strong Henry).

Windmills

Kruisvest. A collection of four historic windmills lining the canal. Two of these are still operational and can be visited during the summer:

De Koeleweimolen. *Open June–Sept daily 9.30–12 and 1.15–5; adm 40 BF.*

Sint-Janshuysmolen. *Open May–Sept daily 9.30–12 and 1.15–5; adm 40 BF.*

Churches

Heilig Bloedbasiliek, Burg 10. *Open April–Sept daily 9.30–11.45 and 2–7.45; Oct–Mar 10–11.45 and 2–3.45, closed Wed afternoon; Schatkamer museum adm 40 BF.* Two-storey church: the one below from the 12th century, and robustly gloomy; the one above sparkling with 19th-century neogothic. The tiny museum contains the reliquary of the Holy Blood and other treasures.

Jeruzalemkerk, Peperstraat 3. *Open Mon–Fri 10–12 and 2–6, Sat 10–12 and 2–5; closed Sun; combined adm 60 BF with the Kantcentrum next door.* Splendidly odd-ball 15th-century church built as a private chapel for the Adornes family, with replicas of various sacred places in the Holy Land.

Onze-Lieve-Vrouwekerk, Mariastraat. *Open Mon–Fri 9–11.30 and 2.30–5, Sat 9–11.30 and 2.30–4, Sun 2.30–5; adm 60 BF for the museum only (open from 10am).* Fine Gothic church, containing the *Madonna and Child* by Michelangelo. The choir behind is fenced off as a museum, with various paintings and monuments, supreme among which are the tombs of Charles the Bold and his daughter, Mary of Burgundy.

Onze-Lieve-Vrouw ter Potterie, Potterierei 79. *Open daily April–Sept 9.30–12.30 and 1.15–5; Oct–Mar 9.30–12.30 and 2–5; closed Wed; adm 60 BF.* Adjacent to a medieval hospital (and still an old people's home), this richly ornate baroque chapel houses a miraculous statue of the Madonna. The small museum attached contains an interesting collection of paintings, church treasures and furniture.

Sint-Annakerk, Sint-Annaplein. *Open April–Sept Mon–Fri 10–12 and 2–4, Sat 10–12; closed Sun.* One of Bruges' most endearing parish churches, with few changes since its reconstruction in the 17th century.

Sint-Gilliskerk, Sint-Gilliskerkhof. *Open May–Sept Mon–Sat 10–12 and 2–5, Sun 11–12 and 2–5.* A triple-aisled parish church, with original wooden vault, noted above all for its 18th-century paintings of the Trinitarian Brotherhood by Jan Garemijn.

Sint-Godelieveabdij, Boeveriestraat 45. *Open Mon–Sat 9–12 and 2.30–6.30, Sun 10.30–12 and 2.30–6.30.* Modest but attractive convent church, mainly in 18th-century baroque.

Sint-Jakobskerk, Sint-Jakobsplein. *Open July and Aug Mon–Fri and Sun 2–5.30, Sat 2–4.* The richest of Bruges' smaller churches, with some 80 paintings, and the elaborate tomb of Ferry de Gros and his two wives.

Sint-Salvatorskathedraal, Steenstraat. *Open Mon 2–5.45, Tues–Fri 8.30–11.45 and 2–5.45, Sat 8.30–11.45 and 2–5.30, Sun 9–10.15 and 3–5.45.* Bruges' cathedral by default, but still an impressive building. It has a small museum of miscellaneous church treasures (*open Mon–Fri 2–5, Sun 3–5; closed Sat; adm 60 BF*).

Sint-Walburgakerk, Sint-Maartensplein. *Open Easter–Sept daily 8pm–10pm.* A fine baroque Jesuit church, built in the early 17th century.

Food and Drink

So prodigiously good was the eating and drinking on board these sluggish but most comfortable vessels [between Bruges and Ghent], that there are legends extant of an English traveller, who, coming to Belgium for a week, and travelling in one of these boats, was so delighted with the fare there that he went backwards and forwards from Ghent to Bruges perpetually until the railroads were invented, when he drowned himself on the last trip of the passage-boat.

Vanity Fair William Makepeace Thackeray (1847–8)

It is now a well-known secret that Belgium's food ranks among the best in Europe—even the French are prepared to admit it. It has an armful of garlanded restaurants over which even the most hardened international gastronomes will bill and coo, and, more importantly, it is almost impossible to eat badly. Since virtually everyone is an expert on food, restaurants serving sub-standard fare simply cannot survive.

Belgians have a great enthusiasm for eating out: decent restaurants are well patronized and are able to keep their prices competitive. Standards are invariably high—in the humble chip-stand on a street corner as well as at the pinnacles of *haute cuisine*.

Some Belgian Specialities

Belgian food is solidly northern European, hearty and copious—with a touch of genius that lifts it above the ordinary. Clearly it is closely allied to French cuisine, and even in Flanders French is the language of food, but its most famous dishes are still firmly rooted in burgher traditions and by and large the Belgians have little patience with the over-priced preciousness to which *la haute cuisine française* can so easily fall victim.

Steak and chips is virtually the national dish. The steak will be first class and the chips, of course, have no rival in Europe. Mussels and chips comes a close second: no dainty soup bowls scattered with mussels, but a kilo per person, which comes in a casserole the size of a bucket. *Moules marinière/gestoomde mossels* is the standard preparation: cleaned live mussels are cooked on a bed of sweated celery, onion and parsley until the shells open. Few elaborations improve on this formula.

Lighter dishes may include delicately flavoured soups, such as *soupe de cresson/ waterkers soep* (watercress); excellent fish; tasty, substantial salads, such as *salade Liégeoise/warme Luikse sla* (a warm salad of green beans or *salade frisée* and bacon pieces); and *steak à l'américaine* (or *américain préparé*), raw minced steak with capers, chopped raw onion, Worcestershire sauce and a raw egg.

The most typically Belgian dish is *waterzooi*, a soothing soup-like creation in which chicken is cooked with cream and vegetables. The *waterzooi* formula has recently been applied to fish. Other classic Belgian dishes include *vlaamse stoverij*, a hearty, sweetly flavoured beef stew cooked in beer; and various vegetable and meat purées known as *stoemp*. In the spring, you can try Dutch-style raw herrings, *maatjes*, held by the tail and dropped into the mouth. Maytime is the season of asparagus raised on the sandy polders, and known locally as 'white gold'.

There is a wide variety of pork dishes: *andouillettes* (rich sausages made of offal) and the excellent *boudin blanc* and *boudin noir* (soft meat and blood sausages). Game (*wild*) in season includes pigeon, hare, pheasant and venison, often with berries, raisins or braised chicory. Look out for unusual seasonal vegetables, such as salsify and hop shoots—served in spring with a peppery cream sauce and poached eggs.

Chicory

The French-speaking Belgians call them *chicons*, the French call them *endives*, the Flemish call them *witloof*, the English-speaking world refers to them as chicory in the UK and Belgian endives in the US—a suitably mysterious confusion for this bizarre little vegetable. Chicory consists of a head of firm, bullet-shaped leaves—white, yellow and pale green—with a crunchy texture and a distinctive, bitter flavour. It is often eaten raw, in salads, but with simple cooking, chicory is transformed into one of the most delicious and surprising of Belgium's foods. Melt some butter in a saucepan, drop in a handful of chicory, put on the lid and cook very slowly until it has collapsed into its own aromatic juices and transmogrified into a sweet, succulent delicacy. Chicory wrapped in slices of ham and baked in a cheese sauce (*chicons gratin*) is a classic, warming Belgian dish.

Chicory is essentially a winter crop. The roots of the *chicorée* lettuce are replanted and allowed to shoot, but are kept in the dark to make the shoots white. The process was apparently discovered by accident in about 1840 by the head gardener at the botanical gardens of Brussels, who was simply trying to overwinter some rootstock. He kept the shoots in the dark by gently piling up the earth over them, and this is the method still used in the *potagers* today. Commercial growers, however, use darkened sheds and hydroponics to maintain a thriving export industry.

Chips

If you want a quick snack in Belgium, you could do worse than stopping at a *frituur* van and ordering a cone of chips (French fries). Belgian chips—*frietjes*—are quite simply the best: no thicker than your little finger, served piping hot, golden brown and crispy. The traditional accompaniment is a dollop of heavenly Belgian mayonnaise. One of the reasons Belgian *frietjes* are so good is the choice of potato—usually a sweeter one such as Bintje, and old enough to have the right quantity of starch. Belgians bring critical appreciation to their potatoes, just as they do to any other aspect of food: hang the shelf life. Take, for instance, the Saint-Nicholas, a delicious, waxy potato with a yellowish hue and an aromatic, nutty flavour; this is not just a lump of carbohydrate filler but a vegetable of distinction.

So what is the secret of making good Belgian chips? First select an appropriate potato variety; cut the potatoes to size, keeping them fairly thin. Lastly, fry them *twice*: the first time so that they are cooked but not brown; then, after allowing them to cool, cook them a second time until golden brown. They do not always have to be crispy, by the way: chips served with stews, such as *vlaamse stoverij* are sometimes deliberately left soft—the better to soak up the sauces. Traditionally, *frietjes* were cooked in the rendered fat of beef kidneys; but if beef kidneys are hard to come by, sunflower or corn oil is a lighter, modern alternative.

Chocolate

When it comes to chocolate, 'Belgian' is synonymous with quality—so much so that unscrupulous foreign operators will use the term liberally as a sales tool when their product contains only the merest fraction of Belgian chocolate, or is simply prepared in Belgian style. Imitation may be a form of flattery, but do not be misled: only the Belgians produce the chocolates that are responsible for this reputation. This is partly because freshness counts: Belgian chocolates are sumptuous, fresh cream confections with a limited shelf life (three weeks or so in the fridge); furthermore, because the Belgians themselves are enthusiastic consumers of handmade chocolate, turnover is high and the price is remarkably low.

Three factors have given rise to the unassailable reputation of Belgian chocolate: the cream fillings, white chocolate, and—most important of all—the quality of the plain chocolate. The Belgians may not have been the first to put fresh cream in chocolates, but they pioneered fresh-cream fillings for the mass market. White chocolate is a comparative newcomer; in fact it is barely chocolate at all, but a milk-based confection mixed with cocoa butter and sweetener. The best plain Belgian chocolate contains a very high proportion of cocoa solids—at least 52 per cent, usually more like 70 per cent (90 per cent is the feasible maximum). These cocoa solids are the crushed and ground product of cocoa beans (usually from West Africa), from which some of the oily cocoa butter has been extracted. This valuable cocoa butter is later reintroduced to make high-quality chocolate (in poor-quality chocolate, vegetable fat is substituted for cocoa butter and there is also a much lower percentage of cocoa solids). Cocoa butter makes a significant difference, as any chocolate addict will tell you: the natural oils in the cocoa butter evaporate in your mouth, provoking a slight cooling, refreshing sensation.

Leonidas, Godiva, Corné de la Toison d'Or and Neuhaus are the most famous manufacturers in Belgium, but there are many more, some of them tiny individual concerns with just one outlet. Of the big names, Leonidas is probably the cheapest, but this has little bearing on quality: many Belgians actually prefer Leonidas and find the others too rich. Leonidas appears to produce chocolates on an industrial scale, and has numerous outlets. Some have large counters opening directly on to the street, so that the staff can shovel out boxes of chocolates to passing customers with the minimum of delay. Only in Belgium could chocolates be treated as a kind of fast food. Godiva, however, has the greater international reputation: the company now has 1400 shops worldwide, selling 120 different kinds of chocolate at the luxury end of the market. Why, you may ask, is a Belgian chocolate company named after Lady Godiva, the nobleman's wife who rode naked through the streets of Coventry in the 11th century? The answer is simply that, in 1929, the founders of the business liked the image, which seemed to represent the qualities of their chocolates: elegant, rich, sensual and daring.

Other Sweet Treats

Belgian biscuits are almost as famous as their chocolates. S*peculoos*, a hard, buttery biscuit, is a well-known speciality of Flanders, but the Bruges speciality is *Brugge Kletskoppen*, 'lace cookies', which resemble the lace for which the city is famous.

At the other end of the scale, you can sink your teeth into a luscious, freshly cooked *wafel* (*gaufre* in French), the original Belgian holiday food, generously sprinkled with icing sugar. Waffles appear at country fairs, or by the sea, at street cafés, and in homes whenever there is something to celebrate. The waffle iron is brought out, polished up, and set to work to stack up piles of steaming *wafels* for hungry guests. *Koeken* are another Flemish favourite—sweet, buttery pastries flavoured with spices or drizzled with sugar or topped with raisins and nuts. They are eaten with pots of strong coffee in the afternoon, or as part of a lazy Sunday morning breakfast ritual.

Beer

Belgian beer enjoys an unparalleled reputation. For beer-lovers, it is the object of pilgrimage and reverence. For others it can be a revelation. Belgium has some 400 different kinds of beers produced by 115 breweries (in 1900 there were 3223 breweries). Each has its own distinctive style, and even the ubiquitous Stella Artois (when brewed in Belgium) and Jupiter, made by the brewing giant Interbrew, are a cut above your average lagers.

A word first of all about how beer is made. The essential ingredient is grain—usually barley, but sometimes wheat. The barley is soaked in water to stimulate germination, then dried in a kiln to produce malt. The malted barley is then crushed and boiled before being left to ferment, during which process the natural sugars (maltose) and any added sugars are converted into alcohol. Yeast is the agent of fermentation. Some yeasts rise to the top of the brew, forming a crust that protects the beer from the air; this process creates a richly flavoured 'top-fermented' ale. Other yeasts sink to the bottom to make a lighter, clearer, lager-type 'bottom-fermented' beer. The choice of barley, the preparation of the malt, the quality of the water, and the type of yeast used all influence the final taste of the beer. Hops provide a spicy, bitter tang and may be added at various stages of brewing.

With Belgian beer there is no great concern about whether it is served from the keg or in bottles. The labels on the bottles give the vital statistics, including the all-important alcohol content. By and large Belgian beer has a higher level of alcohol by volume than equivalent British or American beers. Specialist bottled beers start at about 5 per cent; stronger brews measure 8 or 9 per cent. The maximum alcohol content for beer is about 12 per cent—four times the strength of most lager. Bush beer is one of several brands that claims to be Belgium's strongest beer: after two bottles you feel as though your knees have been hinged on backwards. Some breweries classify their beer as *double/dubbel* (dark and sweet, about 6.6 per cent) or *triple/tripel* (paler and lighter, but stronger, about 8 per cent). Labels also instruct you about the correct temperature at which to serve the beer and the shape of glass to be used. Every brew is assigned its own glass shape, from tumbler to goblet, and this is something that any bartender instinctively understands. Only in the appropriate glass can the merits of a particular beer be fully savoured.

The most famous bottled beers are those produced by the Trappists—the order of Cistercian monks which observes the strict (these days not quite so strict) order of silence. In the 19th century the monasteries produced beer for the consumption of the monks, but then they began to sell it to the outside world in gradually increasing quantities. Trappist beer has become a major income-earner for the monasteries, nowadays produced largely by lay workers rather than monks. Nonetheless, the monasteries retain strict control over their product and have resisted offers of expansion into the large-scale export markets, which would rapidly lap up any increased production. These Trappist beers are top-fermented ales, with extra yeast added at bottling to produce a second fermentation in the bottle. Allow the beer to stand to let the sediment settle, then pour the entire contents off all at once to avoid disturbing it (it's not harmful, just rather yeasty).

The most famous Trappist beer is probably Chimay, produced by the abbey of Notre-Dame de Scourmont, the first to release its beers to the public. Today Chimay is available as 7, 8 and 9 per cent alcohol by volume. Kept for several years, Chimay Bleu becomes ever richer, its flavour drifting towards port.

The Beers of Bruges

Beer is good for you. This was the message spread by St Arnold, who founded the Benedictine abbey of Oudenburg Abbey, to the west of Bruges, in the 11th century. During a bout of plague, he plunged his cross into a vat of beer, and told the people to drink it, instead of water. It was a miracle cure: people started getting better immediately, and St Arnold was made the patron saint of beer. There were sound scientific reasons for St Arnold's cure: beer was boiled and drinking water wasn't, but it took another eight centuries to discover how this worked, and the Belgians were prepared to take it on trust. To this day, Steenbrugge Abdijbier (abbey beer) features St Arnold himself on the label.

Before the First World War, there were 31 breweries in the city; today, there are just two: De Gouden Boom and De Halve Maan (Straffe Hendrik). Both produce excellent beers, and you can visit them to watch it being made.

Brouwerij 'De Gouden Boom', Verbrand Nieuwlandstraat 10 (*open May–Sept Wed–Sun 2–6; adm 150 BF, including one free drink*). The name De Gouden Boom (The Golden Tree) recalls a trophy awarded in jousting tournaments held in the Markt. The brewery was founded in 1584, and moved to this site, called 't Hamerken (Little Hammer) in 1902. The museum is in the old malthouse, used until 1976, while the brewery itself is on Langestraat 47.

Huisbrouwerij De Halve Maan 'Straffe Hendrik', Walpein 26 (*guided tours April–Sept daily 10–5; Oct–Mar daily 11 and 3; adm 140 BF, including one free drink*). Founded in 1856 beneath the sign of De Halve Maan (the Half Moon), this brewery was run by four generations of the Maes family, all called Henry. It now specializes in one brand called Straffe Hendrik (Strong Henry), with a picture of a cheery carouser on the label straining the beer through his copious moustache. The brewery has been developed with its own museum and tavern.

't Brugs Beertje, Kemelstraat 5 (off Steenstraat), stocks 300 sorts of beer, and is run by enthusiasts who even hold seminars on the subject.

Den Dyver, Dijver 5, ✆ 050 33 60 69, is an elegant retaurant whose speciality is dishes cooked in beer, served with beer of all kinds. This is a good place to discover the extraordinary range and nuances of Belgium's national drink. Some, like 'the red beers' of Rodenbach of Roeselare, edge decidely towards wine. *Closed Wed and Thurs lunch.*

For a refreshing change, try the remarkable 'white' beers—*witbier*—made with wheat. De Gouden Boom Brewery in Bruges produces a fine *witbier* called Brugs Tarwebier, but the most famous is produced at Hoegaarden, to the east of Brussels. Hoegaarden (also a brand name) is a wheat beer flavoured with a touch of coriander; it has a delicious peppery tang and a modest alcohol content (5 per cent)—excellent for that jaded moment in the late afternoon. Some *witbier*-drinkers even add a slice of lemon to their glass. It is often a little cloudy—don't send it back: that is how it should be!

One of the most unusual of all Belgian beers is *lambic*, a wheat beer unique to the valley of the River Senne. What makes *lambic* so special is that it is 'spontaneously' fermented by the agency of naturally occurring airborne yeasts—tiny fungi called *Brettanomyces* that are found only in Brussels itself and in the countryside to the west. Fermentation begins within three days, but the beer is allowed to age for a year or more. *Lambic* is a fairly strong (about 5.5 per cent), still beer with a distinctive sour, winey flavour—something of an acquired taste. Cherries (formerly from the Brussels suburb of Schaerbeek) may be macerated in *lambic* to produce the fruity beer called *kriek*; raspberries are added to make *framboise*; and sugar and caramel are added to make *faro*. Blended *lambic* of different ages is allowed to ferment a second time in bottles to become the slightly fizzy sour beer called *gueuze*.

Restaurants ●

1. De Castillion
2. De Karmeliet
3. De Lotteburg
4. Den Braamberg
5. Den Dijver
6. Den Gouden Harynck
7. De Snippe
8. De Visscherie
9. Patrick Devos 'Zilveren Pauw'
10. De Witte Poorte
11. Die Swaene
12. Duc de Bourgogne
13. Hermitage
14. Kardinaalshof
15. 't Pandreitje
16. 't stil Ende
17. Tanuki
18. Breydel–De Coninc
19. Cafedraal
20. Cornee
21. De Paspartout
22. Lotus
23. Maria van Bourgondië
24. Marieke van Brugghe
25. Pietje Pek
26. 't Begijntje
27. 't Kapoentje
28. 't Ketelje
29. Toermalijn
30. 't Pallieterke
31. 't Voermanshuys
32. Zen
33. Bistro De Schaar
34. Bistro 't Gezelleke
35. Boterhuis Brasserie
36. Café 'De Versteende Nacht'
37. De Beurze
38. De Bron
39. De Serre–Eetcaf 'De Vuyst'
40. De Watermolen
41. De Wintmolen
42. Het Dagelijks Brood
43. Maximiliaan Van Oostenrijk
44. 't Vorske Malpertus
45. Van Eyck

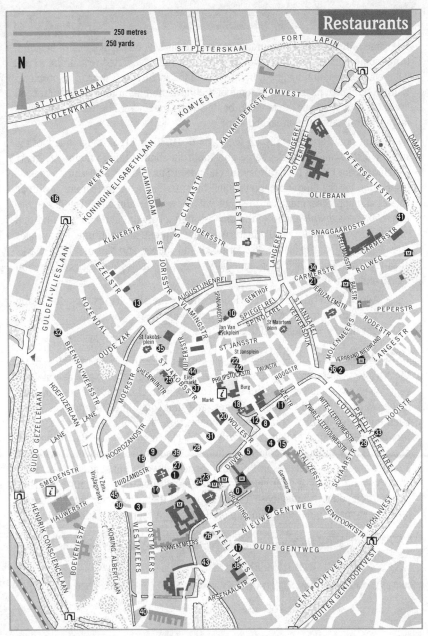

Restaurants

250 metres
250 yards

N

FORT LAPIN
ST PIETERSKAAI
ST PIETERSKAAI
KOLENKAAI
KOMVEST
KOMVEST

16

WERFSTR
KONINGIN ELISABETHLAAN
VLAMINGDAM
CLARASTR
ST CLARASTR
BIDDERSSTR
BALIESTR
LANGEREI
POTTERIEREI
PETERSELIESTR
OLIEBAAN
DAMPO

41

KLAVERSTR
ST JORISSTR
SNAGGAARDSTR
SPEELMANSSTR
CARMERSTR
ROLWEG

GULDEN-VLIESLAAN
EZELSTR
ROZENDAL
AUGUSTIJNENREI
VLAMINGSTR
SPANJAARDSTR
GENTHOF
SPIEGELREI
SPINOLAREI
CARMERSTR
JERUZALEMSTR
BALSTR
PEPERSTR
RODESTR
LANGESTR

34
21

13

32

10
Jan Van
Eyckplein
St Maartens
plein
ST ANNAREI
VERVERSDIJK
MOLENMEERS

BEENHOUWERSSTR
OUDE ZAK
MOERSTR
GHEERWIJNSTR
ST JAKOBSSTR
ST JANSSTR
ST JANSSTR
St Jansplein
TWIJNSTR
HOOGSTR
VERRRAND NIEUWLAND

St Jakobs-
plein
35

36 2

HOEFIJZERLAAN
LANE
NOORDZANDSTR
44
Eier
markt
25
37
PHILIPSTOCKSTR
Burg
WESTR
COUTURE
PREDIKHERENREI
HOOISTR

HENDRIK CONSCIENCELAAN
GUIDO GEZELLELAAN
SMEDENSTR
't Zand
Vrijdagmarkt
ZUIDZANDSTR
31
28
Markt
18
20
WOLLESTR
12
8
11
WITTE-LEERTOUWERSTR
ZWARTE-LEERTOUWERSTR
STALIJZERSTR
SCHAARSTR
29
33

9
39
27
1
19
5
4
15
DIJVER

45
30
3
11
14
24
23
0
GROENINGE
NIEUWE GENTWEG
GENTPOORTSTR
BONINVEST
GENTPOORTVEST

HAUWERSTR
BOEVERIESTR
KONING ALBERTLAAN
WESTMEERS
OOSTMEERS
ZONNEKEMEERS
26
KATELIJNESTR
17
7
OUDE GENTWEG
BUITEN GENTPOORTVEST

43
38
40
ARSENAALSTR

The fame of Bruges' best restaurants has spread far beyond the borders of Belgium. It has some outstanding chefs working in beautifully decorated restaurants. Treat yourself. Besides, finding good, inexpensive food in Bruges is more of a problem: tourism has taken its toll, and in some of the more prominent tourist restaurants on the main tourist circuit the fare can be decidedly mediocre. Plasticized, formulaic menus in four languages are a bad sign!

Restaurant hours are generally 12–2.30 and 6–10.30 or 11, although many of the smaller *bistros* and brasseries serve nonstop from about 11am to midnight. Many restaurants are closed for Saturday lunch and on Sunday. It's advisable to make a reservation for the more upmarket establishments. There are restaurants to suit all palates and appetites; menus at the door will show what's on offer. The fixed-price *dagschotel/dagmenu* (menu of the day) is often a bargain, and you will find that even luxury restaurants usually feature a cheaper menu at lunchtime. Many cafés serve a limited range of light dishes for lunch and supper, and bars may offer snacks or sandwiches. Some food shops and *pâtisseries* have tables and chairs where you can sit and eat a snack.

Value Added Tax (TVA/BTW) at 21 per cent is generally already included in the price of restaurant meals. A 16 per cent service charge is also usually included, so no further tipping is required. If in doubt, ask.

Vegetarians

Meat plays a central role in Belgian cuisine, but it would be wrong to assume that vegetarians are completely left out in the cold. Belgian chefs have become increasingly aware of the call for lighter dishes, and that sometimes means vegetarian. Even traditional Belgian cooking includes noted vegetarian dishes, such as *flamiche aux poireaux*, a kind of flan filled with leeks in a cream sauce. Egg dishes are excellent, and although vegetarians often get tired of being fobbed off with yet another omelette, omelettes in Belgium are actually extremely good. Asparagus, chicory and hop shoots often feature in meatless dishes. In restaurants, you may fare better if you pick and choose from the edges of the menu, ordering two starters instead of a main course and filling up on delicious, substantial puddings.

Price for 3-course meal (without wine) for one person

∞∞ over 1,500 BF

∞ 700–1,500 BF

◊ below 700 BF

De Castillion, Heilige-Geeststraat 1, ✆ 050 34 30 01, 🖨 050 33 94 75. *Closed Mon and Tues lunchtimes and Sun eve.* Dignified and traditional hotel-restaurant serving rich, elegant French cuisine. Menus from 995 BF.

De Karmeliet, Langestraat 19, ✆ 050 33 82 59, 🖨 050 33 10 11. *Closed Sun eve, Mon and for Sun lunch June–Aug.* Chic restaurant in patrician house with terrace. Among the best restaurants in Belgium, awarded three Michelin stars in 1996. Lunch menu 2,600 BF.

De Lotteburg, Goezeputstraat 43, ✆ 050 33 75 35, 🖨 050 34 04 04. *Closed Mon and Thurs exc hols.* Regional specialities and exceptionally fresh fish dishes at this friendly establishment. Lunch menu from 1,195 BF.

Den Braamberg, Pandreitje 11, ✆ 050 33 73 70, 🖨 050 33 99 73. *Closed Fri, Sun and 2 weeks in July.* Elegant restaurant in an 18th-century house, with award-winning cuisine. Lunch 1,780 BF including wine.

Den Dyver, Dijver 5, ✆ 050 33 60 69. *Closed Wed and Thurs lunch.* Sumptuous historic backdrop: dishes cooked with beer; perfect for beer enthusiasts. Menus from 1,400 BF.

Den Gouden Harynck, Groeninge 25, ✆ 050 33 76 37, 🖨 050 34 42 70. *Closed Sun, Mon, 1st week after Easter, last week in July, 1st 2 weeks in Aug.* Elegant restaurant serving inventive French cuisine with the emphasis on seafood. Open fire and faultless service. Lunch menu at 1,500 BF.

De Snippe, Nieuwe Gentweg 53, ✆ 050 33 70 70. *Closed Sun, Mon* lunch, 3 weeks in Feb and 2 weeks in Nov. Hotel-restaurant with orangerie overlooking a garden. Superb *haute cuisine française—queues de langoustines à la ciboulette.* Lunch menu at 1,950 BF; four-course evening menu 3,400 BF (with wine).

De Visscherie, Vismarkt 8, ✆ 050 33 02 12. *Closed Tues, last 2 weeks of Nov, first 2 weeks of Dec.* Fish gastronomy of high renown, overlooking the fish market. *Waterzooi van de Noordzee* especially recommended. Menus upwards of 1,250 BF (lunch), 1,950 BF (evening).

Patrick Devos 'Zilveren Pauw', Zilverstraat 41, ✆ 050 33 55 66. *Closed Sun and 2 weeks July–Aug.* Much-fêted restaurant in an elegant turn-of-the-century house with garden. Noted for French cuisine prepared with an ingeniously light touch. Lunch menu at a bargain 1100 BF, gourmet menu 3,000 BF.

De Witte Poorte, Jan van Eyckplein 6, ✆ 050 33 08 83. *Closed Sun, Mon (except public hols), 2 weeks in Feb and last 2 weeks of June.* Specialists in Belgian cooking of exceptional quality. Lunch menu 1,050 BF, evening menus from 1,950.

Die Swaene, Steenhouwersdijk 1, ✆ 050 34 27 98. *Closed Wed and Thurs lunch.* Elegant hotel-restaurant which prides itself on its French-style cooking. Lunch menu 1,250 BF.

Duc de Bourgogne, Huidenvettersplein 12, ✆ 050 33 20 38. *Closed Jan and 3 weeks in July.* Classy hotel-restaurant in former palace gatehouse, overlooking the canal at the heart of the city. Lunch menu 1,250 BF. Sunday menu 2,200 BF including wine. Gastronomic menu 2,150 BF.

Hermitage, Ezelstraat 18, ✆ 050 34 41 73. *Closed mid-July to mid-Aug.* Delightful 17th-century mansion serving light French favourites. Menus from 2,000 BF. **⑬**

Kardinaalshof, Sint-Salvatorskerkhof, ✆ 050 34 16 91, ✉ 050 34 20 62. *Closed Wed and Thurs.* Attractively restored restaurant, relaxed and intimate; emphasis on seafood, imaginatively prepared. Menus from 1,100 BF. **⑭**

Pannenhuis, Zandstraat 2, Brugge (Sint-Andries), ✆ 050 31 19 07, ✉ 050 31 77 66. *Closed last 2 weeks of Jan and first 3 weeks of July.* A mock-Tudor stylish hotel-restaurant on the outskirts. Delightful terrace and flower-filled garden; interesting French classics. Menus from 1,050 BF.

't Pandreitje, Pandreitje 6, ✆ 050 33 11 90, ✉ 050 50 34 00 70. *Closed Sun, Wed, 1st 2 weeks in July, last week in Feb, 1st week in Nov.* Louis XV décor, terrace and garden. Excellent wine list and inventive French cuisine. Menus from 2,200 BF. **⑮**

't stil Ende, Scheepsdalelaan 12, ✆ 050 33 92 03, ✉ 050 33 26 22. *Closed Sat lunch, Sun eve, Mon, last 2 weeks of July.* Crisp modern interpretations of classic French dishes served in a stylish, modern setting. Menus from 950 BF (lunch). **⑯**

Tanuki, Oude Gentweg 1, ✆ 050 34 75 12. *Closed Mon and Tues.* *Teppanyaki*, *tempura*, *sashimi* and *sushi* and a Japanese garden. Menus from 580 BF (lunch) to 1,800 BF. **⑰**

Breydel–De Coninc, Breidelstraat 24, ✆ 050 33 97 46. *Closed Wed.* Hearty portions of mussels and seafood; easy-going, modern ambience. Very central, favoured by locals and extremely well priced. Menus from 1,000 BF. **⑱**

Cafedraal, Zilverstraat 38, ✆ 05 34 08 45. French brasserie and bar in a lovely 15th-century building (the Vasquezhuis). The house specialities include lobster (750 BF for a half) and *bouillabaisse* (850 BF). **⑲**

Cornee, De Garre 2, ✆ 050 33 95 88. *Closed Wed.* Friendly, intimate restaurant down a tiny alleyway off Breidelstraat. French and Belgian cuisine (eels in green sauce, dishes with *witloof*). Lunch menu 995 BF. **⑳**

De Paspartout, Jeruzalemstraat 1, ✆ 050 34 66 13. *Open Fri and Sat eve and Sun lunch.* Romantic and intimate little gabled restaurant, serving delicious game in winter and seafood in summer. Seasonal menu 1100 BF. **㉑**

Lotus, Wapenmakersstraat 5, ✆ 050 33 10 78. *Closed eves exc Fri.* Relaxed, elegant vegetarian restaurant, with inventive and well-priced dishes, including some fish. **㉒**

Maria van Bourgondië, Guido Gezelleplein 1, ✆ 050 33 20 66. Solid Belgian cooking (soup, ham, pâté, *vlaamse stoofkarbonaden* (beef stew in beer), *waterzooi*) in a comfortable and spacious townhouse with an open fire. 'Regional' lunch menu 595 BF. **㉓**

Marieke van Brugghe, Mariastraat 17, ✆ 050 34 33 66, ✉ 050 34 33 60. Reminiscent of the galley of a Spanish galleon, with a modern designer twist. The *vlaamse stoverij met kasteelbier*, a succulent stew, comes with **㉔**

delicious soft-fried chips, perfect for soaking up the juices. The all-in 995 BF menu is especially good value.

∞ **Pietje Pek**, 13 Sint-Jakobsstraat, **25** ✆ 050 34 78 74. *Open 5.30–11pm only, closed Tues and Wed.* Atmospheric bistro specializing in fondues (meat, cheese); open early to cater for families. 'Eat-as-much-as-you-like' fondue 795 BF; children under 10 can share with adults for free.

∞ **'t Begijntje**, Walstraat 11, ✆ 050 33 **26** 00 89. *Closed Wed and Sun evening.* Minuscule and charming family-run restaurant serving good home-cooked Flemish food. Menus 880–1450 BF.

∞ **'t Kapoentje**, St Salvatorskoorstraat **27** 3, ✆ 050 34 02 30. *Closed Wed lunch and Sun.* Relaxed ambience with arty décor; specializes in meat and fish fondues: fish pieces simmered in a *bouillon*, fished out with a little net. Good fun for children. Good South African wines.

∞ **'t Keteltje**, Oude Burg 20, ✆ 050 34 **28** 68 20. *Closed Sun.* Fresh linen, fresh flowers and an unfussy atmosphere for nicely judged, inventive French-style cuisine: North Sea fish soup with *rouille*, snails in a creamed curry sauce, fine fillet steaks or mixed fish brochettes. Lunch menu 490 BF, evening menus 950–1250 BF.

∞ **Toermalijn**, Coupure 29a, ✆ 050 34 **29** 01 94, @ 050 34 35 39. Vegetarian restaurant in the Hotel Dante, overlooking the canal, with a range of creative menus using organic produce. *Waterzooi* with tofu is particularly recommended. Menus from 1,050 BF.

∞ **'t Pallieterke**, 't Zand 28, ✆ 050 34 **30** 01 77. *Closed Tues.* Pleasant, friendly French-style restaurant and tea room

in the west of the city, serving mussels, game, fish and *waterzooi*. Menus 495 BF–980 BF.

∞ **'t Voermanshuys**, Oude Burg 14, **31** ✆ 050 33 71 72. *Closed Tues.* Robust grilled dishes and filling fondues in 16th-century cellars.

∞ **Zen**, Beenhouwersstraat 117, ✆ 050 **32** 33 67 02. *Open 12–2 only; closed Sun.* Inventive home-made vegetarian cuisine dished up in suitably minimalist surroundings.

◌ **Bistro De Schaar**, Hooistraat 2, **33** ✆ 050 33 59 79. *Open 12–2.30 and 6–11; closed Sun.* Agreeable bistro with some tasty starters: fish soup, stuffed mushrooms with snails (300 BF), and wholesome main courses of lamb, duck, monkfish, etc. (600 BF).

◌ **Bistro 't Gezelleke**, Carmersstraat **34** 15, ✆ 050 33 81 02. *Open 12–12, Sat 6pm–2am; closed Sun.* Agreeably wacky bistro-bar. Pastas, salads and fish dishes.

◌ **Boterhuis Brasserie**, Sint-Jakobs-**35** straat 38, ✆ 050 34 15 11. Warm welcome in traditional brasserie. Steaks, brochettes, pasta and snacks.

◌ **Café 'De Versteende Nacht'**, **36** Langestraat 11. Friendly, lively bar. Free jazz in the evenings. Bar meals: scampi, steaks and copious chips (250–500 BF).

◌ **De Deurze**, 22 Markt, ✆ 050 33 50 **37** 79. Laid-back *bistro* with wooden tables and an open fire. Mussels, grilled fish and meat, light snacks. Lunch menu 495 BF.

◌ **De Bron**, Katelijnestraat 82, ✆ 050 **38** 33 45 26. *Open 12–2 only; closed Mon.* Agreeable vegetarian restaurant in an old town house built in 1647.

De Serre–Eetcaf 'De Vuyst',
Simon Stevinplein 15, ✆ 050 34 22
31. *Closed Tues*. Friendly and bright.
Quick lunch menu 525 BF.

De Watermolen, Oostmeers 130,
✆ 050 34 33 48. *Closed Tues eve
and Wed*. Bistro with terrace, specializing in fish. Menus from 555 BF.

De Windmolen, Carmersstraat 135,
✆ 050 33 97 39. *Open 10–9; closed
Sat*. Charming, folksy, family-run
bistro and bar. Pasta, sandwiches and
garnaalkroketten.

Het Dagelijks Brood,
Philipstockstraat 21. *Open 7–6, Sun
8–6; closed Tues*. A branch of the successful *Pain Quotidien* chain. Bakery

snacks and upmarket sandwiches.
Seating around a big central table.

Maximiliaan Van Oostenrijk,
Wijngaardplein 17, ✆ 050 33 47 23.
Straightforward Flemish food at good
prices in an attractive tavern.

't Vorske Malpertus, Eiermarkt 9,
✆ 050 33 30 38. Solid Flemish food,
including rabbit dishes and delicious
waterzooi, in medieval cellars which
once formed part of a monastery.

Van Eyck, 't Zand 23, ✆ 050 33 41
48. *Closed Thurs*. Tiny restaurant,
brasserie and tea room with vaguely
Art Nouveau décor, and reasonably
priced menus.

Cafes and Bars

Café Hoegaarden, Steenstraat 10. Sleek,
modern bar named after its main product,
served on tap. Salads and sandwiches.

Café Vlissinghe, Blekersstraat 2. *Open
11am–midnight; closed Tues*. Artists apparently used to gather here to meet Van Dyck.
Atmospheric, wood-panelled bar, with a cast-
iron stove. Boules court in the garden. Soup,
cheese, ham platters, pasta (100–220 BF).

Charlie Rockets, Hoogstraat 19, ✆ 050 33
06 60. Lively, relaxed, fun bar attached to a
youth hotel. Loud music. Tex-Mex dishes
(395 BF), nachos, burgers (95 BF).

Cohiba, Zilverstraat 38A. Lively Cuban bar
for rum and tight rhythm in a crush.

Craenenburg, Markt 16. Café, with stained
glass and heavy brass chandeliers, on the site
where Archduke Maximillian was imprisoned
for three weeks in 1488. Good snacks.

De Garre, De Garre 1. Cosy *staminee* (pub),
in a passageway off Breidelstraat. Good beer
and light snacks, including savoury *taart*.

De Kogge, Braamergstraat 7. Built in 1637
as a trading house for fish porters, little
changed, although they now play live music.

De Medici Sorbetière, Geldmuntstraat 9.
Good coffee served with sorbets and *petit-
fours* in genuine Art-Nouveau setting. Also
does tasty lunch dishes (300–350 BF).]

L'Estaminet, Gevangenisstraat 5. *Open
from 11.30; closed Mon lunch and Sun*.
Quaint pub with low-beamed ceilings: a
trusty *drankhuis* since 1900.

Straffe Hendrik–De Halve Maan,
Walplein 26. The brewery tavern. Snacks
include beer soup (*see* p.163).

Taverne Erasmus, Wollestraat 35. Popular
and friendly bar in a hotel, favoured by beer-
enthusiasts.

't Brugs Beertje, Kemelstraat 5. *Open
4pm–1am; closed Wed*. Mecca for beer-
lovers; more than 300 brews. Astoundingly
knowledgeable owners: follow their advice!
Pâté and cheese snacks (about 200 BF).

Where to Stay

Bruges has hotels to suit all tastes—and over 100 of them. They range from small family-run guesthouses, with their own ways of doing things and quirky charms, to the large, efficient, comfortable you-could-be-anywhere hotels of the international chains.

The really special hotels are the small and luxurious ones in the centre of town, occupying beautifully restored and converted historic mansions and town houses. The rooms look like photographs from glossy interior-design magazines, with plush and tasteful comfort down to the last pampered detail—backed by impeccable service. Cheaper hotels are more run-of-the-mill, but it may be worth sacrificing comfort for a more central location.

Note that Bruges' cobbled streets are noisy with traffic, horse-drawn carriages and revellers. In summer you may want to insist on a room with double glazing and air conditioning, unless you can put up with the noise and mosquitoes coming through open windows.

Virtually everyone in the hotel business speaks English, so booking is easy. Check that the price quoted includes breakfast (charged separately, it can be surprisingly expensive). Establish if the hotel has its own parking or is close to a public car park. Parking can be very tricky anywhere in the city, especially in summer.

Hotels

1. De Castillion
2. De Orangerie
3. De Tuilerieën
4. Sofitel
5. de' Medici
6. Die Swaene
7. Holiday Inn Crowne Plaza
8. Prinsenhof
9. Relais Oud Huis Amsterdam
10. Walburg
11. Alfa Dante
12. Aragon
13. Azalea
14. Bryghia
15. De Snippe
16. Duc de Bourgogne
17. Hansa
18. Jan Brito
19. Navarra
20. Park Hotel
21. Portinari
22. Romantik Pandhotel
23. Ter Brughe
24. Ter Duinen
25. Adornes
26. Albert I
27. Biskajer
28. Botaniek
29. Boterhuis
30. Bourgoensch Hof
31. Cordoeanier
32. Egmond
33. Grand Hotel du Sablon
34. Groeninghe
35. Ibis Brugge Centrum
36. Karos
37. Montovani
38. Patritius
39. 't Putje
40. Asiris
41. Cavalier
42. De Pauw
43. Het Gulden Vlies
44. Imperial
45. Jacobs
46. Lucca
47. Rembrandt-Rubens
48. Ter Reien
49. 't Koffieboontje
50. Van Eyck

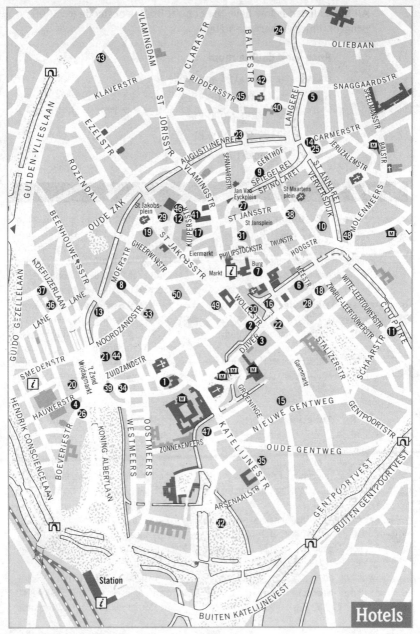

Hotels

173

All hotels listed below have the central Bruges postcode (✉ 8000 Brugge), unless otherwise stated.

Price for a double room

⌘⌘⌘⌘⌘	8,000 BF and above
⌘⌘⌘⌘	6,000–8,000 BF
⌘⌘⌘	4,00–6,000 BF
⌘⌘	2,500–4,00 BF
⌘	under 2,500 BF

Hotels

⌘⌘⌘⌘⌘ **★★★★De Castillion**, Heilige-
1 Geeststraat 1, ✆ 050 34 30 01, 🖷 050
33 94 75. Once a prince's residence.
Opulent hotel-restaurant furnished
with heavy turn-of-the-century
grandeur. Near St-Salvatorskathedraal.

⌘⌘⌘⌘⌘ **★★★★De Orangerie**, Kartuizerin-
2 nenstraat 10, ✆ 050 34 16 49, 🖷 050
33 30 16. Central Bruges. Delightful,
elegant and sumptuous small hotel,
sister to De Tuilerieën. 16th-century
former convent overlooking the canal
with canalside breakfast terrace.
Private garage.

⌘⌘⌘⌘⌘ **★★★★De Tuilerieën**, Dijver 7,
3 ✆ 050 34 36 91, 🖷 050 34 04 00.
Pampered luxury in a 15th-century
town house on a pretty stretch of
canal near the centre. Private garage
and swimming pool. One child under
12 stays free.

⌘⌘⌘⌘⌘ **★★★★Sofitel**, Boeveriestraat 2,
4 ✆ 050 34 09 71, 🖷 050 34 40 53.
Comfortable modern hotel behind the
façade of a 17th-century monastery.
Swimming pool.

⌘⌘⌘⌘ **★★★★de' Medici**, Potterierei 15,
5 ✆ 050 33 98 33, 🖷 050 33 07 64. A
sympathetic fusion of modern and traditional design. Gym, sauna,
solarium, Turkish baths, jacuzzi.
Lounge bar leading onto a Japanese
garden, and excellent Japanese restaurant specializing in teppanyaki.

⌘⌘⌘⌘ **★★★★Die Swaene**, Steenhouwers-
6 dijk 1, ✆ 050 34 27 98, 🖷 050 33 66
74. Part of the Small Luxury Hotels of
the World group. Delightful 15th-
century mansion, with a much-lauded
gastronomic restaurant, overlooking
the canal. Louis XV-cum-Laura Ashley
style décor with four-poster beds.

⌘⌘⌘⌘ **★★★★Holiday Inn Crowne Plaza**,
7 Burg 10, ✆ 050 34 58 34, 🖷 050 34
56 15. Sleek modern hotel, with pool,
parking and an archaeological site in
the basement. Children free if sharing
with parents.

⌘⌘⌘⌘ **★★★★Prinsenhof**, Ontvangersstraat
8 9, ✆ 050 34 26 90, 🖷 050 34 23 21.
Very plush, antique-furnished rooms
in the heart of the city. A Relais du
Silence hotel.

⌘⌘⌘⌘ **★★★★Relais Oud Huis Amster-
9 dam**, Spiegelrei 3, ✆ 050 34 18 10,
🖷 050 33 88 91. Four 17th-century

mansions combined to offer idiosyncratic luxury, with antique-furnished rooms, many overlooking the canal or a garden. Feels like a large, grand but relaxed family home.

10 ****Walburg**, Boomgaardstraat 13–15, ℗ 050 34 94 14, @ 050 33 68 84. Elegantly restored 19th-century mansion in the heart of Bruges with impossibly high ceilings and frothy neoclassical décor. Restrained and spacious; backs onto a sunny garden and terrace.

11 ***Alfa Dante**, Coupure 29A, ℗ 050 34 01 94, @ 050 34 35 39. Large, imposing and modern with mellow interior. Vegetarian restaurant, 'Toermalijn' comes recommended.

12 ****Aragon**, Naaldenstraat 24, ℗ 050 33 35 33, @ 050 34 28 05. Spacious 18th-century noble's house, opposite the Hof van Bladelin.

13 ****Azalea**, Wulfhagestraat 43, ℗ 050 33 14 78, @ 050 33 97 00. Very elegant, traditionally decorated central hotel with beautiful, sweeping wooden staircase. Private car park.

14 ****Bryghia**, Oosterlingenplein 4, ℗ 050 33 80 59, @ 050 34 14 30. Central yet peaceful family-run hotel with traditional décor of exposed brickwork and beamed ceilings.

15 ***De Snippe**, Nieuwe Gentweg 53, ℗ 050 33 70 70, @ 050 33 76 62. Hotel-restaurant with celebrated cuisine. Sympathetically restored 18th-century house; comfortable elegance, polished wood floors, soft drapes.

16 ***Duc de Bourgogne**, Huidenvettersplein 12, ℗ 050 33 20 38, @ 050 34 40 37. Hotel-restaurant

with just ten traditionally decorated rooms in a very central historic house. Excellent restaurant.

17 ****Hansa**, Niklaas Desparsstraat 11, ℗ 050 33 84 44, @ 050 33 42 05. Elegantly restored 19th century mansion with air conditioning, fitness centre, sauna, steambath and solarium. Crisply efficient.

18 ****Jan Brito**, Freren Fonteinstraat 1, ℗ 050 33 06 01, @ 050 33 06 52. 16th-century gabled mansion, near the centre, beautifully restored, in Louis XVI style. Breakfast only, no restaurant.

19 ****Navarra**, Sint Jakobsstraat 41, ℗ 050 34 05 61, @ 050 33 67 90. Gleaming white hotel, recently renovated—once the medieval trading house of the merchant of Navarre. Wicker armchairs scattered in the lovely enclosed garden. Sauna, fitness area and indoor pool.

20 ****Park Hotel**, Vrijdagmarkt 5, ℗ 050 33 33 64, @ 050 33 47 63. Comfortable modern hotel on 't Zand.

21 ****Portinari**, 't Zand 15, ℗ 050 34 10 34, @ 050 34 41 80. Relaxed and comfortable with excellent service and pleasant terrace.

22 ****Romantik Pandhotel**, Pandreitje 16, ℗ 050 34 06 66, @ 050 34 05 56. Fine central 18th-century burgher's house, now a cosy, elegant hotel, with canopied beds and Ralph Lauren fabrics. Part of the Romantic Hotels chain.

23 ****Ter Brughe**, Oost-Gistelhof 2, ℗ 050 34 03 24, @ 050 33 88 73. Renovated, typical 16th-century narrow Flemish mansion; breakfast in the vaulted medieval cellar. Overlooks the canal.

24 ***Ter Duinen**, Langerei 52, ✆ 050 33 04 37, 🖷 050 34 42 16. Welcoming, family-run hotel, with views over the canal. Conservatory, real open fire, air-conditioned rooms, heavily double glazed. Nothing too much trouble. Free car parking.

25 ***Adornes**, Sint Annarei 26, ✆ 050 34 13 36, 🖷 050 34 59 39. A cluster of softly coloured gabled 16th–18th-century houses, tastefully restored and overlooking the canal. Friendly and welcoming. Free bicycle rental. Some car parking.

26 ***Albert I**, Koning Albertlaan 2–4, ✆ 050 34 09 30, 🖷 050 33 84 18. A warm red-brick building on the busy 't Zand, with pleasant rooms and hearty breakfasts.

27 ****Biskajer**, Biskajersplein 4, ✆ 050 34 15 06, 🖷 050 34 39 11. Quiet, cosy, personable hotel, a short walk from the Markt. Bright, modern furnishings.

28 ***Botaniek**, Waalsestraat 23, ✆ 050 34 14 24, 🖷 050 34 59 39. Small, comfortable 18th-century town house. Central.

29 ****Boterhuis**, Sint-Jakobsstraat 38, ✆ 050 34 15 11, 🖷 050 34 70 89. Lovely, whimsical hotel with a turret in the old dairy market. Quirky charm and friendly welcome.

30 ***Bourgoensch Hof**, Wollestraat 39, ✆ 050 33 16 45, 🖷 050 34 63 78. Traditional Flemish architecture overlooking the canal. Good restaurant and brasserie serving classic regional dishes.

****Campanile**, 20 Jagerstraat, 8200 Brugge (St Michiels), ✆ 050 38 13 60, 🖷 050 38 45 42. Friendly, modern family-run hotel, south of the station.

31 ****Cordoeanier**, Cordoeaniersstraat 16–18, ✆ 050 33 90 51, 🖷 050 34 61 11. Small, central good-value family-run hotel.

32 ***Egmond**, Minnewater 15, 8000 Brugge, ✆ 050 34 14 45, 🖷 050 34 29 40. Gabled, sprawling and utterly romantic. Also surprisingly reasonable. Beautiful gardens and free car park.

33 ***Grand Hotel du Sablon**, Noordzandstraat 21, ✆ 050 33 39 02, 🖷 050 34 20 18. Turn of the century décor with an Art Deco glassed cupola in the entrance hall. Handily placed for shopping.

34 ***Groeninghe**, Korte Vulders-straat 29, ✆ 050 34 32 55, 🖷 050 34 07 69. Small guesthouse with the atmosphere of a private home, not far from Sint-Salvatorskathedraal.

35 ***Ibis Brugge Centrum**, Katelijnestraat 65A, ✆ 050 33 75 75, 🖷 050 33 64 19. Large hotel with all mod cons in a 15th century convent; near the Begijnhof.

36 ****Karos**, Hoefijzerlaan 37, ✆ 050 34 14 48, 🖷 050 34 00 91. New, well-equipped hotel on a busy road near 't Zand with Breton-style façade, swimming pool, sauna and solarium.

***Kasteel Cateline**, Zandstreet 272, ✉ 8200 Brugge (Sint Andries), ✆ 050 31 70 26, 🖷 050 31 72 41. Located on the outskirts of Bruges. Small, turretted castle in the middle of a pretty park. Inventive cuisine.

37 ***Montovani**, Schouwvergers-straat 11, ✆ 050 34 53 66, 🖷 050 34 53 67. Near 't Zand. Family-run hotel with patio and attractive interior veranda.

***Novotel Zuid**, Chartreuseweg 20, ✉ 8200 Brugge (Sint-Michiels),

© 050 40 21 40, ✆ 050 40 21 41. Functional family hotel 4km south of the city. Woodland setting with outdoor pool. Near the A17 motorway but good double-glazing.

∞ *****Olympia**, Magdalenstraat 16, © 050 39 05 78, ✆ 050 39 01 13. Just outside the town ramparts. 30 quiet rooms and cheerfully efficient approach.

∞ *****Pannenhuis**, Zandstraat 2, 8200 Brugge (Sint Andries), © 050 31 19 07, ✆ 050 31 77 66. Black and white gabled former notary's villa on the outskirts. Expansive terraced garden and good seafood restaurant.

∞ **38** ****Patritius**, Riddersstraat 11, © 050 33 84 54, ✆ 050 33 96 34. A big old mansion, converted into a medium-priced hotel, spacious and central but with few frills.

∞ **39** ***'t Putje**, 31 't Zand, © 050 33 28 47, ✆ 050 34 14 23. Central, well-run, clean and friendly modernized hotel.

∞ *****Wilgenhof**, Polderstraat 151, ✉ 8310 Brugge (Sint Kruis), © 050 36 27 44, ✆ 050 36 28 21. On the banks of the Damme canal outside the city centre. Attractive cottage-style hotel set amidst the green polders. Good opportunities for walking and cycling.

◊ **40** ****Asiris**, Lange Raamstraat 9, © 050 34 17 24, ✆ 050 34 74 58. Former aristocrat's home near Sint-Gillis church, colourfully renovated. Free car parking.

◊ **41** ****Cavalier**, Kuipersstraat 25, © 050 33 02 07, ✆ 050 34 71 99. Just behind the theatre, with eight cosy rooms and a touch of 19th-century grandeur.

◊ **42** ****De Pauw**, Sint Gilliskerkhof 8, © 050 33 71 18, ✆ 050 34 51 40. Traditional, cosy, sturdy brick house in a quiet street.

◊ **43** ****Het Gulden Vlies**, Koningin Elisabethlaan 40, © 050 34 12 70, ✆ 050 34 73 00. Pleasant, straightforward, no-frills establishment on a busy road Good value for money. 20 mins' walk from the Markt.

◊ **44** ****Imperial**, Dweersstraat 24, © 050 33 90 14, ✆ 050 34 43 06. Tucked down a side street east of 't Zand, with gleaming stepped gables and flourishing window boxes. Friendly and comfortable.

◊ **45** *****Jacobs**, Baliestraat 1, © 050 33 98 31, ✆ 050 33 56 94. Comfortable quiet rooms. Family-run for almost 50 years.

◊ **46** ****Lucca**, Naaldenstraat 30, © 050 34 20 67, ✆ 050 33 34 64. Neoclassical building in the centre, on the site of the trading house of the merchants of Lucca. Breakfast in the 14th-century cellar. Friendly and relaxed. Rooms have heavy blinds which cut down the street noise.

◊ **47** ****Rembrandt-Rubens**, Walplein 38, © 050 33 64 39. A gabled 17th-century house set back from the canals, near the Begijnhof.

◊ **48** *****Ter Reien**, Langestraat 1, © 050 34 91 00, ✆ 050 34 40 48. Much-praised, well-located small hotel, overlooking the Sint-Annarei canal. Excellent value for money. Recent pretty renovation.

◊ **49** ****'t Koffieboontje**, Hallestraat 4, © 050 33 80 27, ✆ 050 34 39 04. Atrractive little hotel in the heart of the city. Also reasonably priced holiday apartments for 1–6 people.

◊ **50** ****Van Eyck**, Korte Zilverstraat 7, © 05 33 52 67, ✆ 050 34 94 30. In a quiet yet central street; businesslike, but comfortable.

Youth Hostels and Youth Hotels

There are several *jeuglogies* in Bruges, where you can find cheap and cheerful accommodation—fine if you don't mind sleeping in a dormitory.

Bauhaus International Youth Hotel, Langestraat 135–137, ✆ 050 34 10 93, ✉ 050 33 41 80. Room for 81 people, about 20 mins' walk from the centre, or bus no.6 from the station. 430 BF per person.

Charlie Rockets, Hoogstraat 19, ✆ 050 33 06 60, ✉ 050 33 66 74. Funky and very central youth hotel. Rooms shared by 2, 4 or 6. 495 BF without breakfast; 595 BF with.

Passage, Dweersstraat 26, ✆ 050 34 02 32, ✉ 050 34 01 40. Capacity for 50, a stone's throw from Sint-Salvatorskathedraal. Dormitories from 380–430 BF excluding breakfast (100 BF). Double room 1,200 BF including breakfast.

Snuffel Sleep In, Ezelstraat 47–49, ✆ 050 33 31 33, ✉ 050 33 32 50. Cheap lodgings close to the centre. Easygoing regime. 350–490 BF per person.

International Youth Hostel, Baron Ruzettelaan 143, ✉ 8310 Assebroek, ✆ 050 35 26 79, ✉ 050 35 37 32. The modern youth hostel, located in a suburb east of the city. Bus no.2 to the city centre, or from the station out to the hostel. 420–495 BF with a Youth Hostel card, 100 BF more without.

Bed and Breakfast

The tourist office publishes a list of approved bed and breakfast accommodation. Double rooms are available in central locations for 1,500 BF upwards, family rooms sleeping four for around 2,500–4,500 BF. Contact the tourist office for more details and reservations (*see* p.xxx). The excellent, comprehensive website, *www.bruges.be*, lists all the Bed and Breakfast accommodation in the city.

Camping

Memling, Veltemweg, Sint Kruis 109, ✆ 050 35 58 45, is in the east of the city and has places for tents and caravans. Tents 110 BF per person; caravans 135 BF per person. Discounts in low season.

Sint-Michiels, Tillegemstraat, Sint-Michiels 55, ✆ 050 38 08 19. Camp site located southwest of the city. From 110 BF per person.

Shopping

The shops in Bruges are excellent: stylish, enticing, competitively priced. You can buy anything you like, from a new outfit to a Tintin watch, designer shoes to Trappist beer—all elegantly displayed in individual shops, most run by knowledgeable experts.

The main shopping streets are to the west of the Markt: Steenstraat, which leads into Zuidzandstraat, and Noordzandstraat, which continues into Smedenstraat. These are all good for clothes, shoes, designer household wares and mouth-watering specialist food shops.

Between Zilverstraat, Zuidzandstraat and Noorzandstraat there is a warren of shops called the Zilverpand, a mixture of covered arcades and pedestrianized courtyards (mainly clothes boutiques).

Katelijnestraat also has plenty of shops but, as this is a major tourist thoroughfare, many of them sell chocolates and other goods to appeal exclusively to the tourist trade.

Most shops are open Mon–Sat 9–6, and many are open on Sunday too, especially during the summer. Supermarkets tend to be open later, 9am–8pm, and 9am–9pm on Fri.

Value Added Tax

All shop prices include Value Added Tax (BWT) where applicable (currently 21 per cent). Non European Union visitors may claim it back on purchases in excess of 5001 BF made in any one shop, by asking for a form called a Tax-free Shopping Cheque. When you reach the airport, have the Shopping Cheque stamped by customs (who may wish to inspect the goods) and take it to the refund office, which will refund you the VAT, less an administration charge. You can also apply for a refund by sending your stamped Shopping Cheque by post to a refund office. Further information is available in any major shop, or from **Global Refund Belgium**, Avenue Sobieskilaan 13–1, ✉ B-1020 Brussels, ✆ 02 479 94 61, 🖷 02 478 36 64, *www.taxfree.se/belgium.*

Markets

Bruges' main markets sell fruit, vegetables, flowers, cooked meats, cheeses, fresh fish and household wares. They are visually ravishing—worth sampling for the ambience and the salesfolks' cries. The main markets are in the Markt and 't Zand.

Markt: *Wednesday 7–1.*

't Zand: *Saturday 7–1.*

Dijver: Flea market. *Mar–Oct Sat and Sun afternoon.*

Vismarkt: Fresh fish. *Tues–Sat.*

Christmas Market: Markt. Festive stalls selling Christmas goods around an open-air skating rink. *First week Dec–first week Jan.*

Beer

Good bottled beers are widely available in supermarkets and food shops.

Brugs Bierpaleis, Katelijnestraat 25–27, ℰ 050 34 31 61. Comprehensive selection of Belgian beers, as well as other beer-drinking accoutrements: correctly shaped glasses for each brand, and T-shirts with beery slogans.

Books

De Reyghere Boekhandel, Markt 12, ℰ 050 33 34 03. A fine bookshop. Good for books on Bruges and Belgium. Also has English-language books and newspapers.

Marc van de Wiele, Sint-Salvatorskerkhof 7. Art and antiquarian bookshop; the only source of *Bruges: The City Behind the History* (*see* p.xxx). *Closed Wed and Sun.*

Chocolates

Godiva, Zuidzandstraat 36. Leading name in Bolgian luxury chocolates, sumptuously rich. 250g for 320 BF, 1kg for 1280 BF.

Honfleur, Noordzandstraat 31. Traditional artisan-style chocolates and delicious hand-made biscuits.

Leonidas, Steenstraat 4. One of the best, and the least expensive. 250g for 125 BF; 1kg for 500 BF. *Open daily till 7pm* (so you can load up with *pralinen* as you head home).

Neuhaus, Steenstraat 66. Up-market and pricey. 250g for 370 BF; 1kg for 1330 BF.

Clothes and Accessories

Christophe Coppens, Genthof 3, ℰ 050 34 40 62. High-style hats and accessories, designer vases and candles.

Esprit, Steenstraat 20. Good quality men's and women's off-the-peg clothes.

InWear/Matinique, Steenstraat 42. Smart off-the-peg clothes for men and women.

Quorum, Noordzandstraat 30. Men's clothing: tweedy English elegance injected with Continental panache.

Clothes for Children

Belgium does some fabulous ranges of children's clothes. Why do they have to grow so fast?

Kids' Corner, Noordzandstraat 24. Designer children's clothes for all ages.

Katimini, Smedenstraat 4. Beautiful outfits for 0–14 year olds.

Department Stores

Inno, Steenstraat 15. Large, up-market department store, with clothes, luggage, household goods, toiletries, etc.

Hema, Steenstraat 73. Clothing, house-wares, toiletries.

Flowers

Flowers are almost as much a part of Belgian life as chocolates, chips, beer and *pâtisserie*. Florists conjure up spectacular confections with flowers and plants—more sculpture than simply flower arranging. Here are just two of many:

De Vier Seizoenen, Langerei 65.   **Myosotis**, Sint-Jakobsstraat 16.

Food

There are numerous specialist food shops in Noordzandstraat, Zuidzandstraat and Smedenstraat, selling hams, sausage, smoked eels, cheese. Even the vegetable shops take trouble to put on a show to gladden the eye. For cheese, try:

De Brugse Kaashove, Eiermarkt 2. A good selection of well-conditioned cheeses, including many of Belgium's finest such as Herve and Limburger.

Lace

There are numerous shops selling lace, notably in Breidelstraat, between the Markt and the Burg. If you want proper handmade lace, be sure to ask for a certificate of authenticity. Here are two reliable sources:

Kantcentrum, Peperstraat 3a, ✆ 050 33 00 72. The shop in the Lace Centre, with fully authenticated handmade lace, plus everything for the lace-maker: bobbins, cushions, yarn, work stands. *Open Mon–Fri 10–12 and 2–6, Sat 10–12 and 2–5; closed Sun.*

't Apostelientje, Balstraat 11. New and antique handmade lace, along with lace-making equipment. The owners make wooden bobbins, and are launching a line in chocolate bobbins as well.

Supermarkets

Profi, Langestraat 55. Medium-sized, but with a full range of food, drink, toiletries, stationery etc. *Open Mon–Thurs 9–12.30 and 1–6.30, Fri 9–12.30 and 1.30–7, Sat 9–6; closed Sun.*

Delhaize, junction of the Expressweg (main road linking Zeebrugge to the E40) and Exit Sint-Andries/Olympiastadion. One of several large out-of-town supermarkets, conveniently placed for the route to the Channel ports.

Tintin

The Tintin Shop, Steenstraat 3. The little Belgian hero and his pals in figurines, towels, postcards, posters, chess sets, cutlery—and books, of course.

BRUGGES SCHOONSTE DAG

Entertainment and Nightlife

Bruges is not a city famed for its throbbing nightlife—and no one would expect it to be otherwise. The young head off for the clubs of Antwerp, Ostend, Ghent and Brussels, leaving Bruges to its more sedate entertainments.

Sitting on a terrace at a café, or cradling a Trappist beer by a log fire in winter is perfectly sufficient entertainment for many of Bruges' visitors, especially after a day of walking around the city's sights.

That said, Bruges does provide a fair bit of fun after dark, ranging from friendly jazz bars to a couple of rock and jazz venues that attract highly respectable line-ups at weekends and during the summer season.

For listings, look for the free newspaper called *Exit*, available from the tourist office and many pubs, cafés, restaurants, shops and places of entertainment.

Theatre

Stadsschouwburg, Vlamingstraat 29, ✆ 050 44 30 60. The premier city theatre, offering mainstream or highbrow plays, usually in Dutch. Also the venue for dance and classical music concerts.

Theater De Korre, Sint-Jacobsstraat 36, ✆ 050 33 51 97.

Theater De Werf, Werfstraat 108, ✆ 050 33 05 29.

Cinema

Foreign films are almost always played in the original language, with Dutch and French subtitles.

Cinema Lumière, Sint-Jakobsstraat 36. Part of the Sint-Jakobsstraat/Boterhuis complex. Rolling agenda of impressive, upmarket and current films from Europe and the USA.

Chaplin, Ziverstraat 45

Ciné Liberty, Kuipersstraat 23

Kennedy, Zilverstraat 14

Van Eyck, Smedenstraat 12

Classical Music

Stadsschouwburg, Vlamingstraat 29, ✆ 050 44 30 60.

Joseph Ryelandzaal, Achiel van Ackerplein.

Concerts also take place in the **Provinciaal Hof**, **Sint-Salvatorskathedraal**, **Sint-Jakobskerk**, **Kapel 't Keerske** and the **Sint-Walburgakerk**.

Contemporary Music

Cactus Club, Sint-Jakobsstraat 36, ✆ 050 33 20 14. Part of the Sint-Jakobsstraat/Boterhuis complex. Interesting line-ups for music, including world music, rock, jazz and folk. The club also organizes the *Cactusfestival* of music in the Minnewater Park in mid-July.

De Werf, Werfstraat 108 (to the northeast of the town centre). Venue for cutting-edge jazz, as well as theatre. Also has its own record label.

Café 'De Versteende Nacht', Langestraat 11. Jazz (often free of charge) in the evenings in a friendly and lively bar, which also serves food and snacks. Seems to appeal to all age ranges.

Celtic Ireland, Burg 8, ✆ 050 34 45 02. Irish pub and restaurant offering regular free live music, usually along the Celtic theme.

Est Wijnbar, Noordzandstraat 34. *Closed Wed.* Bar offering an extensive choice of wines, plus cheese platters and raclette, frequently to the accompaniment of live jazz-blues.

Jazz-Club 'The Duke', Hotel Navarra, Sint-Jakobsstraat 41. Occasional jazz, gratis. Look out for announcements.

Historical Banquets

**Brugge Anno 1468/
Bruges Celebrations**, Vlamingstraat 84, ✆ 050 34 75 72, ✆ 050 34 87 28. *Nov–Mar Sat 7.30–10.45pm; April–Oct Thurs, Fri and Sat 7.30–10.45pm; 2095–2695 BF per head, discounts for children. Advance booking essential.*

The extravagant marriage festivities of Charles the Bold and Margaret of York in 1468 provide the theme for ye olde four-course medieval feast (with beer and wine included), accompanied by minstrels, jesters, fire-eaters, falconers, sword fights, set in a neogothic former Jesuit church.

Belgium has three official languages: Dutch, French and German, which is spoken on the eastern border. The language of Bruges is Dutch (sometimes still referred to as Flemish). The Dutch spoken in Flanders varies strongly from area to area, but all children at school learn a standard form called *Nederlands*, the common language of both Flanders and the Netherlands.

It is strangely rare to hear any French at all in Bruges, given that this is Belgium. English, by contrast, is widely spoken. Most people connected to the tourist industry will speak it a bit, and many speak it very well indeed. That said, some knowledge of Dutch will come in handy, if only to read signposts and decipher labels. Also, a little Dutch, even if just in an exchange of greetings, is almost always appreciated: few visitors make the effort.

A Guide to Dutch Pronunciation

Two main problems confront anyone trying to learn even just the rudiments of Dutch. One is the grammatical structure—although if you know German you will be familiar with the broad pattern of the postponed verb. The other is pronunciation. It is a phonetic language, but you have to begin by shedding any preconceived notion about how written vowels should be pronounced. *A, e, i, o* and *u* are pronounced in a broadly similar way to English—although the a is much throatier and ends up more like the o in the English 'odd'. When it comes to combination vowels, however, any attempt to interpret them in an English or, worse, a French manner, will end in failure. Wipe the slate clean and relearn! Names of places, or familiar words, will often provide useful aids to memory. For instance *huis* sounds similar to the English word 'house', which is what it means (although the 'ow' sound is more complex, making it more like 'ah-oohss').

Combination Vowels

aa	like aa in the English 'aardvaark'; e.g. *waar* (= where; pron. 'wahr')
ae	like ar in the English 'part'; e.g. Verhaeren (Belgian poet; pron. 'Verharen')
au	like ow in the English 'cow'; e.g. *kabeljauw* (= cod; pron. 'cabbelyow')
ee	like ai in the English 'hail'; e.g. *een* (= one; pron. 'ayn')
ei	like ij (*see* below); e.g *trein* (= train; pron. 'trayne')
eie	like ay in the English 'say'; e.g. Reie (name of a river; pron. 'Ray')
eu	like the English 'err'; e.g. Leuven (place name; pron. 'Lerven')
eeu	ay-ooh; e.g. *leeuw* (= lion; pron. 'lay-oohv')
ie	ee in the English 'three'; e.g. *drie* (= three; pron. 'dree')
ieu	ee-oo; e.g. *nieuw* (= new; pron. 'nee-oo')
ij	like ay in John Wayne; e.g. *wijn* (= wine; pron. 'wayne')
oe	like oo in the English 'pool'; e.g. *soep* (= soup; pron. 'soup')

oo	like oa in the English 'boat'; e.g. *Te koop* (= For sale; pron. 'Te cope' or 'Te cohp')
ou	like ou in the English 'out'; e.g. *zout* (= salt; pron. 'zout')
ui	like ow in the English 'house'; e.g. *huis* (= house; pron. 'ouse' or 'ah-oohss')
uu	like oo in the English 'hoot'; e.g. *Te huur* (= For rent; pron. 'Te ooer': but round your lips, or you risk enquiring about a *hoer*, a prostitute)

Consonants

Most consonants sound the same as they do in English, although some combinations present their own difficulties. Here are some of the more troublesome ones:

ch	pronounced like the *ch* in the Scottish 'loch'.
g	pronounced like a gutteral *h*—something similar to the *h* in 'hotel' or (again) like the *ch* in the Scottish 'loch'.
j	pronounced like the English *y*.
v	closer to the English *f*.
w	in Dutch is like a soft English *w*.
sch	at the end of a word is pronounced *s*. At the start of the word it sounds more like *sr*, with a bit of gutteral throat-clearing.

Numbers

0	*nul*	12	*twaalf*	40	*veertig*
1	*een*	13	*dertien*	50	*vijftig*
2	*twee*	14	*veertien*	60	*zestig*
3	*drie*	15	*vijftien*	70	*zeventig*
4	*vier*	16	*zestien*	80	*tachtig*
5	*vijf*	17	*zeventien*	90	*negentig*
6	*zes*	18	*achttien*	100	*honderd*
7	*zeven*	19	*negentien*	101	*honderdeen*
8	*acht*	20	*twintig*	200	*twee honderd*
9	*negen*	21	*een en twintig*	thousand	*duizend*
10	*tien*	30	*dertig*	million	*miljoen*
11	*elf*	31	*een en dertig*		

Useful Words

very	*erg/zeer*	enough	*genoeg*
much/too much	*veel/te veel*	expensive	*duur*
little/few	*weinig*	cheap	*goedkoop*

Language

old	*oud*	big	*groot*
new	*nieuw*	quickly	*snel*
little	*klein*	slowly	*langzaam*

Dates and Holidays

Monday	*maandag*	Friday	*vrijdag*
Tuesday	*dinsdag*	Saturday	*zaterdag*
Wednesday	*woensdag*	Sunday	*zondag*
Thursday	*donderdag*		

Shopping and Services

open/closed	*open/gesloten*	clothes	*kleding*
entrance	*toegang/ingang*	shoes	*schoenen*
exit	*uitgang/uitrit*	lace	*kant*
No smoking	*Niet roken*	bank	*bank*
shop	*winkel*	post office	*postkantoor*
bakery	*bakkerij*	postage stamp	*postzegel*
cake shop	*banketbakkerij*	letter	*brief*
grocer	*kruidenierswinkel*	postcard	*ansichtkaart*
bookshop	*boekhandel*	air mail	*luchtpost*
pharmacy	*apotheek*		

Time

What is the time?	*Hoe laat is het?*	night	*nacht*
today	*vandaag*	day	*dag*
yesterday	*gisteren*	week	*week*
tomorrow	*morgen*	month	*maand*
morning	*morgen/ochtend*	year	*jaar*
afternoon	*namiddag*	century	*eeuw*
evening	*avond*	early/late	*vroeg/laat*

Directions and Transport

Where is...?	*Waar is...?*	return/round trip	*heen en terug*
left/right	*links/rechts*	car	*auto*
straight on	*vooruit*	car hire	*auto verhuur*
near/far	*dichtbij/ver*	driving licence	*rijbewijs*
airport	*luchthaven/vliegveld*	petrol	*benzine*
railway station	*station*	petrol station	*benzinestation*
platform (five)	*spoor (vijf)*	unleaded	*loodvrij*
ticket	*kaartje*	car park	*parkeerplaats*
single/one way	*enkel*	bicycle	*fiets*

Emergencies

police	*politie*	I'm not feeling well.	*Ik voel niet lekker.*
doctor	*dokter*	ambulance	*ambulance*
dentist	*tandarts*	hospital	*ziekenhuis*
ill	*ziek*	medicine	*geneesmiddel*

Greetings, Responses and Getting By

I am...	Ik ben...
Britain/British	Groot Brittannië/Brits
America/American	Amerika/Amerikaan
Canada/Canadian	Canada/Canadees
Australia/Australian	Australië/Australisch
yes/no	ja/nee
please	alstublieft (abbrev. a. u. b.)
thank you (very much)	dank u (wel)/bedankt
hello, good day	goedendag, or simply dag
good morning	goedemorgen
good evening	goedenavond
good night (at bedtime)	goede nacht
goodbye	tot ziens
How are you?	Hoe maakt u het?
Very well, thank you.	Goed, dank u.
My name is...	Mijn naam is...
mister/sir	mijnheer
mrs/madam	mevrouw
how much?	hoeveel?
I can't speak Dutch	Ik spreek geen Nederlands.
Do you speak English?	Spreekt u engels?
a little	een beetje
I do not understand.	Ik begrijp het niet.
I don't know.	Ik weet het niet.
Go away!	Ga weg!
Where is the toilet?	Waar is het toilet?
ladies/gents	damestoilet/herentoilet
Watch out!	Pas op!
Sorry!	Sorry!/Het spijt me.
Cheers!	Gezondheid!/Proost!

Food and Drink

to eat	eten	soft drinks	limonaden
to drink	drinken	orange juice	sinaasappelsap
the bill	de rekening	mineral water	mineraalwater
breakfast	ontbijt	soup	soep
lunch	middagmaal/noenmaal	starter	voorgerecht
dinner	avondeten	main course	hoofdgerecht
beer	bier	dish of the day	dagschotel/dagmenu
a bottle of wine	een fles wijn	bread	brood
red/white wine	rode/witte wijn	butter	boter
glass	glas	cheese	kaas
tea/ coffee	thee/koffie	egg	ei
milk	melk	filled chocolates	pralinen

The language of cuisine in Flanders is traditionally French, and in restaurants French terms are still often used for the dishes, although this is changing. Dutch terms are used in food shops. Both Dutch and French versions are given here.

Fish (poisson/vis)

cod	*cabillaud*	*kabeljauw*
haddock	*aiglefin/églefin*	*schelvis*
lobster	*homard*	*kreeft*
mussel	*moule*	*mossel*
oyster	*huître*	*oester*
salmon	*saumon*	*zalm*
scallop	*coquille Saint-Jacques*	*Sint-Jacobsoester/Jacobsschelp*
shrimp/prawn	*crevette*	*garnaal*
squid	*calamar*	*calamar/inktvis*
trout	*truite*	*forel*
tuna	*thon*	*tonijn*

Meat (viande/vlees)

game	*gibier*	*wild*
beef	*boeuf*	*rundvlees*
chicken	*poulet*	*kip*
duck	*canard*	*eend*
ham	*jambon*	*ham/hesp*
lamb	*agneau*	*lamsvlee*
pork	*porc*	*varkensvlees*
snails	*escargots*	*escargots/slakken*
venison	*cerf/chevreuil*	*ree(bok)*
leg	*gigot*	*bout*
sausage	*saucisse/saucisson*	*worst*

Vegetables (légumes/groenten)

asparagus	*asperges*	*asperges*
Belgian endive/chicory	*chicon*	*witloof*
carrots	*carottes*	*worteltjes*
cauliflower	*choufleur*	*bloemkohl*
chives	*ciboulette*	*bieslook*
garlic	*ail*	*knoflook*
green beans	*haricots princesse*	*princesbonen*
leek	*poireau*	*prei*
mushroom	*champignon*	*champignon*
onion	*oignon*	*ui*
peas	*petits pois*	*erwten*
potatoes	*pommes de terre*	*aardappelen*
potato chips/french fries	*frites*	*frieten*
rice	*riz*	*rijst*
spinach	*épinard*	*spinazie*

Fruit (fruits/fruit; vruchten)

apple	*pomme*	*appel*
banana	*banane*	*banaan*
cherry	*cerise*	*kers*
chestnut	*marron*	*kastanje*
orange	*orange*	*sinaasappel*
peach	*pêche*	*perzik*
pear	*poire*	*peer*
pineapple	*ananas*	*ananas*
plum	*prune*	*pruim*
raspberry	*framboise*	*framboos*
strawberry	*fraise*	*aardbei*

Dessert (dessert/nagerecht)

cake	*gâteau*	*koek*
cheesecake	*tarte au fromage*	*kaastaart*
tart	*tarte*	*taart*
whipped cream	*crème Chantilly*	*slagroom*
ice cream	*glace*	*ijs*
pancake	*crêpe*	*pannekoek*
waffle	*gaufre*	*wafel*

Preparation

rare	*saignant*	*rood*
medium	*à point*	*half doorbakken*
well done	*bien cuit*	*gaar*
plain (without sauces)	*nature*	*natuur*
minced	*haché*	*gehakt*
stuffed	*farci*	*gevuld*
grilled	*grillé*	*geroosterd*
steamed	*à la vapeur*	*gestoomd*
smoked	*fumé*	*gerookt*

French/Walloon Dishes and Specialities

à l'ardennaise	cooked with Ardennes ham (and sometimes cheese)
à la liégeoise	cooked or prepared with strips of bacon
à la nage	(fish) served in a delicately flavoured stock
andouillettes	rich sausages made of offal
anguilles au vert	eels in green herb sauce
assiette anglaise	a selection of cold meats
boudin/boudin noir	sausage/black pudding
boulettes	meatballs
carbonnades flamandes	beef stew cooked with beer
civet (de lapin, etc.)	game stew enriched with blood and red wine
cramique	raisin bread
cuisses de grenouille	frogs' legs

entrecôte à l'os	a huge rib steak
(poissons) en escavèche	(cold fish) cooked in a jellied stock flavoured with herbs
jets de houblon	hop shoots
navarin d'agneau	lamb stew
oiseaux sans tête	slices of beef rolled around a meat stuffing
plateau de fruits de mer	platter of mixed cold shellfish and other seafood
quenelles (de brochet)	rolls of poached paste flavoured with pounded fish (pike)
salade liégeoise	green salad made with green beans and bacon pieces
steak à l'américaine	raw minced steak
steak tartare	raw minced steak (*steak à la américaine* is the usual term)
tartare (de thon)	raw and minced (tuna)
tourte	savoury pie made with meat and vegetables

Flemish Dishes

boterham	a slice of bread and butter (for open sandwich)
fricandel	meatballs
garnaalkroketten	potato croquettes with shrimps inside
Gentse stoverij	rich beef stew from Ghent cooked with beer and mustard
gueuze	beer made from matured and blended lambic (*see* below)
hutsepot	hearty stew (perhaps oxtail or pig's trotters) with root vegetables
paling in 't groen	eels in green herb sauce
speculoos	hard biscuits made with butter, brown sugar and spices
karbonaden	braised beef with onions, usually cooked in beer
koeken	pastries
lambic	beer brewed in the Senne Valley, fermented by natural yeasts
Noordzee vissoep	thick fish soup, with North Sea fish and vegetables
rijstpap	rice pudding flavoured with cinnamon
stoemp	mashed potato mixed with vegetable and/or meat purée
waterzooi	chicken (now also fish) cooked in a soup-like cream sauce

Place Names

Many places in Belgium have two versions of their name: Dutch and French. Signposts tend to be based on the assumption that you know both. Below is a list of the principal cities and towns in Belgium (and France) where the two versions are noticeably different and might cause confusion.

Dutch/English	French	Dutch/English	French
Aalst	Alost	Ieper	Ypres
Antwerpen/Antwerp	Anvers	Kortrijk	Courtrai
Bergen	Mons	Leuven	Louvain
Brugge	Bruges	Mechelen	Malines
Brussel/Brussels	Bruxelles	Namen	Namur
Doornik	Tournai	Oostende/Ostend	Ostende
Furnes	Veurne	Rijsel	Lille (in France)
Gent/Ghent	Gand	Zeebrugge	Zeebruges

59 BC	Julius Caesar begins his campaign against the Gauls (Celts).
54 BC	Revolt against the Romans suppressed by Caesar, and the Belgae are subdued.
AD **15**	Creation of Roman province of Gallia Belgica.
Late C5th	Collapse of the Roman Empire.
c. **620**	Christianity is brought to the Bruges region by St Eloi and St Amand.
843	Treaty of Verdun splits Frankish Empire along the line of the River Scheldt: first division of Belgian lands into what will become Flanders and Wallonia.
862	Charles the Bald, King of France, makes Baldwin Iron-Arm the first Count of Flanders. Baldwin establishes a fortress at Bruges.
1127	The murder of Charles the Good, Count of Flanders provokes a political crisis in Flanders. Derick of Alsace becomes Count of Flanders.
1127–8	Defensive walls, with moat, built around Bruges (now the inner ring of canals).
1134	Storm creates the Zwin, a navigable inlet accessible to Bruges on the River Reie.
1297	Philip the Fair, King of France, annexes Flanders. Bruges is fortified with a new (outer) ring of walls, the Brugse Vesten.
1302	Revolt in Bruges led by Pieter de Coninck and Jan Breydel. French supporters are massacred in the 'Bruges Matins' (18 May). Flemish victory over the French at the Battle of the Golden Spurs (11 July).
1327	The French take revenge by massacring the Flemish at the Battle of Cassel.
1337	Start of the Hundred Years' War (to 1453).
1338	Revolt in Flanders against the French, led by Jacob van Artevelde.
1384	Philip the Bold, Duke of Burgundy, inherits Flanders through his marriage to Louis de Male's daughter.
1406	Dukes of Burgundy inherit Brabant and take over most of the Low Countries.
1419–67	Reign of Philip the Good, Duke of Burgundy. Era of Jan van Eyck.
1468	Philip the Good's successor, Charles the Bold, marries Margaret of York, sister of Edward IV of England, celebrated with lavish festivities in Bruges.
1477	Charles the Bold is killed at the Battle of Nancy. Succeeded by his daughter, Mary of Burgundy, who is forced to grant privileges to the Flemish cities.
1477	Mary of Burgundy marries Maximilian I of the German-Austrian Habsburg family; beginning of Habsburg rule of the Low Countries (until 1794).
1482	Mary of Burgundy dies in a hunting accident, aged 25. Maximilian takes over as regent, but his rule is resisted by the Flemish cities.
1488	Maximilian held prisoner in Bruges and wins release through concessions, which he fails to honour. Antwerp becomes new focus of North European trade.
1506–55	Reign of Charles V: Brussels is at the hub of his mighty empire, which includes much of Spain, Germany, Austria and Italy.
1529	Treaty of Cambrai: France hands over control of Flanders to Charles V.

Chronology

1556–98	Philip II rules the Low Countries from Spain, using the Inquisition.

1562	Canal to Damme extended 10km to Sluis, on the edge of the retreating Zwin.
1578–84	Bruges is ruled by Protestants; many of the churches are wrecked by iconoclasts.
1579	United Provinces (modern Netherlands) declare independence.
1584	Bruges is recaptured by Spanish forces under Duke of Parma.
1585	Creation of the Spanish Netherlands (approximately equivalent to modern Belgium; lasts until 1713), with Brussels as the capital.
1598–1633	Rule of the Infanta Isabella and Archduke Albert. Age of Rubens.
1622	The Ghent–Bruges–Ostend Canal is completed.
1648	Peace of Münster: Spain formally recognizes United Provinces.
1656–7	The future Charles II of England in exile in Bruges, prior to the Restoration.
1701–13	Bruges changes hands twice during the War of the Spanish Succession. Under Treaty of Utrecht (1713) the Spanish Netherlands are assigned to Austria. Belgium is known as the Austrian Netherlands until 1794.
1741–80	Rule by Charles of Lorraine: a period of prosperity and stability.
1780–90	Unpopular rule from Vienna by reformist Emperor Joseph II.
1782–4	The city walls of Bruges are demolished, leaving just four city gates.
1790	French Revolution of 1789 inspires the Brabançon Revolt; the United States of Belgium declared independent; the revolt is crushed by the Austrian army.
1795	Belgium is incorporated into France. Many of Bruges' churches and religious institutions are sold off, vandalized or destroyed.
1815	Final defeat of Napoleon at Waterloo. The Congress of Vienna makes Belgium a part of the United Kingdom of the Netherlands (until 1831).
1830	On 25 August a revolt in Brussels leads to the expulsion of Dutch troops. A Provisional Government declares Belgium independent on 4 Oct.
1831	At the London Conference the international community accepts Belgium's independence. Leopold of Saxe-Coburg becomes King Leopold I (r. 1831–65).
1865–1909	Reign of King Leopold II, marked by rapid economic and industrial development, grand building projects, and the acquisition of the Congo.
1892	Publication of Georges Rodenbach's symbolist novella *Bruges-la-Morte*.
1907	The Boudewijn Canal is completed, linking Bruges to Zeebrugge.
1909	Accession of King Albert I (r. 1909–34).
1914–18	First World War: Germany ignores Belgian neutrality to overrun much of the country. King Albert I leads spirited resistance in northwest Belgium.
1934	Death of Albert I in a climbing accident; accession of Leopold III (r. 1934–51).
1940–5	Second World War: Germany again ignores Belgian neutrality.
1951	Abdication of Leopold III in favour of his Baudouin I (r. 1951–93).
1958	The European Economic Community (EEC) is created; Belgium is a founder member, and Brussels is established as the EEC headquarters.
1962	The Belgian Congo (later Zaire) wins its independence.
1993	The 'Saint-Michel Accords' formalize the on-going devolution of government to the three regional governments: Flanders, Wallonia and Brussels.
1999	Marriage of Prince Philippe to Mathilde d'Udekem d'Acoz.
2002	Bruges becomes a Cultural Capital of Europe.

History

Blyth, Derek, *Flemish Cities Explored*, The Bodley Head, London, 1990. Well-informed, affectionate book on Bruges, Ghent, Antwerp, Mechelen and Brussels, with history, walks, anecdotes and historic illustrations.

Geirnaert, Noël, and Ludo Vandamme (English translation by Ted Alkins), *Bruges: Two Thousand Years of History*, Stichting Kunstboek, Bruges, 1996. A solid, locally produced history in paperback, with some good insights into various facets of Bruges, past and present.

Goffin, Joël, *Sur les Pas des Écrivains de Bruges à Damme*, Les Éditions de l'Octogone, Brussels, 1999. One of the neatly presented *Promenades Découvertes* series, in which the author relates the literary connections to landmarks in the city. Contains many delightful anecdotes.

Jacobs, Roel, and Jan Vernieuwe (English translation by Ted Alkins), *Bruges: The City behind the History*, Marc van de Wiele Publisher, Bruges, 1999. A large format book, beautifully illustrated with photographs by Jan Vernieuwe. The serious, well-researched text unmasks the myths of Bruges' history, and analyzes the city's changing face since its medieval heyday. The best book for anyone who wants to take a deeper look at Bruges.

Art and Architecture

Dictionnaire de la Peinture Flamande et Hollandaise, Larousse, Paris, 1989. Well-illustrated paperback, with brief accounts of all significant Belgian painters.

Souillard, Colette, *Kunst in België*, Lannoo/Tielt, 1986. A good introduction to Belgian art and architecture, with plenty of large colour illustrations. There is an English translation of the Flemish text at the end of the book.

Treasures of Bruges, Stichting Kunstboek, Bruges, 1998. Small, but perfectly formed—page after page of colour photos of paintings and artefacts: the full richness of Bruges' cultural heritage. Like opening a jewellery box.

Literature

Dunnett, Dorothy, The *Niccolò* Series, Michael Joseph, London, 1986. Historical novels set in 15th-century Burgundian Bruges, with meticulously researched background.

Further Reading

Gezelle, Guido (English translations by Paul Claes and Christine D'haen), *The Evening and the Rose*, Guido Gezellegenootschnap, Antwerp, first published 1971. A selection of 30 poems with the Dutch text set out next to the English verse translations. An excellent introduction to Gezelle's work.

Rodenbach, Georges, *Bruges-la-Morte*, Flammarion, Paris, 1998. A new edition of the infamous 1892 novella, complete with original photographs.

Rodenbach, Georges (English translation by Thomas Duncan and Terry Hale), *Bruges-la-Morte*, Atlas Press 1993. An excellent translation, first published in 1903 and upgraded for this edition, which includes the original photographs, plus Khnopff's frontispiece, and Lévy-Dhurmer's portrait of Rodenbach.

Food and Drink

Jackson, Michael, *The Great Beers of Belgium*, Prion Books, London, and Media Marketing Communications, Antwerp, new edition 1997. The definitive work by the greatly respected international 'Beer Hunter'. Lavishly illustrated, in an approachable style and packed with anecdotes. An essential tool for any Belgian beer-lover.

Van Waerebeek, Ruth, *Everybody Eats Well in Belgium Cookbook*, Workman Publishing Company, New York, and Weidenfeld & Nicholson/Orion Books, London, 1996. Visually appealing and very thorough cookbook by a Ghent-born chef now teaching in New York. It also contains some fascinating personal recollections and culinary nuggets which makes the book a real pleasure for enthusiasts of Belgian food.

Belgian Background

Mason, Antony, *Brussels, Bruges, Ghent and Antwerp*, Cadogan Guides, London, second edition 1998. Same series as this guide, focussing on Brussels, but with chapters on the Flemish cities.

Mason, Antony, *Xenophobe's Guide to the Belgians*, Oval Books, London, second edition 1999. One of a series of light-hearted books designed to cure xenophobia by describing what makes a nation tick. Even Belgians like this book.

Pearson, Harry, *A Tall Man in a Low Land*, Abacus Books/Little, Brown, London, 1998. Delightful, affectionate, well informed and funny—a good introduction to the Belgians, even if the author does not go to Bruges.

Main page references are in **bold**. Page references to maps are in *italics*

Index

197